No Small Change

No Small Change

Money, Christians and the Church

by

ADRIAN MANN

The Canterbury Press
Norwich

First published 1992 by The Canterbury Press Norwich
(a publishing imprint of Hymns Ancient & Modern Limited
a registered charity)
St Mary's Works, St Mary's Plain,
Norwich, Norfolk, NR3 3BH

A catalogue record for this book is available
from the British Library

ISBN 1–85311–057–4

*Typeset by Cambridge Composing (UK) Ltd
and printed in Great Britain by
St Edmundsbury Press Limited
Bury St Edmunds, Suffolk*

Foreword

Money, or rather the lack of it, is threatening the very life of the Churches, and therefore of their ministry in and to our society. For a generation, we have been misled by those who have avoided the challenge of a money-ethics by subordinating it within a wider debate about talents. Yet economics in general, and money in particular, cannot be so subjected to supposedly higher moral values. They are too important *in their own right*, and therefore they make such Christian moralising increasingly irrelevant. For money and economics are perhaps the supreme moral currency of our age.

What Adrian Mann has done is to recognise this challenge. To his task he has brought a wealth of practical experience from his work for the Anglican Stewardship Association, and combined it with a broad-based disciplined reflection on his economic involvements.

This is not a book for the mythical 'person in the pew', or 'Guardian reader'. It is rather for those Christians concerned about money: in other words, it applies to each and everyone of us! For we are all inextricably enmeshed with the reality of money in our lives in society, and in the Church. And Adrian Mann rightly recognises that the two worlds are intimately related. Indeed, it is out of 'the conversation' between the two that a new Christian stewardship can most hopefully and realistically emerge. It will therefore be at home equally with the reality of money in both society and Church. So it will avoid that dreadful departmentalisation between the two, which has been the hallmark of Christian stewardship to-date. His guidelines seek to help us to do precisely that. I do hope this book is widely read by Christians concerned about the ministry of and about money in our modern society and Church. It should be essential reading for local church members as well as the Church Commissioners.

JOHN ATHERTON
Canon Theologian, Manchester Cathedral
(Author of *Christianity and the Market*, SPCK, 1992)

Contents

Acknowledgements

This book draws upon a wide range of sources and experience, and I am grateful to a large number of people for their work, writings, help and encouragement. Any contribution the book is able to make often comes from the way in which I have juxtaposed the work of others – the responsibility for this is entirely mine, but the credit is not. The notes and bibliography give as full a list as possible, and I am grateful for the permission granted to use these sources.

Naming names fills me with the dread of inadvertent omission, but particular people must be acknowledged. I apologise unreservedly to anyone I have left out.

Two groups in particular must be thanked. Firstly, there are my friends and colleagues of the Anglican Stewardship Association, with whom I have shared much which has ended up in or between these lines: Peter Fahy, John Eastwood, Carol Sims, Ann Middleton, Gordon Strutt, Ronald Jones, John Willmington, Peter Ralston, Graham Hallam, Adrian Dorber, John Cole, Tony Bowering and others. Secondly, there are those at and around the William Temple Foundation in Manchester, who supplied the disciplines which analysed the experience and then supported as it was set down: Roger Clarke, Brian Cordingley, Jo Saunders, Paul Bilton, David Beverley, Duncan McClements, Andrew Nash and others.

It was through the William Temple Foundation that I came to know John Atherton, who has helped me beyond measure. I thank him for his generosity in sharing his time and knowledge, for his encouragement and for his honesty.

The text and notes reveal that I have gleaned much from the writings, research and reports of others. Some should be mentioned in particular: Charles Gore, R. H. Tawney, William Temple, Reinhold Niebuhr, J. P. Wogaman, Ronald Preston, Brian Griffiths, Ulrich Duchrow and John Atherton in the field of Christian social ethics; David Marquand and Robin Murray for important insights into our changing society; Frank Prochaska for his clear exposition of the history of voluntarism, and the Charities Aid Foundation for a variety of valuable publications; William Countryman and Martin Hengel for insights into the world of the New Testament and the early Church; Avery Dulles, Robin Gill, John Macquarrie, Sara Maitland and John Hull for a variety of striking thoughts about the Church's relationship with the world; and the Church Commissioners, the Central Board of Finance of the Church of England, Douglas McKean and others for maps and guides of the labyrinthine structures of the Church of England.

I am grateful for permission to quote from articles: in various issues of *Charity*, published by the Charities Aid Foundation; in *Church Times*, 9 September 1988 and 17 March 1989; in various issues of *Crucible*, published by the Church of England's Board for Social Responsibility; in *The Guardian*, 11 March 1989, 29 June 1989, 11 March 1991 and 11 November

1991; in *The Independent*, 6 February 1990; in Industrial Christian Fellowship Theme Pamphlets; in *The Observer*, 29 May 1988 and 23 February 1992; in *New Statesman and Society*, 10 March 1989; in the Spring 1988 edition of *Christian Action Journal*; in various issues of *Theology*, published by SPCK. I also acknowledge with thanks the following publishers for their kind permission to reproduce material: from *Clergy Attitudes towards Christian Stewardship* by Clive Barlow – The Revd Clive Barlow; from *How to be a Christian in Trying Circumstances* by Hugh Buckingham – Epworth Press; from BCC Stewardship Committee: *Christian Stewardship in the 1980s* – CCBI Publications; from *The Voluntary Impulse* by Frank Prochaska – Faber and Faber Ltd; from *The Unprincipled Society: New Demands and Old Politics* by David Marquand – Fontana/Cape; from *Where Moth and Dust Corrupt* by Maurice Coombs – Forward Movement Publications, 4125 Sycamore St, Cincinnati, OH 45202, USA; from *Property: Its Duties and Rights* edited by Charles Gore – Macmillan Press Ltd; from *Moral Man and Immoral Society* by Reinhold Niebuhr – Charles Scribner's Sons, an imprint of Macmillan Publishing Company; from *Morality and the Market Place*, and *The Creation of Wealth*, both by Brian Griffiths – Hodder & Stoughton; from *The Parish Church?* edited by Giles Ecclestone – Mowbray (a division of Cassell plc); from *Religion and the Rise of Capitalism* by R. H. Tawney – John Murray; from *The Political Theory of Possessive Individualism* by C. B. Macpherson – Oxford University Press; from *Sustainable Consumerism* by Paul Ekins – New Consumer; from *A Map of the New Country* by Sara Maitland – Routledge; from *Letters and Papers from Prison*, and *Ethics*, both by Dietrich Bonhoeffer, *Beyond Decline: A Challenge to the Churches* by Robin Gill, *A Theology of Liberation* by Gustavo Gutierrez, *What Prevents Christian Adults from Learning?* by John M. Hull, *Economics and Ethics* and *A Christian Method of Moral Judgment* by J. P. Wogaman, *The Future of Christian Ethics*, *Church and Society in the Late Twentieth Century*, and *Religion and the Persistence of Capitalism* by Ronald H. Preston – SCM Press Ltd; from *Faith in the Nation* by John Atherton, *Meaning and Truth in II Corinthians* by Frances Young and David F. Ford, *Holding Fast to God* by Keith Ward – SPCK, London; from *Global Economy: A Confessional Issue for the Churches* by Ulrich Duchrow – WCC Publications, Geneva, Switzerland; from *Following Christ in a Consumer Society* by John Francis Kavanaugh – Orbis Books, Maryknoll, New York; from various official reports and publications – the Central Board of Finance of the Church of England; from his lecture Incarnation and Social Vision – Rowan Williams.

Every effort has been made to make due acknowledgement. Inadvertent errors or omissions will be corrected in any future editions.

Bury St Edmunds, March 1992   ADRIAN MANN

Preface

Problems of Possession

This book is a response to questions which have arisen in my mind out of the experience of working with the Anglican Stewardship Association for some twelve years. The questions are familiar: 'Why does the Church only teach about money when it wants some?'; 'Why does finance always dominate meetings of PCCs and Deanery Synods?'; 'Why do discussions about money in the Church seem to bring out the worst in people?'; 'Why does this whole area in life, so important to us all, seem to be dealt with so inadequately by Christians and the Church?'.

Naturally, I started with some fixed points, some intuitions and some preconceptions about the conclusions I would be likely to reach. Some of these have indeed remained constant. Others have shifted a great deal as the study has progressed.

Money is a many-headed Hydra in both the world and the Church. It is a subject we try to avoid, but it keeps popping up. It speaks far more eloquently of our priorities and desires than any amount of self-justification. It can short-circuit any self-deception back into reality with devastating effect. It is like an onion – the more layers we cut through, the stronger the smell, the harder it is to see what we're doing, the more tears we shed and the tighter we shut our eyes.

In fact our attitudes to money and wealth are ambivalent. We like to think we are realistic about it, and we certainly like to have what we consider to be an adequate quantity of it. At the same time, we suspect our attachment to it, and glance nervously at those passages in the Bible which warn us about it. The result is that we find it all too easy to succumb to spirit/matter dualism.

We feel that a too energetic application of Christian principles to the world of the bank balance, the mortgage, the pension, would be fundamentally threatening to the comfort and security with which we have managed to surround ourselves. We have a problem of possession, but we like to shelter from it by keeping our religion spiritual and abstract.

So it seems to be left to the surrounding culture to define our conceptions of money and wealth. In the underlying ethos and motivations of a consumer society value seems so often to be defined subjectively. What do I want? How much do I desire this or that? What I value is valuable – justification by desire alone.

We think, and certainly behave, as if wealth is *my* business, but wealth is also a relative term. It is a community matter, packed with relatedness, with *other* people. But we protect the money compartment of our lives, if we think about it at all, by conniving with the niceties of conventional religion and labelling money as somehow 'unspiritual'. Ironically, we protect our own consumerism as we bewail the prevailing 'materialism'.

The fact is that money is of such importance that, for Christians, it must present a serious test of credibility and integrity. In the first part of this study, to begin to face up to this test, I examine the secular economic world within which we all live, Christian and non-Christian alike, and consider the ethical response which Christians have made to that world. I conclude that it is of urgent importance for the Church to open up and honestly come to terms with economic change and the role of money in our society. This leads me to propose five important questions or guidelines for the Church to consider, which should help it towards that end.

In the second part I go on to look at ecclesiastical economics – the world of the Church set within society at large – to see how its practice matches up to its principles and to the five guidelines suggested.

This leads on to a final part in which I set out a possible way ahead. Here one of the five guidelines, regarding the Church as a 'third kingdom' which interacts with the kingdom of God and the world, is further developed. The 'third kingdom' provides an overall structure within which the major issues raised by this study can be addressed. I then offer suggestions and give examples of how such recommendations might work out in practice.

This book has been written out of my experience as an Anglican. It is therefore primarily and specifically related to the life of the Church of England – dealing first with the beam in my own eye, so to speak. However, this does not mean that the same principles and precepts will not apply elsewhere. Friends in other denominations have certainly recognised features of their own Church life in what I have written. I therefore hope that what is offered here will be, at least by analogy, a challenge and a help to Christians from all backgrounds.

PART ONE
Economics and Ethics

1. Introduction

Every generation feels that the pace of change in its society is more rapid than the changes undergone by its predecessors. This is particularly striking when we look at the part played by money, and the way we handle it, in our culture. Christians share this experience of change with everyone else; they are not exempt from it, nor should they seek to be.

Here Christians are presented with an opportunity to relate their experience to their faith in a way which will witness to the whole of society, showing them to be creatively and realistically engaged with the issues which dominate people's lives. However, the truth is that for many of us these changes are happening beyond the boundary within which the Christian moral view normally operates.

The temptation is to jump straight out of one compartment of life, the *religious*, into another, the *worldly*, without attempting to draw the compartments together in any way. This produces prophets who point out to us the mismatch between the values of the kingdom of God and the values of modern society, and they are right in what they say.

All the same, we must recognise that an exclusively idealistic or utopian approach is insufficient, for it leaves most of humanity and the world behind it in its quest for perfection. Although we shall always need visionaries and their message of hope, the whole body of the Church has to take seriously the job of building bridges which connect idealism and realism. People, including many active and professing Christians, are living their lives in the mainstream of economic life. The Church must address their dilemmas both in its preaching and teaching of the gospel *and* in the way it conducts its own affairs.

Most Christians are secular, in the world, and their experience must be part of the process of constructing a contemporary Christian approach to handling money. They can be part of a dialogue, both listening to and speaking to the world – making a renewed structure out of which the Church can serve the world and express the sacred through the ordinary things of life.

The task in this first part is therefore to identify and examine some key trends in the ways that we experience and handle money. These trends can be said to exemplify or symbolise contemporary changes, and so are appropriate areas in which to study the relevance of Christian views on economics and ethics.

The examples of economic change I have chosen for this are (1) debt and credit, (2) property and home ownership, and (3) charitable giving and philanthropy. All of these have to do with people, families and communities and the ways in which they relate and live. All, therefore, have particularly important ethical, and practical, implications for Christians and the Church.

Before looking at these examples of change it will be helpful to survey the general background against which they are set. I will do this, firstly, by looking at the pressure of change on economic culture and the posture of the Church towards such change. Secondly, I will identify some key features of our economic culture and the pressures put upon people by the workings of that culture. Thirdly, I will look at the interplay between Christians, the Church, Christian ethics and economic culture.

Some conclusions are then drawn at the end of Part One which lead towards the issues I address in the remainder of the book.

2. Pressure of Change

Church and Change

Christians often appear to be the most conservative group in society. The vigilance of their efforts to preserve cherished values is often their most distinctive group characteristic. Seeing this, it would probably be difficult for an independent observer to come to the conclusion that Christian faith holds the concept of *metanoia*, a radical turning round and setting off in a new direction, in some esteem.

The task of the Church in society is often expected to be that of guarding standards of personal morality. It is less likely to be thought to have the role of questioning public, corporate or structural morality. Such expectations tend, in practice, towards making a presumption in favour of the present established order.

Stability and quality of personal morality are important ingredients in any economic system. In providing them the Church can find itself presenting a conservative profile, whether it wishes to or not. However, the Church cannot be content to concentrate on personal morality without integrating with it a complementary critique of society. It must take account of the context within which people have to make their day-to-day decisions. Life is becoming more plural, the influence of the Christendom heritage of Western Europe is diminishing, and much less in the way of social order and values can be taken for granted.

This puts the Church under some pressure, because the questioning approach which is now necessary conflicts with the expectations of many people. A Church which has questions and talks of life as a journey is a problem for people, both inside and outside its worshipping life, who expect answers and stability.

This is not new, indeed Western Christianity has been recovering a place for its social theology for well over a century. But the exercise is still novel to many and it is increasingly complex and stretching to all. Rates of change accelerate and make even more disturbing F. D Maurice's comment that it is folly to oppose the spirit of the age with the spirit of a former age. The spirit of the age is now so quickly obsolete, so rapidly changing, that it is indeed difficult to choose pilgrimage rather than stability.

This is quite natural. Cultural change often feels as if it is substituting the inferior and shallow for the superior and substantive. Andy Warhol's vision of a world where everyone will be famous for fifteen minutes is not, to most people, obviously the outcome of healthy forms of progress. They react against the insecurity implied by such anarchic egalitarianism. They feel perhaps that it undervalues the importance of sustained work and use of skills and thus undermines the values on which their lives are built.

Economic change has often presented to the Church the sharp edge and primary example of its instinctive feeling that what is new is worse. This happened with the enclosures and with the excesses of the industrial revolution, and it has happened again more recently with the resurgence of market-led economics in the 1980s. The Church will always wish to defend those who are damaged or disadvantaged in the process of economic change. In doing so its questions will often be directed towards and against people, movements and social forces which propagate change. New is not by definition better.

'The certainties of one age are the problems of the next.'[1] For example, the post-war construction of broad-based social provision by successive British governments is now seen as problematic, even by those who remain committed to it. Nevertheless, the Welfare State, in particular the National Health Service, is still 'owned' at a deep emotional level by the bulk of the population. Change may be accepted as necessary, or 'realistic', but nobody thinks things improve.

It is all too easy, in our state of accelerating change, for the Church to become the sacrament of, and the priest to, that in all of us which remains convinced that life is bad and steadily getting worse. But it is not enough to deplore the world and retreat into a conserving ghetto.

Pace of Change

The speed of change undergone by human beings in western society grows with each generation. The pace of advances in technology and communications makes knowledge and skill appear more and more transitory. Rapid change has become a constant in people's lives, and security is sought in new ways, from burglar alarms to inflation-proof pensions. The human capacity to adapt to all this is remarkable, but it does imply a parallel rapid adaption of the values by which lives are lived. Nihilistic crime and violence could be the jagged edge of this negative adaption.

As change becomes a constant, the future begins to come within the compass of the present. Expertise in prediction, forecasting and planning is greatly valued, along with fashion, youth and style, novelty and innovation, doing tomorrow's thing today. Society is on the move, flexible, diverse and decentralised. Points of reference are less definitive or objective and our sense of identity and self is less sure.

Post-industrial patterns of work revolving around services, information and leisure are replacing patterns based primarily on manufacturing, just as those industrial patterns had themselves replaced the earlier, agricultural ones. A 'waiting workforce'[2], and all that implies in terms of unemployment and its social consequences, is needed to serve this new pattern's appetite for flexibility and change. Many of our theories, beliefs and values remain those developed out of and favoured by industrial society, such as commitments to the work ethic and full employment. It remains to be seen whether they will continue to be of use in new circumstances. Perhaps they will emerge again in adapted form, as agrarian values have found a new expression in such diverse forms as suburban gardens, organic produce and the continuing quest of many for a rural idyll.

For a time, economic liberalism appeared to be adapting better than most of the values of the industrial era, but it is too early to say if that adaption can be sustained. The signs are that social and ecological factors will cause the collapse, abandonment or qualification of economic liberalism, but that is not the point at issue. The point is that many people are adrift on a sea of change without a set of values which can reconcile realism and idealism.

Social authority of all types is subject to stringent questioning. Guidance from traditional sources is no longer accepted as objective. Although specialisation increases as there is more and more division of labour, we are sceptical of experts. We do not find their skills easy to comprehend, and we are not sure enough of their values to trust them. We suspect that, as our new elites reach their peaks at ever-earlier ages, so technique triumphs over wisdom. 'When a thing is intelligible you have a sense of participation; when a thing is unintelligible you have a sense of estrangement.'[3]

In the Church, and across the whole spectrum of politics and economics into ecology, it does not seem that anyone has a reliable idea of the consequences of the changes which are under way and to which we are already irrevocably committed. All scour the past for signs of the future. Many only find old arguments to repeat, although some are recognising the need not just to restate. As the scouring becomes more intense and the specialisation of skills increases, so does their compartmentalisation.

People are also having to adjust to striking changes in the patterns of family life. The number of households has risen, but average household size has reduced. Single parent households have increased dramatically. Relatives from the preceding generation no longer tend to live as close by. Traditional and extended family patterns are eroded at the same time as their virtues are extolled.

In the face of the pace of change people clutch at the security of their 'compartment', that part of life which can be defined and understood: home, family, job, car, garden, holiday. If we travel, we take our compartment with us, and so all hotel rooms look the same wherever in the world they are. If we live in a plural society, we do so whilst retaining our compartment as an inner sanctum. But a 'compartment' needs economic resources. The poor are not properly equipped with one of these compartments and are consequently not protected from the effects of change in the same way as their contemporaries.

Money and change

A striking example of the rate of change is the accelerating role of money in our economy and in the overall ambience of our society – this is qualitative, not just quantitative, a change of character, not just one of speed. The movement from subsistence and agricultural to capitalist and industrial economies was accompanied by a change in the role of money away from barter and exchange towards investment and growth. Money began to earn its own living, to move from metal to paper.

Similarly, the movement to a post-industrial society is accompanied by money changing gear again. Money now needs to move faster than paper will allow and has become electronic, future-orientated, finding the flexibility of cable and satellite. It exists in its own right and becomes increasingly dislocated from that which it theoretically represents.

In this context the monetarists' call for honest, straightforward, easily comprehended, housekeeping-type money can be seen to be as utopian, even romantic, as any other ideology. Refraining from printing extra money may not be enough to eliminate inflation if credit, human expectations and information technology combine in a ratchet effect to increase the speed of circulation. Alternatively, in a time of recession, it may simply be politically impossible to keep to such simple rules as public spending on social benefits inevitably rises with numbers unemployed, independently of specific government decisions.

Post-industrial trends

Compartmentalism and the accelerating influence of money combine to produce some disturbing effects as Britain's post-industrial society develops. John Atherton[4] has pointed out that our changing economy is creating a situation where poverty for a large minority exists within an overall state of increasing affluence for the majority. This in turn exists within the possible long-term relative decline of the nation as a whole vis-à-vis its peers. Out of great complexity a pattern emerges which shows the poor minority paying the price of movements in the industrial base, being excluded from the benefits gained by the majority in its material lifestyle, and being unable to approach, let alone sustain, the way of life generally presented as normal and desirable.

Flexibility is a key word, leading to changes in work and living patterns. This can manifest itself as increasing part-time work for women at the expense of full-time work for men. Alternatively, it can mean having to move to another area where the costs of housing increase along with the availability of work. For the more affluent it can mean the opportunity, provided by information technology, to adopt flexible work patterns or to work at home. Population shifts from north to south, from city to dormitory village or riverside development. A neighbourhood watch scheme takes the place of the extended family.

In all this the divisions in society are emphasized and deepened. Those who can make it are able to move further and further away from sight and sound of those who cannot, aided by the compartmentalism both of society at large and of their own way of life.

Adjusting to change

What posture should Christians adopt in the face of change? How should the true nature of any change be discerned? Is it possible, or even desirable, for us to untangle selfish preferences from principles as we make the choices which set the course for our way of life? If we adopt a positive attitude to changes taking place in the world, how can we guard against allowing our insights to be so influenced by change that they are taken over and lose their specifically Christian nature?

The British Churches continue to have difficulty in adjusting to the recent renaissance of market economics. In this, are the Churches standing for timeless moral values? Or are they perceptively discerning trends in economic activity which are not sustainable in terms of the created order and not justifiable in terms of the disadvantaged? Or are they reacting conservatively as institutions which have made considerable emotional investments in the priorities of the welfare state, and have failed to take note of the experience of many of their members who live their lives in the market place? The answer to *all* of these questions is probably 'yes'. There is a big psychological difference between adopting a stance of grudging acknowledgement and taking a positive attitude, even if qualified.

In a society of increasing pluralism and decreasing Church attendance it is not surprising to find the Churches at the forefront of questioning the new priorities people are giving to their lives. They point out that people are losing visions and ideals to live by, and finding purpose in the workings of the economic system rather than seeing it as a function in the service of more important values. If means take over from ends, they can become ends in themselves, and many feel that this is happening to money.

It is very easy to feed our own presuppositions into an analysis and to reproduce them as our findings or as the evidence of our experience. At the same time as society is doing this by asserting that a market economy is the only way to provide a fulfilling standard of life, the Church apparently attacks the same subject from the other end and asserts that the market is bound to be damaging to the cohesion of society.

In the midst of the change going on all around us it seems that the age-old tension, between God as the centre of value and money as the centre of our values, is as strong as ever, with the added twist that the Church is now a generation behind with its language and its terminology.

So it is that the Church has several problems facing it as it tries to adjust to economic change, and these are all in some sense problems of communication, of blockages between compartments of life, difficulties in making necessary connections between people or ideas.

Firstly, there is an unreconciled conflict between those who stress wealth creation and those who stress wealth distribution. This is a division of ideas which may well have something to do with the way of life or of earning a living of different people within the Church. It must be reckoned unfortunate if many Christians participating in industry and commerce do not take seriously the positions on wealth creation taken by their Churches and do not feel in turn that their way of life is properly relevant to Christian faith.

Secondly, the Church remains reluctant to apply the same standards in the specifics of its own situation that it proclaims in the abstract of its wider pronouncements. Money as a moral issue is all too often kept safely in the sphere of political economy and social justice, away from the challenge of personal faith to individual and ecclesial ways of life.

Consequently a detached laissez-faire fatalism develops. This accepts increasing restrictions on the areas of life to which the Christian concepts of justice, love and forgiveness can be allowed to apply. The handling of money by Christians and the Church is undertaken all too often in such a way as to subtly undermine the application of Christian ethics. The greater truths of value judgements are circumscribed by the lesser truths of financial expediency, even though the lesser depends on the greater for its long-term viability. The common good is undermined as people compartmentalise and seal off from their decision-making broader interests beyond self-interest. This happens even though these are the things, such as the interests of community or ecology, which give self-interest its real foundation and justification, and even though self-interest is only sustainable within common interest.

3. Society and Economic Culture

Background

The insecurities of modern life provide fertile ground for all sorts of escapism and apocalyptic paranoia. In this context it is important for the Church to keep its feet planted firmly on God's earth; it needs to know what is going on so that it can avoid becoming escapist. As change pushes ahead of our ability or moral capacity to cope, it is important not to make unjustifiable or unsustainable claims. Instead, the emphasis should be on reality; on the Word made flesh and present in the here and now; on using what we have been given to discern the nature and content of the pressures on the present. I now look, therefore, at some important features of wealth and money in our culture.

Money and power

Tawney defined power as the capacity to modify the conduct of other individuals or groups in ways which we desire, and to prevent our own conduct being modified in the ways in which we do not[1]. Power does not exist in a vacuum; it is about relationship. Although not all power is economic, much is, and an accumulation of money is also an accumulation of power. History shows us that there is an innate human tendency to accumulate power. Although in a planned economy power can be accumulated bureaucratically or politically, in a western-style free economy power can more easily be accumulated economically.

The possession of money gives us power over our own lives, makes us less vulnerable to the choices of others, and gives us power over the lives of others, makes them more vulnerable to our choices. The possession of money gives us greater capacity to express our values, to impart and quantify value to people and things, and to communicate that value to others. With this power comes responsibility.

The economic development of a society tends to produce a shift in emphasis from agriculture to industry to technology to services, accompanied by increasing levels of specialisation. Money gives the capacity and power to direct and control these changes and not be subject to them. This becomes increasingly evident as the gap between rich and poor widens both nationally and internationally. The power of money can be used negatively, for example through fear of unemployment, to apply coercion to social behaviour and to control events to the benefit of those who hold that power.

An obvious connection between money and power is shown by the enormous amount of money which is directed towards military expenditure. Apart from the contrast and conflict between this type of expenditure and expenditure directed towards the world's apparent needs, this also raises questions of economic sustainability and politial abuse, and the anti-democratic tendency of high military expenditure.

Money is also powerful in the international dimension, where debt and resource depletion are issues which highlight the power wielded by financial institutions, setting conditions for the granting of vital loans, and transnational companies, planning their activities where labour is cheap.

The use of advertising, and its political cousin propaganda, is a startling modern example of the power of money at work. It is impossible to quantify the extent to which money thus gives the power to affect, perhaps subtly or unconsciously, apparently free choices being made by others.

Power of money

Money is a medium, a means and an expression of power. But it is more than this, more than a mechanism, more than a simple mechanistic measure of quantities of wealth. Money has a power of its own which can be applied to people through desire. 'Nothing can be more certain than this: daily experience shows the more (money desires) are indulged, they increase the more.'[2] This cannot be quantified or proven, but it is, as Wesley said, a commonplace of human experience, even if it is one which we can tend to leave out of many of our theories and analyses.

We are all able to feel the power of money acting upon us, be it through personal desire or through accumulated capital. We are usually capable, too, of identifying the problem as being wholly outside ourselves rather than partially within. It is all too easy to blame the forces of wealth and greed for social circumstances of which we disapprove, without acknowledging the extent to which we are ourselves in thrall to that power.

The power of money to induce self-deception and the subsequent rationalisation of decisions is remarkable. It is the often unmentioned motivation behind many actions, be they moral, immoral or criminal. And its influence on attitudes should also be noted. Reinhold Niebuhr perceptively wrote: 'The moral attitudes of dominant and privileged groups are characterised by universal self-deception and hypocrisy.' There is 'unconscious and conscious identification of their special interests with general interests and universal values . . '³ In addition, the compartments in which we do so much of our thinking are a most effective aid for any sort of self-deception.

It may be that the capacity to deceive ourselves in matters of money is accumulating and accelerating exponentially along with money's role in society. All human beings want to be accepted and valued according to the particular emphases of the society in which they are set. In our case that means economic culture. The tendency is towards conformity and following the crowd. This has the potential to be a heady and complex cocktail when mixed with self-deception. Neither following the herd nor self-deception are any the less powerful for the difficulty or impossibility of identifying or isolating them.

Problems in the Marketplace

The market economy constitutes a large and, some would say, formative part in the lives of individuals, communities and whole societies. It is important for the Church, therefore, to develop a thoughtful, sensitive and discerning attitude towards the marketplace which can be communicated to Christians living their daily lives in the world and to that world itself.

The characteristic features of market economies are, firstly, private property, protected by law; secondly, freedom of enterprise, encouraging experiment and innovation; and thirdly, freedom of consumer choice, allowing the price mechanism rather than any structured agency to control the distribution of scarce goods. People make their own choices and pay directly themselves. No pretence of objectivity needs to be made. The value placed on goods and services depends on the wealth and preferences of those who are buying and selling.

The problems of inefficiency, and often tyranny, afflicting state-controlled economies have led to an increasing acceptance of the market mechanism in recent times. Former communist countries have been variously seeking ways of increasing the amount of economic activity undertaken within the market environment, and of handling the concomitant political change and volatility.

Nevertheless, the market system is not without problems of its own. Criticism is often levelled at the market because of its concentration on the profit motive. It is impossible to know at which point the desire to make money ceases to be justifiable or enlightened self-interest and becomes greed. This motivation applies to all in society, for money is needed to take part in the activities of society. Without making money or profit, it is not possible to exercise consumer choice, to acquire property, to spend or to save and invest. These activities are limited only by wealth and allowed only by wealth – freedom of choice in what is needed or wanted, good or bad, is up to the individual consumer, whose position is therefore one of responsibility, a responsibility which can be well or poorly exercised.

The emphasis on the individual in a market economy is often extended to include the family. Providing for the present and future needs of one's family is seen as a healthy justification for and logical extension of the profit motive. However, it is certainly open to question whether the family is not much more necessary for the survival of market capitalism than market capitalism is for the future of the family. Many of the pressures which bear destructively upon families are economic ones, mediated by the market. Modern market economies require mobile and flexible workforces, and this requirement is not always compatible with settled family life, especially extended family life, and the development of local communities. The market place's sentimental advertising image of the family contrasts with many of the real effects of the market on family life.

Much has been written about market capitalism's common heritage with puritanism[4], and it can be a notable expression of the stewardship ideal in practice: 'Puritanism in its essence meant an increased sense of personal responsibility, and an assertion of the right of the conscience, under grace, to guide the individual . . .'[5] Along with this went the idea that wealth and property come from character. Obviously, the puritan virtues of rigorous honesty, diligence, thrift, sobriety and prudence give an advantage in the world of business. However, the danger is that this elevates the observance and interpretation of cause and effect into a matter of principle and takes it further than it can be sustained, to the point where a self-righteous middle class pride prevails.

A problem arises when the market economy loses its anchorage in grace and in responsibility as an expression of that grace. Brian Griffiths is a strong proponent of the free market and therefore his criticisms of it should be taken seriously; it is notable that they are written from a modern puritan perspective. He sees the 'crisis of capitalism' as being 'nothing less than the crisis of humanism as a religion being played out in economic life'[6] and he is not surprised to note that decline in economic performance often runs simultaneously with moral decline[7]. He regards humanism as leading to hedonism, and thus rejects the New Right's libertarian defence of market capitalism. Griffiths' defence of the free market is based on values, stewardship and a sense of human participation in the creative purposes of God. Accordingly, prosperity is good, but must be distinguished from luxury[8], and biblical warnings about the dangers of wealth must be heeded[9].

Underlying this is the paradox that capitalism requires many social virtues which can only be laid down and maintained in a different type of society. A full and rounded form of self-interest implies such things as social ties, religious teaching and a sense of civic duty[10]. None of these is created or sustained by market mechanisms which emphasize differentials, individual preferences and compartmentalised transactions. Transactions affect other people and the environment as well as the prime participants, and they affect the long-term as well as the short.

Dualism, compartments and contradictions

Brian Griffiths notes that 'we live in a society in which there are very great pressures on us to keep (Christianity and economics) in watertight compartments'[11]. He follows Arthur Bryant in identifying a landmark in the development of this situation as the Companies Act of 1862 which 'completed the divorce between the Christian conscience and the economic practice of everyday life.'[12] Increased regulations now qualify this assertion, but the basic meaning of the structure remains the same. The limited liability company does not adequately express interdependence, it undervalues our responsibility for people and creation. Of course, there is a need to limit individual liability in complex situations, but, if no vacuum is to result, this requires adequate accountability and regulation within the corporate responsibility thus implied.

Tawney reached similar conclusions: 'Religion has been converted from the keystone which holds together the social edifice into one department within it . . .' Decisions become primarily economic and a dualism is formed which 'regards the secular and the religious aspects of life . . . as parallel and independent provinces, governed by different laws, judged by different standards, and amenable to different authorities.' Christian ethics and economic activity are kept in separate compartments. 'They cannot collide, for they can never meet.'[13]

It is necessary for clarity of thought sometimes to separate out ideas and concepts from one another, but it is equally necessary to put them back together into the whole at the end of the thought process. This we often fail to do, especially in the area of popular communication, which forms a large part of our culture. Here the demand is for simple and digestible concepts, and so compartmentalised thinking and ideas often become the end product instead of a valid but temporary part of an overall process. Slogans can replace thought.

In this context the quasi-Christian dualism between the spiritual and the material, bypassing the doctrine of the incarnation, becomes quite dangerous in the influence it can have on our way of thinking. The tendency to condemn 'materialism' as the source of all our problems is an example of this. It is as if we just label the parcel and leave it unopened, shut away from our decisions.

Sometimes we try to be a bit more precise and we use the word 'consumerism' pejoratively instead. This introduces another dualism, where production is somehow 'good' and consumption, by implication, 'bad'. What is consumed cannot be saved and invested, and cannot therefore create wealth. This is the implicit descant behind much puritanism, socialism and Christian moralism, but it is only half the truth. The contradiction in this way of thinking is that it is so incomplete and fails to recognise anything beyond the individual, particularly the fact that production and consumption are related, forming a complex web of giving and receiving, within social relationships. One person's consumption is another person's production. Respectable, cautious, compartmentalised Christianity often fails to recognise that it has as much in its heritage advocating spontaneous expenditure and irrational or generous consumption as it has supporting prudence, saving and investment.

It is these dualisms and compartments, between spiritual and material, between religious feeling and social concern, between social concern and personal decision or action, which allow the situation to persist in which reasonably affluent people can live out their lives as if the poor do not exist. It is possible for us to be blissfully unaware that the plight of others has anything to do with us and our responsibilities and opportunities.

Consumer choice and post-industrial society

The free market gives sovereignty, choice and creativity to the individual consumer, and in doing so it channels many social relationships into the area where they are expressed by the use of money. Market decisions can be more powerful than electoral decisions. In post-industrial society power is shifting away from production towards consumption, and the need to exercise control of the power of the monopoly producer over the consumer is generally recognised. The consumer with money is in an increasingly well-protected and powerful position.

This change of emphasis has been called the shift to 'post-Fordism', a shift away from the factory and mass-production towards the office and the shop[14]. An important feature of this is the use of computers by retailers in their distribution systems, allowing them to hold the minimum optimum amount of stocks. For a retail chain such as Sainsbury's, ordering can now be done overnight on the basis of today's sales. This ultra-sensitivity to demand gives increased power, variety, creativity and effectiveness to consumer choice. Manufacturing has also become more flexible in response – computer controlled production in the car industry, where technology has replaced mass production with differentiated response to demand, is a striking example of this. Such developments are as important within sectors of the economy as changes between them.

A great deal of this is positive, allowing the possibility of decisions and responsibility devolving towards people living their lives more flexibly and creatively. Commonly, political parties now espouse a concept of citizenship which further affirms and empowers the consumer. Much is heard, too, of the 'green consumer'. The possibilities of flexibility brought by information technology can also be built into the provision of public services, which do not have to be centralist and bureaucratic.

On the negative side, the scope for manipulation by advertising and for victory of style over content is also extended. Many workplace decisions are delegated, not to people but to computer programmes. Job satisfaction can be reduced as microchips respond to consumer choice, bypassing the responsibility of human decision by workers in the retail trade. Money is required to exercise the growing opportunities for consumer choice, and thus the divisions in society are increased and emphasised.

Accumulation and acquisition

Wesley's comment that to fulfil the appetite for acquisition only leads to its increase has already been noted. For Wesley this presented a problem for the soul and so it remains, perhaps increasingly so, for us. Furthermore, we no longer have the eighteenth century's luxury of comparative ignorance concering the finite nature of the space and resources provided by this world. We cannot continue to perceive the whole of creation as, in a positive sense, awaiting exploitation. We have to consider the probability that continuous, long-term, universal, consumption-orientated economic growth may be physically as difficult to sustain as it is spiritually.

Our capacity for self-deception over matters of wealth gives plenty of scope for environmental problems to creep up on us and give us a nasty surprise. This happens regularly and with increasing frequency. Is it possible for consumers to exercise oppression – over themselves, over the poor, over the environment – by their overweening, even addicted, demands?

It is worth looking at the problem of inflation in this context. Reacting to the rapid rises in prices during the 1970s, monetarists produced a simple, clinical, empirical answer – a direct connection between money supply and inflation. Here Brian Griffiths, himself a strong advocate of honest money, parts company and asks whether this diagnosis is not itself simplistic and amoral[15]. It certainly seems possible that the monetarist solution brought only temporary relief, and that at a heavy human price in terms of unemployment. Griffiths sees a spiritual element, as well as a technical one, in the problem of inflation. In order to describe the nature of this spiritual problem, he interestingly chooses the analogy of addiction[16]. He asks if we are not becoming addicted to consumption. It is certainly worth noting that the classic symptoms of addiction – denial, deception of self and others, money problems, suppression of moral values – are all present in varying degrees. The effect of the compartmentalism we have already noted is to exacerbate these by providing an environment in which denial and self-deception can flourish.

This is an outworking of what C. B. Macpherson has called

'possessive individualism'[17], part of a line which can be traced back via Burke, Smith, Kant, Rousseau, Howe and Locke to the Stoics, who considered each individual to be possessed of divine reason, giving life its meaning[18]. This line of thought has very little place for the community. Nevertheless it has social consequences, a social contract protecting the rights of individuals and leading towards a possessive market economy and a possessive market society. Locke therefore argued that a person 'necessarily and legitimately' becomes the owner of whatever he or she 'removes out of the state that nature hath provided'. In its day this was a call for justice, for people to enjoy the fruits of their own labour and initiative, free of feudal vested interests such as Church or aristocracy. But it has now been overtaken by the reality of living in a finite world where exploitation can no longer provide the rationale for the justification and conduct of ownership.

Human beings have always been subject to the danger of the possession possessing the possessor. The teaching of Jesus is alive to this possibility. We need to consider whether this might not now be happening in western society on a broader and wider scale than previously, and in a way which is supported by and is supportive of the social, political and economic status quo. The Jesuit J. F. Kavanaugh calls this pattern 'the commodity form', and asserts: 'the commodity . . . achieves an independent existence over and against men and women.'[19]

This sets up a cumulative cycle of cause and effect which disorients people, fragments community, accelerates material expectations, presupposes values of consuming and marketing, defines being in terms of having. 'Possessions which might otherwise serve as expressions of our humanity, and enhance us as persons, are transformed into ultimates.'[20] The idea of greater accumulation is taken for granted and comes to underlie the whole culture.

Values in economic culture

Not everyone believes that the material and the spiritual can be kept in separate compartments of life. 'Economics are the method; the object is to change the soul', Margaret Thatcher said in 1981[21]. Brian Griffiths stresses the importance of values and rejects the 'value-free' concept of modern economics as seen, for example, in Hayek's and Friedman's libertarian theories of the free market. He deplores its secular humanism.

Although Griffiths is clear that creation is good and that any platonic dualism is to be rejected[22], he then comes much too close to making a Church/world dualism of his own to replace it. In this the reformation, the puritan tradition, a vocational work ethic, stewardship, savings and the family are good; the Renaissance, the Englightenment, secular humanism, deficit financing and the State are bad. This is surely an oversimplification which attempts, for example, to attribute the credit for the wealth creation of the industrial revolution entirely to puritanism, whilst ignoring the complementary scientific and political contributions made, in the enlightenment period, to a complex web of developments.

This dualism, separating out interconnecting components of historical developments and failing to put them back together again, allows the argument in defence of market capitalism that '. . . we should not judge the legitimacy of the process by its abuse'[23], whilst denying socialism the benefit of any such doubt. Here Brian Griffiths' clarity of thought is led astray by his political agenda.

In fact many of the values of economic determinism and positivism are shared by both capitalism and socialism, *both* of which tend to undervalue those things which have not been made by humankind. This happens both in the individualist view of property, which is that things belong to the exploiter, and in the Marxist labour theory of value, which disagrees about who should own the title deeds, but not about the fact that value inheres in production. Consequently each type of economic culture tends towards compartmentalism and values the quantifiable judgement above the qualitative, the short-term benefit above the long-term safeguard, market relations above personal relationships, the individual's contribution to society above society's contribution to the individual and measurable means above conceptual ends.

As post-industrialism shifts the emphasis away from production and towards consumption, a shift in values also takes place away from actions and towards possessions. Advertising is growing in importance as information technology develops, and it is not free of value. The 'commodity form' of culture conditions us to relate to such things. Market forces come to represent more than a network of individual choice. They also express a subliminal system of values and conditioning which ironically and paradoxically undermines the freedom and choice they symbolise.

By putting the market into a separate compartment of life, we fail to recognise the hidden set of values affirmed by our economic

culture. We see it simply as a mechanism which can only be judged
by its efficiency. However, the hidden values exist, and they deeply
affect our lives.

Money and divisions in society

An emphasis on money-orientated values pulls society's centre of
gravity towards what works economically. A dose of realism is no
bad thing in itself, but in practice the balance simultaneously tilts
away from the disadvantaged and the poor, whose contribution to
society is harder to measure than their dependence upon it.

Divisions between the better off and the worse off increase as
society gives more weight to economic efficiency. Taxes for the well
off are lowered, benefits for the badly off are restricted, both in
order to sharpen the cutting edge of financial incentive. Pay
differentials increase for the same reason. The effect is compounded
by an increase in low-paid and part-time work. Proponents of the
free market argue that this is necessary in order to sort out the
economy for the benefit of all, but fail adequately to acknowledge
the corrosive social effects of relational poverty. The pattern which
emerges is one of greater inequality, with a majority benefiting from
economic prosperity, but with a significant minority living much
nearer the margin.

Money divisions are superimposed upon the traditional differences of class. There are now greater economic differentials within
the working class itself. Recent trends in industrial relations point
in this direction – private pension schemes, medical insurance,
flexible working, less protection for low-paid and part-time staff,
single-company unions, union-organised training, the reluctance of
skilled unions to accept a minimum wage, and so on.

There is security for some, insecurity for others, as a direct result
of the power of money in the market – the differentials required to
enhance market flexibility and productivity.

This division exists between regions, and between areas within
regions, as well as between people. It is more desirable and more
costly in money terms to live in some areas than in others. The
divisions in our cities are symbolised and reinforced by the images
on our television screens. We need the trappings of affluence in
order to survive in the stark and threatening city. In the designer
loft of the converted warehouse, goods and services for sale become

part of a protective cocoon between the consumer and the potential hostility of the rest of society.

Fred Hirsch used the concept of 'positional goods' to point out that 'the paradox of the relative affluence we have achieved is that it is unsatisfying when widely spread . . . if everyone stands on tiptoe no-one sees better.'[24] This may well help to feed our modern obsession with style. Beyond the necessities of life there are 'positional goods' which remain scarce, or which are damaged if they don't, as in the cases of rural or urban environment and access to leadership.

Market capitalism, as with any economic system, presupposes scarcity of goods, and scarcity by definition means not everybody can have it. The modern market economy also presupposes access, aspiration and incentive for all – it posits that all should achieve their maximum as producers in order to find fulfilment as consumers. In doing so it encourages expectations which often cannot be fulfilled or sustained, and division in society is the inevitable outcome. It encourages growth, yet is limited to the finite world.

In theory the post-industrial or post-Fordist model of society, in which freedom is released from structures into the hands of the individual by means of maximisation of consumer choice, is an attractive one. It offers more subsidiarity, more devolved power, than any other system. However, pressures are inevitably created by consumer expectations, access to 'positional goods' and ecological sustainability. These pressures mean that the freedom generated can be transitory and illusory. It melts away as people and groups seek safety and security, relegating others to the periphery and centralising political power in the process. The pressure of reality means that utopian free market ideas inevitably need to be qualified by regulation, just as socialist idealism has found itself superceded by a more realistic assessment of the place of the market economy in society.

4. Christians and Economic Culture

Christians and Social Debate

'The modern mind . . . calls any moral method unpractical, when it has just called any practical method immoral.'[1] The Church's reaction to wider changes in society and economic life always runs up against the accusation of being 'unrealistic' or 'too idealistic'.

Quotations from bishops in the mass media always attract the most attention if they can be labelled as being critical of government. This is accentuated if the government is identified with economic changes which can be said to be disadvantageous to the poor. For example, the Bishop of Shrewsbury points out that '. . . the style of Jesus in making judgements about social order is almost always that a social system, or a religious tradition, must be judged by how well it works for those who have least advantage.'[2]

There is a debate taking place, initiated in the 1980s but still continuing, in which the Church feels rightly it should make its voice heard. On the one hand there is the call for maintenance and improvement of the quality of public services such as health, education and welfare. Against this there is set the argument that the trend towards universal social provision undermines individual choice and responsibility, encourages dependency, discourages initiative, and is economically impractical. Christians are to be found on both sides of this argument, defending public services in the name of the poor and criticising them in the name of individual responsibility.

Similarly, there are those who see the well-being of society in terms of community provision from the arts to the universities, and everything in between. This is set against those who set greater store by wealth creation and the ability of individuals to participate in the community through the medium of their own private property unconditionally under their own control. Here there is an underlying divergence between those who give priority to a communal motivation and those who give priority to an individual motivation. This, too, exists in the Churches where emphases differ from those who stress social involvement and action to those who give much more weight to individual stewardship and responsibility.

24

In parallel with this run differing views of what the Church is and what it should be doing, and these differing views are held both inside and outside the Church. This divergence is at its most striking between those who stress the communion and fellowship of the Church in terms of its universality and its inclusiveness, and those whose emphasis is on personal salvation. The latter tend to take a much more exclusive view of the role of the Church, leading to a more sectarian or gathered view of Christian fellowship.

In turn these varying viewpoints within the Church can be seen against a society where wider views and perceptions of family and community are gradually being superceded by the smaller, tighter, more isolated and more mobile, sealed unit family. Ironically, such perceptions may in themselves lack a degree of reality if the increasing numbers of single-parent and step-family households are taken into account.

Similarly again, in a global context, there is a divergence between a stress on internationalism and a stress on nationalism. Internationalism sits comfortably within a viewpoint which stresses social justice and allows a longer-term ecological angle to influence economic decision making. Nationalism is more in tune with the pursuit of self-interest in a free market, discounting the longer-term to a greater extent; it is a concept readily understood by those who give priority to the role of the individual. It is notable that a resurgence of nationalism in Eastern Europe and the republics of the former Soviet Union has accompanied the free market reforms in those areas.

The multi-faceted pluralism of modern society is perhaps more readily accepted and accommodated by those whose sympathies lie with the communal, the social, the international and the interrelational. Christians, too, are divided amongst those who are ready to assent to pluralism and those who would resist it. Here the pattern becomes much more complex than these few sentences would allow. Suffice it to say that Christians are as divided as anyone else over these issues.

What Christians must face up to is the need to examine the ideology and interrelatedness of the various priorities they espouse in terms of political options, social policy, family life, international questions, consumer decisions, the place of the Church in society, personal stewardship and so on. Reality must be faced, not concealed behind a complicated network of compartments which allow different standards to be applied in considering different aspects of life.

The Gospel of Prosperity

At the extreme fringe of a Christianity which comes down hard on the side of biblical fundamentalism and a very individualistic view of salvation are those who proclaim the 'Gospel of Prosperity'. In this gospel, highly influential in the United States and gaining ground in parts of Africa, wealth is preached as God's will for those he has saved and poverty is the result of personal sin or deficient faith. This is a view of the gospel which is irrational, emotional, indefensible and often fraudulent. Nevertheless, it is a view which historically has often been attractive to the affluent and to those seeking material improvement.

It is not easy to justify the 'Gospel of Prosperity', but it is important to note its existence and to realise how it extends to the extreme and the absurd many of the arguments used by some mainstream Christians. It is a serious warning of the consequences of unquestioning biblical literalism called into the service of self-interest and self-deception.

Its attraction for large numbers of people is unqualified by any challenge to the idea that the acquisitive money aspirations of society are anything other than God's measuring rod of faith. If we think that idea is ridiculous then we owe it to ourselves to note in passing just how open to self-deception human beings can be when money becomes the object, the ends and the criterion. There is a long history of linking prosperity and God's favour, and the 'Gospel of Prosperity' is simply a striking contemporary manifestation of a danger which is real for all of us.

Christian Ethics and the Free Market

Christian social thought has always questioned the legitimacy of the free market. 'Competition.' wrote F. D. Maurice, 'is set forth as the law of the universe. That is a lie.' The suspicion that the market is an idol is implicit or, at times, explicit. 'Society is not to be made anew by arrangements of ours, but is to be regenerated by finding the law and ground of its order and harmony, the only secret of its existence, in God.'[3]

Tawney reflected upon the relationship between puritanism and economic conduct: 'What is significant is the change of standards which converted a natural frailty into a resounding virtue.'[4] Nevertheless he could not be reconciled to it: 'But the question, to what end the wheels revolve, still remains.'[5] So it is that for many Christians the verdict on the free market has to be that it is inimical to the teachings of Jesus because it encourages greed and results in social injustice.

Ulrich Duchrow[6] criticises the free market as being a product of our scientific world-view and as such a 'mechanistic distortion of reality' which leads to an increasing neglect of people's real needs. He sees the economic theories which support the free market as ignoring questions of power, domination, justice and the social effects of individual decisions, together with the cultural, social and political context within which the market operates. The market responds to the possession of wealth, to purchasing power, not to human need. Consequently, the material consumption aspect of human needs is made absolute and is infiltrated by the profit motive via the powerful medium of advertising. 'The behaviour which follows from this is a constant "desire for more" on the part of some and a failure to meet the basic needs of others, and this is . . . the inevitable result of the system itself.'[7]

However, it is not the free market itself which Duchrow criticises so much as its absolutization, which destroys its capacity to be 'an instrument in the service of humanity' and 'a place of exchange where human needs are met in accordance with rules of comparable benefit.'

What to Duchrow appears as the absolutization of the market appears to Christians of the New Right to be an acceptance of its impersonality, allowing full scope for individual freedom and thus offering the most effective mechanism for distributing scarce resources. In this pattern of thought economic decisions made by consumers are preferred to, and considered to be more moral than, democratic decisions made by voters, which are felt to be open to irresponsibility. People make decisions more responsibly, it is thought, if they have to pay for the outcome.

The tendency of the free market is therefore to trust people as consumers, rather than as voters. Accountability is due to those who pay, rather than to those who participate, in society. Many Christians are critical of this tendency because of the special place given to the poor in the Bible and in much of the Christian tradition. The poor are by definition those least able to claim accountability and take responsibility by being able to pay for things, but it is difficult to avoid the conclusion that for Christians accountability is owed to the poor, who are said to personify Christ in the lives of his followers.

Brian Griffiths does not concur with the tendency to defend the free market along libertarian lines. Instead, he restates the importance and biblical basis of puritan and family values and claims that the free market is the best environment known to our experience in which such values can thrive.[8] Luxury is distinguished from prosperity, and discerning the difference is the responsibility of the individual. Materialism is deplored along with covetousness and the idolatry of wealth, but the battle against these things is a private one. The relief and elimination of poverty is a Christian concern, but the pursuit of equality is spurious and counter-productive because it hinders the creation of wealth.

Griffiths deplores determinism and rejects any 'attempt to present economic life as something which is impersonal, amoral, which can be expressed as a "system" and which, as a system, has a natural tendency to equilibrium'.[9] This relegates God either to a deist non-participant or to nowhere at all and is unacceptable to trinitarian, personal faith. The market must be a means, not an end, and must be rescued from secular capitalist ideology.

The case for the free market can be overstated and thus become open to the charge that it is Pelagian – a practical expression of the belief that human beings are able to attain their own salvation, separate from the grace of God. Brian Griffiths rigorously avoids this dangerous ground, but in his proper emphasis on individual responsibility and stewardship he allows some corporate arguments and rejects others. Broadly, the communal, with the *exception* of the Church, is regarded as a source of idolatry and corruption and as such as a threat to the salvation of the individual.

It is possible to acknowledge the usefulness of the market as a method for the distribution of goods whilst calling to attention its limitations and disadvantages. J. P. Wogaman points to the tendency for 'the best stewardship of our own personal resources' to become the *only* moral question, rather than *an* important one, and that in practice social planning has to be used to dilute the consequent bad effects such as poverty, low pay and environmental pollution.[10] Free market economic efficiency can be social inefficiency. Unrestrained market forces can have devastating effects as they exploit the natural resources of the world.

In environmental questions the limitations of the free market and its tendency to overvalue the short-term are very apparent. 'It is very difficult for the market mechanism to provide a rational way for consumers to indicate their preferences about the overall state of the environment when it is in competition with jobs and consumer goods.'[11] However, it is possible for the market to be used as a tool of regulation by grading goods for VAT, or something similar, according to their social or ecological effects. Rigorous free-marketeers would deplore this fiscal interference, but reality may soon require it.

The self-interest of competition and the profit motive in the free market is often criticised by Christians. However, it is quite possible for self-interest to be a proper expression of the self-worth and self-love which is quite compatible with, indeed necessary to, Christianity. An affirmed sense of self is needed for us to relate to others and to give and receive in our relationships with others.

Nevertheless, whilst acknowledging a proper self-interest of one's self and family, it must be pointed out that there is a boundary between this and selfishness. Free market apologists pay insufficient attention to this boundary.

They consequently give too little regard to the need for regulation to control those aspects of the market which operate contrary to the common good.[12]

Underlying much of this debate is a dualism which Tawney traces back to Luther: 'He preaches a selfless charity, but he recoils with horror from every institution by which an attempt had been made to give it concrete expression . . . God speaks to the soul, not through the mediation of the priesthood or of social institutions built up by man, but *solus cum solo*, as a voice in the heart and in the heart alone. Thus the bridges between the worlds of spirit and of sense are broken . . .' The soul is separated from human community, 'that it may enter into communion with its maker.'[13] The modern stress on the free market as a value system leaves the job of putting the soul in the community still to be done.

Christian Ethics and Private Property

Rights to private property are a cornerstone of the free market. They are defended in the puritan tradition by reference to the decalogue, stewardship of God-given resources and the importance of inheritance to family life. Historically, however, other Christians have been much more equivocal, particularly pointing to the prophetic tradition in the Old Testament and to the teaching of Jesus himself, both of which include a strong critique of wealth.

Gore and Scott Holland distinguished between 'property for use', a limited amount sufficient to maintain true freedom, and 'property for power', which is accumulated and used to dominate others.[14] In the same symposium A. J. Carlyle noted that the views of the Fathers and the Schoolmen were 'opposite to that of Locke, that private property is an institution of natural law, and arises out of labour. Private property is allowed, but only in order to avoid the danger of violence and confusion.' 'Private property is the result of avarice, but also a restraint upon it.'[15] It cannot override the natural right of people to obtain their needs from the earth's abundance or God's provision.

Gore discerned a strong communal claim overriding private property in the Christian tradition. He felt that this had been obscured in Protestantism by an excessive individualism. He therefore, on grounds of justice and equity, rejected the modern defence of private property.[16] The Roman Catholic Church tends to the same position: '. . . the right to private property is subordinate to the right to common use, to the fact that goods are meant for everyone . . .'[17] Private property is recognised as a means of protecting and defending the person, but there are important qualifications of justice, which are also there to defend the person.

Further limitations on the rights of private property must be set by its effect on character, as well its social effects.[18] Although property rights act as an encouragement to initiative, originality and invention, realism forces us to acknowledge that they bestow power at the same time. Although a democratic society can act to limit the abuse of such power it will often find itself hampered by vested interest. In the modern situation, where the poor are a numerous minority, traditional democracy may not have the resources to resist the exploitation of power by an affluent majority, or to establish the claims of need over and against those of property. More participatory structures may thus be necessary to nurture the common good and to enhance the expression of the Christian view that we hold property only as a result of God's grace.

However, the puritan theologian Baxter refuted the tradition of qualification of property rights as set out by Aquinas and others: '. . . in ordinary cases, the saving of a man's life will not do so much

good, as his stealing will do hurt.'[19] This defence of the decalogue
was based on a differing view of the common good.

For many reformers the tradition of voluntary poverty had been
discredited by their experience of the mendicant orders. The
concept was therefore replaced by a new emphasis on each person's
work, vocation, stewardship and responsibility – much of this being
symbolised by property. This is still a qualified view of property,
but there is a new set of boundaries for it which can only be built
within the individual soul.

The debate continues, often using a functional approach. For
example, Schumacher drew a distinction between property that is
an aid to creative work and property that is an alternative to it[20]. In
emphasizing the importance of private property rights for the
industrial revolution, Brian Griffiths relies on the function of these
rights to ensure that 'reward was related to effort' and that consequently people would be prepared to take risks[21]. For Griffiths the
common good is served by the creation of wealth thus brought
about.

Tawney sees individual property rights, beyond what is required
for necessities, as being diametrically opposed to social function
because of susceptibility to greed and covetousness. They have a
function but it is anti-social and divisive because it nurtures and
encourages such motivations.[22]

The free market is highly developed in the United States and
there are some there who would prefer to speak of a 'theology of
ownership' rather than retain the concept of stewardship[23]. For
many this will be suspect as a capitulation to the prevailing culture,
but it does raise the question of whether our theology of stewardship
has not in fact become one of ownership anyway.

Perhaps what passes for Christian stewardship is simply ownership under a more acceptable or pious name. The name may be less
open to charges of Pelagianism, of placing our own responsibility
higher than God's grace. It may be less likely to be criticised as a
form of deism, of taking complete charge of a product which God
made some time ago but in which he has little further interest. In
defining the term 'steward' Johnson's Dictionary includes a quo-
tation from Swift: 'When a steward defrauds his lord, he must
connive at the rest of the servants while they are following the same
practice.'[24] To what extent does every Christian, in practice and in
common with others in our society, substitute an as yet undefined
and unacknowledged theology of ownership for true stewardship?

Christian Ethics and Economic Individualism

The free market, together with the supporting legal protection of
rights to private property and emphasis on economic competition,
has often been accused by Christians of being excessively individualistic in its influence on human affairs. Others assert that these
rights are necessary for people to be able to exercise full responsibility over their own lives and thus to express as fully as possible
their humanity.

The virtues of individualism in the economic sphere are those of
'standing on your own feet', being independent and so developing a
sense of responsibility and self-worth. These were originally con-
ceived in the eighteenth century as an attack upon aristocratic
privilege, and as such share a common heritage with such things as
economic innovation, intellectual enquiry, scientific discovery, religious dissent (moving towards toleration) and the development of
democratic institutions.

Much of this is positive, but an overemphasis on the virtues of
individualism tends to stress what the individual can do for society
whilst undervaluing what society can do for the individual.

Professor C. B. Macpherson[25] has indicated that there are some
important assumptions which underlie the individualistic world-
view. Freedom from dependence on the wills of others is necessary
in order to be fully human, as is freedom to choose those other
people to whom we wish to relate. Individuals are their own
proprietors, they owe nothing to society and their relationship with
society is defined in terms of a series of market relations. Individual
freedom should only be limited so as to ensure such freedom for
others, consequently the political sphere should not extend beyond
the regulation of property and market transactions. Again, this
contains important elements of truth, but it tends towards a denial
of the relationship between person and community and a failure to
recognise that every person is on the receiving end of a lot of
givenness in terms of family, heritage, infrastructure, education and
so on.

Christians will always need to emphasize the importance of grace
in order to avoid the pitfalls of Pelagianism. They will see the work
of the creator God in so many things which 'are prior to human
decision'[26], and will want to see their own actions and decisions in
terms of response to grace rather than in terms of freedom from

dependence. There is a lot of difference between freedom from and freedom to.

Economic individualism, in particular as expressed in the sanctity of private property, developed out of the human quest for justice – a compensatory justice enabling the benefit to accrue to the person doing the beneficial work of economic exploitation. This was never adequate in Christian terms: 'When grace is considered to be prior to works, it is what we *are* that matters most, not what we *do*.'[27] All people created by God are by definition of infinite importance. In any case, the experience of two centuries has brought a greater awareness of the tendency for property to be accumulated and economic individual success to accrue often irrespective of virtue or hard work. It is now much harder to justify economic individualism on grounds of justice.

Individualism, therefore, has some important insights but it will always require considerable qualification. The whole thrust of consumerism is highly individualistic, and yet consumers' associations have been quick to develop their case for safeguards, limitations and regulations. 'The Consumer' becomes, more than an individual, a collective noun, a role with which many can identify.

In practice, the cliché 'duties go with rights' is quickly revealed to be a truism. The most libertarian of market forces politicians are often the keenest to use this highly communitarian slogan, and thus to give the 'divine hand' a bit of assistance. They are effectively acknowledging that the market does in fact have a context and does in fact depend upon values inherent to the context and not to the market itself. This is not a new insight; Adam Smith similarly acknowledged that people 'could safely be trusted to pursue their own self-interest without undue harm to the community, not only because of the restrictions imposed by the law *but also because they were subject to built-in restraint derived from morals, custom and education.*'[28]

It is therefore dangerous for Christians to wander without qualification too far down the avenue of individualism. Reinhold Niebuhr,[29] pointed out the important distinction between individual responsibility and the behaviour of groups and collectives. The heavy gravitational pull of every type of group interest means that there will always be a need to reform and make more human the structures and institutions of society. There must always be a Christian call to look beyond narrow interest.

Morality cannot be left at the individual level, where issues can be much simpler. Instead, both personal and communal aspects of morality should be tackled, due notice being taken of the need to make vital connections between the two. Pure, isolated, individualism is alien to human personality. True and fulfilling personhood is bound up in relationship, with God, with the world and with others.

Christian Ethics and the Poor and Marginalised

Money tends to accumulate in the same place, and, along with it, power and influence. Ronald Preston puts it well: 'Those who have wealth . . . have a great pull on the market because they can bid more for luxuries than the poor can for necessities, as well as commanding the best attention in the basics of living – food, clothes, houses – and in personal services in education and medicine. Also the possession of capital tends to lead to the accumulation of more in a cumulative way . . .'[30]

Christianity finds this difficult to take, and the case for 'trickle-down', from the successful and wealthy to the aspiring and poor, not proven. The insights of liberation theologians may not be directly transferable to western society, but nevertheless the 'option for the poor' is but one example of the universal question mark Jesus set beside riches. It is a commonly held view in the Judeo-Christian tradition, right up to the present day, that the accumulation of wealth is to a large extent responsible for poverty and injustice. What is not commonly held is any view of what should be done about it.

H. G. Wood noted that '. . . the capitalist class was largely created by men who branded all careless consumption as a sin.'[31] To say that the righteous were careful with worldly goods, and therefore not poor, is perhaps to caricature puritanism at its best, but contains some truth.

Later the demand for asceticism on the part of the rich was developed, for example by William Law and John Wesley. Christians must themselves practise the same level of self-denial they expect from the deserving poor. Nevertheless, there is no explicit statement of any accountability *to* the poor.

Much of the justification for market economics lies in the capacity to create wealth and to allow people to live fuller lives. But the question of distribution of wealth is immediately raised because free operation of the market also produces growing inequalities. Many people simply do not have the capacity to participate at all, let alone fully, and Christians cannot reconcile this with their view of God's purpose for humanity in creation. They are challenged to the limit by both physical poverty, with its enormous worldwide toll of human suffering, and relational poverty, which divides and estranges people from each other and introduces fear into the life of society.

The evils of relational poverty often cause Christians to call an early halt to the widening of income differentials as an instrument of economic policy designed to increase economic efficiency. The price paid for material progress, in terms of loss of humanity in which the poor suffer and the rich are estranged, is too great. Jesus' self-identification with the poor always pushes the Church towards a different order of priority from the society in which it is set, but does not seem to produce any widespread agreement among his followers about where lines should be drawn.

Eschatology and Ethics

'If any man be so addicted to his private, that he neglect the common, state, he is void of the sense of piety and wisheth peace and happiness to himself in vain. For, whoever he be, he must live in the body of the Commonwealth and in the body of the Church.'[32]

Views of Christian social ethics are often underlaid by eschatology, whether it is explicitly stated or merely implied. What is meant by the kingdom of God, and how does it relate to this world and the next, the Church and the powers and dominations? Where is the kingdom, and how and when do we get there? The pitfalls of this area are such that John Atherton posits the use of key intermediary concepts, in particular the corporate images of the Body of Christ and the common good[33].

Ronald Preston criticises liberation theologians such as Gustavo Gutierrez for their use of the saga of the exodus to point to 'a unity between the social-political and the redemptive dimensions of life which was fulfilled and deepened in Christ'[34]. He believes that this ignores the difference between the Old and New Testaments – in the Old there is one kingdom 'which is both Church and state', in the New there are two kingdoms. 'In the kingdom of God the messianic role has been accomplished in the ministry of Jesus. It is quite illegitimate to transfer it to various movements in the kingdom(s) of the world.' This view stands on the same ground as Augustine's two cities and Luther's two realms: 'There are two kingdoms in which Christians live at the same time'[35] – the kingdom of God and the world and its structures.

The warning to beware of undue identification of the kingdom of God and messianic expectation with any particular political or historical movement is well given. But there is a counter-warning from Gutierrez which must also be affirmed: '. . . there is an assumption which should be brought to the surface, namely a certain idea of the spiritual characterized by a kind of Western dualistic thought (matter-spirit), foreign to the biblical mentality . . . This is a disincarnate "spiritual", scornfully superior to all earthly realities.'[36]

Preston is clear that the deuteronomic view, where good nations are rewarded for honouring God and doing his will, lost credibility after the return from exile, which failed to live up to expectations. The apocalyptic strand of biblical thought developed out of this disillusionment, this despair of the world as it is. In the New Testament an apocalyptic 'spiritualizing influence'[37] is common. It is therefore difficult to establish any agreed Christian basis for eschatological fulfilment in this world. Liberation theologians react to this by reaching back beyond the deuteronomic period to the exodus to find an interpretative model.

From an entirely different viewpoint, Brian Griffiths takes this apocalyptic aspect of the New Testament to emphasize the spiritual nature of the teaching of Jesus. He, too, reaches back into the Old Testament for a justification of his position, looking primarily to the law. In doing so he perhaps fails adequately to recognize that it is incomplete to take into account the law without the prophets. Similarly, it is impossible to do justice to the proclamation of Jesus without an eschatology which is *both* present and future. However he does acknowledge, at least in the area of personal obedience, that judgement can be present as well as future inasmuch as accountability is an integral part of economic life, arising from freedom and responsibility[38].

For Griffiths humanity's declaration of autonomy from God in the Fall introduces covetousness and causes work to become toil[39]. The end of history forms a symmetry with its beginning, it is 'a process which will end with the reign of Christ and the establishment of a just society'[40]. In the meantime '. . . those who are members of the Kingdom have a responsibility to live by its laws.'[41] The kingdom is rooted in the supernatural and is spiritual in nature, and therefore contrasts with the kingdoms of this world. 'It is made up of new people with new motives and is brought about by the mysterious influence of the Holy Spirit.'[42] Its 'present manifestation' is the Church. Griffiths here refers to Augustine's two cities, the *civitas dei* and the *civitas terrara*. 'To attempt to translate the principles of the one in terms of institutions for the other is to court disaster.'

There is here a rightly sceptical view of the possibility of attaining an earthly kingdom of God through any existing political programme. However, this seems to tip over into a dualism which is not sceptical enough of the Church's efforts to date to manifest the kingdom of God. The concept of Christendom has been undermined by experience and is no longer viable, whether to be brought about by political action or religious conversion.

The kingdom of God cannot be identified with the world *or* the Church. To banish it to the hereafter contradicts the Lord's Prayer. We cannot ignore the kingdom, but we cannot find it either. Attempts to grapple with, or avoid, this conundrum underlie all Christian social ethics.

Perhaps the signs point to a need for Christians to develop an eschatology which takes three kingdoms into account – the kingdoms of God, of the created order, *and* of the Church. These are three kingdoms which should be in constant interplay and creative tension – a trinity of experience in the lives of Christ's followers. Christianity should be more at ease with a triune model than with a dual one.

The kingdom of God is like a mustard seed, Jesus said. But no seed grows in a vacuum, it must be planted in the earth, in the reality of the world. The Church, in its role as servant of both the kingdom of God and of the world, must nurture the seed. The Church must be the manure. The seed cannot be seen if it is possible for it to grow, for then it is hidden in the ground, and to grow it needs both earth and manure, both world and Church. I shall develop this thought further in later chapters.

5. Debt and Credit

In this and the next two chapters I shall examine in some detail three examples – debt and credit, property and home ownership, charitable giving – of the sort of economic change with which we are having to come to terms. These are changes which show that the role of money is evolving in ways which, if anything, add to its significance and influence. In them we see money present in new forms made possible by communications technology and we see it acting as an increasingly important agency for individual expression. We also see the role of money as it represents relationships within society, with many decisions of day-to-day life conforming more and more to a consumer pattern.

Changing attitudes to Debt

In recent years a credit based way of life has increasingly replaced traditional housekeeping methods for many people. We all bewail the effect that this change has had on the amount of unsolicited mail that comes through our letterboxes, but this mail would not be increasing in quantity if it was ineffective. The long-accepted virtues of household budgeting have been replaced by the wary eye looking over the shoulder at the credit limits obtained from a variety of sources.

Some years ago the Access card was promoted with the claim that it took the 'waiting out of wanting'. The traditional theory is that money is a convenient and transportable modern equivalent of barter, a practical consequence of the division of labour. But credit cards are obscuring the clarity of exchange of value in people's lives. They are taking expenditure a step away from income, what I can buy a knight's move away from what I can afford. Consumption no longer needs to be forgone in order to save or invest – borrowing fills the gap and as it does so reduces the incentive to think beyond the present.

The plastic card has become yet another guide to social status within the complexities of our class system. It is a statement of worth as well as a convenient substitute for cash, dispensing prestige along with purchasing power. For example, the American Express company offers its charge card with advertising which stresses kudos over and above practical advantage. Several companies offer a gold card which provides both more credit and more status.

The traditional values upon which capitalism was based, such as saving and thrift, have undergone an important change. Debt, formerly a source of worry or even shame, has been replaced by credit, which has an altogether more positive set of connotations attached to it. In popular credit card advertising cost and waiting are banished. Credit-worthiness becomes a statement of value, supplanting savings as an expression of values.

There are some interesting comparisons and contrasts to be made here between the lives of nations and the lives of persons. In the early eighties the British Government extolled the virtues of monetarism and proclaimed that its policy would be to eliminate the Public Sector Borrowing Requirement, to run its affairs along the lines of the sort of household budget of which Mr Micawber would have approved. The watchwords were to be realism, efficiency and cost-effectiveness, and the aim was a leaner, fitter, deregulated economy more in tune with the times.

Perhaps, however, economic freedom and possessive individualism have created a new set of expectations and dependencies which are superseding the Butskellite and Welfare State dependencies now out of favour. Realism dictates that these things have to be paid for, too. Even if there is no public debt, the government owing money to the people, there is private debt, resulting in both personal and national balance of payments problems. And for both our personal and national problems the answer tends to be the same, 'The underlying situation is strong.' Our credit-worthiness is sound. Perhaps Keynes was never banished, even in the best of times, but merely privatised.

Whatever the state of the national exchequer, personal borrowing has continued to grow, multiplying by three times during the 1980s, and because it continues to grow the questions remain. These are the questions of sustainability and stewardship which have been the rationale for saying to the public sector 'there is no alternative' to pay as you go.

These questions remain both nationally and personally, starkly posited by the recession of the early 1990s. What does debt say to the steward, at every level from the personal to the international? Is accumulation built on debt morally, ecologically or economically sustainable? Is the underlying situation strong? or hollow? Is our dependence on credit a modern myth, a complete fantasy or a new reality?

Some facts about Debt and Credit

People's lives have changed dramatically. Increased household debt has moved from below 40% of disposable household income in 1979 to above 90% in 1989[1]. This has meant greater property ownership and, along with it, greater vulnerability to changes in circumstances. A large proportion, about four-fifths, of household borrowing is mortgaged, mainly for house purchase, and the remainder is for consumer goods and services[2]. Around two-thirds of people purchase their most basic commodity, housing, through credit in the form of a mortgage and about one third of all consumer items are purchased on credit. The post-war baby boom generation is more numerous, more inclined to spend and less inclined to save than any of its predecessors.

The benefits of this are often overlooked. People are able to obtain goods and services which would otherwise be out of their reach, and this is something of which we are all more willing to be critical than to stop doing ourselves. This feature has been fuelled by liberalisation of institutional lending, enabling people to borrow as much as they had previously wanted to but were constrained from by the austerity of their bank manager. Institutions now compete to lend to people who would have been unable to borrow such amounts previously.

Nevertheless, this overall pattern leaves many people vulnerable to serious debt problems arising out of over-commitment, changes in circumstances, particularly unemployment, and poverty itself. Often these elements build up into a vicious circle which leads people to seek loans from less and less reputable sources at more and more inflated rates of interest. The introduction of the Social Fund into the social security system institutionalised and affirmed personal borrowing in the lives of the poor. Similarly, student loans introduced credit at the very start of many people's adult lives.

The consequences for society as all these factors accumulate are of personal hardship and distress, leading to withdrawal, depression or even suicide, family breakdown and dislocation, and yet more poverty. Since 1979 the number of house repossessions has dramatically increased – 75,000 took place in 1991 and the government and building societies were forced to take action in the face of even higher, six-figure, predictions for 1992. Researchers with the National Consumer Council estimated in early 1992 that 'there may be as many as 600,000 people in multiple debt, defined as having three or more bad debts.'[3]

Many people are ignorant of the relevant costs of different types of credit and unable to make realistic comparisons between different types of loan charges. Few people know the meaning of the term APR (Annual Percentage Rate). It is the common experience of those who deal with offering credit at the point of sale of consumer goods that purchasers are primarily interested in the level of periodic repayment, rather than overall cost, length of repayment period or amount of interest. In other words, short term factors tend to predominate.

The National Association of Citizens Advice Bureaux estimated that half a million people approached CABx with debt problems in the year ended 31st March 1988. So, even during the boom years of the late 1980s, difficulties were increasing at an alarming rate: 'A few years ago, debt problems tended to concentrate in inner city areas . . . Now, CABx in all parts of the country, including relatively affluent districts, are having to cope with debt.'[4] Bureaux in prosperous market towns in East Anglia were not immune from the need to acquire a specially trained debt counsellor, well before the dramatic deterioration into the subsequent recession. Serious debt problems may be a feature of deregulated market economies, even when things are going well.

In today's world debt is not simply a result of bad money management. Debt arises if you are poor and you need to buy essentials for your children. It arises if you have a change of circumstances – illness, marriage breakdown, bereavement, unemployment. It arises if your small business fails due to circumstances beyond your control. It arises out of irresponsible lending which leads the vulnerable into over-commitment. An upward change in interest rates leaves many people in great difficulty, especially if it follows hard on the heels of a period of rapidly rising house prices.

A case history – Usury, Interest and Debt

The payment of interest in Roman times was made as compensation in the case of a late repayment of a loan. This concept has evolved to take recognition of the fact that a sum of money available for use now is worth more than that same sum of money at some time in the future. The value is lowered by passage of time due to additional risk of non-payment together with the lengthening period for which use of the money is forgone. Obviously, inflation is also a factor.

However, the term usury originally meant payment for the use of money, something close to the modern concept of interest. As interest payments achieved legal recognition, so usury came to refer to excessive or extortionate rates of interest. The Church had great difficulty in adapting its theoretical condemnation of usury to the realities of payments of interest as they developed with the rise of capitalism. In the Old Testament lending had been enouraged as a means of assisting the poor, and charging of interest forbidden for the same reason – acknowledging that a lender is someone who has, and a borrower is someone who needs. Christ's teaching did not obviously suggest a relaxation of this principle.

Consequently, usury is a recurrent theme throughout Tawney's 'Religion and the Rise of Capitalism'. Although the highly organised and administratively complex Papacy of the Middle Ages could not do without the services of usurers, it nevertheless maintained a posture of denouncing them[5]. The object of the Church's teaching remained that of protecting the weak from the powerful. This did not come to any abrupt halt with the reformation, and indeed Luther characteristically criticised the status quo for any practical relaxations it made. He wanted a return to orthodox rigour.

It was Calvinism that began to formulate an ethic which took seriously an economic setting more sophisticated than mere subsistence. Calvin was the first to treat the ethics of money-lending 'not as a matter to be decided by an appeal to a special body of doctrine on the subject of usury, but as a particular case of the general problem of the social relations of a Christian community, which must be solved in the light of existing circumstances.'[6]

Interest, although given highly qualified sanction, became an expression of normality and ceased to be an exceptional circumstance requiring its own justification. Ethical attention turned to the individual conscience, people making decisions about rates of interest along with capital, credit and finance. 'Calvinism and its offshoots took their stand on the side of the activities which were to be most characteristic of the future, and insisted that it was not by renouncing them, but by untiring concentration on the task of using for the glory of God the opportunities which they offered, that the Christian life could and must be lived.'[7]

In sixteenth century England the Church, defending communities of peasants and artisans against powerful money-lenders, maintained its opposition to usury, now becoming an all-purpose term for covetousness. Arguments from the Bible, the fathers and the schoolmen were marshalled, but were at the same time being overtaken by social and economic change. The Church's posture was undermined by events, the advent of mass impersonal transactions to which old formulations of personal conduct were ill-suited, and by the movement of lay opinion towards the idea that economics are one thing and Christian ethics quite another.[8] The Church failed to meet this challenge of new circumstances, with the inevitable although undesired result of an effective denial of the practical, societal significance of its 'spiritual', personal, ethical standpoint.

The puritan Richard Baxter was the exception. In his 'Christian Directory' Baxter stood against the new dualism and for the moral responsibility of each person: 'It is not lawful to take up or keep up any oppressing monopoly or trade, which tends to enrich you by the loss of the Commonwealth or of many.' The avoidance of sin must be given priority in every sphere of life.

However, the puritan quest for a Christian code of economic conduct was overwhelmed by the puritan virtues of enterprise and thift. The emphasis on personal self-denial and conduct led inexorably towards the point where 'a halo of ethical satisfaction' was added to 'the appeal of economic expediency'.[9] Poverty lost all merit, became almost a judgement. The poor became the problem, and the arguments against usury and interest, based on protecting the poor, were lost.

Nowadays, the Church accepts the reality of an economic system of which interest is an intrinsic part. Nevertheless, questions are raised, especially at a time when many people suffer greatly through problems related to debt and credit. A recent Grove Ethical Study devotes its second chapter to the role of the rate of interest, and on biblical grounds considers valid only some of the contemporary justifications for charging interest.[10]

The problem here is that the biblical formulations were made in a very different economic climate from our own. Even a very cautious transcription of biblical principles into present realities rapidly produces codes for action which leave Christians working in financial institutions isolated from Christian ethics. As a consequence, dualism once more becomes an attractive option for day-to-day living, with no apparent alternative other than the total asceticism of the desert.

Christian ethics must always be challenged and tested in the light of the Bible and established tradition. They must not cower before the massed ranks of contemporary culture. However, neither can they search after purity at the expense of practical application. If this happens, they cease to be ethics at all by becoming theory separated from the reality of our behaviour.

Implications of Debt and Credit

The modern conundrum is that debt enslaves and credit enables – and yet they are both the same thing. It only takes a small move in interest rates or some other financial circumstance for one polarity to turn into the other.

There is a temptation to oversimplify: 'The Bible cuts through this haze of obfuscation by stating that "the borrower is servant to the lender" (Prov 22:7). That is, any debt places the borrower in effective financial slavery . . .'[11] This may well have an important element of truth in it, but it is one which must be held in balance with the fact that the majority of the population of Britain are housed by means of a mortgage loan. It does not seem enough to say: 'For us, borrowing may be necessary for essentials at times, but we need to retain an uneasiness about being under obligation to someone outside the Church or our family and should be willing to repay at the earliest opportnity.'[12] The fact is that personal credit is now intrinsically part of a very complex economy. As such it cannot readily be separated out from the processes whereby ordinary people are able to obtain the goods and services they require in order to live their lives.

It is very easy for Christians to adopt a patronising tone which oozes middle-class virtue when they try to address the social problem of debt. 'People just aren't responsible enough to borrow on the level they do' is easy enough to say if you are already well equipped with the paraphernalia of a consumer society. The huge increase in the range and availability of loans on offer has led to a backlash and Christians are in the forefront of those who ask for increased regulation and control. If such controls are to dignify and not to discriminate against the already disadvantaged, or those lower down the ladder of acquisition, they cannot easily be introduced in isolation from other measures.

With this proviso, consideration could be given to the introduction of some form of maximum interest rate and/or minimum deposit. However, it might be more helpful to look towards, for example, such things as longer cooling-off periods enabling people to change their minds after entering into a credit agreement, education and high-profile publicity about credit and interest, clearer forms for people to sign and the availability of independent third parties to explain credit agreements. It is important that learning about debt is not left until homes have been repossessed and families subjected to intolerable suffering.

Similarly, on the international level, reforms are needed which relieve the burden whilst enabling trade and investment to grow. This may require routes of action, perhaps analogous to personal bankruptcy, which allow unpayable debt to be written off and a new start made, without abandoning proper financial disciplines.

In the Judeo-Christian tradition the relationship between borrower and lender should ideally be one of mutual relationship, emphasizing mutual obligation, rather than one of buyer and seller of a financial product. In fact, in most cases a financial institution will act as agent or intermediary for the lender, and this makes it difficult for the personal to prevail over the bureaucratic. It also conceals the fact that behind the panoply of the financial services industry the better-off are lending to the less well-off, the tendency of this being towards increasing divisions in the distribution of wealth. In these circumstances the use of credit unions could be encouraged so that saving and lending can both take place based in the local neighbourhood.

The area of credit and financial services is changing as rapidly as the rest of our society, if not more so. In a decade the market has opened up enormously, much more is available for people, but there are more risks and pitfalls, too. The whole question of the advertising and promotion of credit and the effect of such publicity on the expectations and aims of people in society is very problematic. Banks use both gifts and donations to charity in order to encourage people to use their cheque or credit card.

All this is part of the wider post-industrial trend to give greater emphasis to the consumer and to make the point of consumption the key point of decision in economic life. The Church is bound to be uneasy about the concomitant idolatory of money and vulnerability of the poor, but it will do no-one any good by rending its clothes and wailing: 'Let it not be so!' That way lies just another chance to capitulate to dualism. Instead the Church must learn to relate to economic institutions and structures. The alternative is an existence on the margins of people's real lives.

At every level, personal, corporate, national, international, the question of debt is one of vital importance in people's lives, and particularly in the lives of the poor. It cannot be ignored.

6. Property and Home Ownership

The property owning democracy

As part of the pattern of post-war material progress, the 1960s and 1970s saw Britain become self-aware as a nation of home owners. The council house sales of the 1980s further established this trend, the policy being both in tune with people's aspirations and formative of them.

In our rapidly changing society the requirements of both security and participation tend to pull towards property ownership. The last two decades of the century are therefore seeing more and more people become owners of all sorts of financial assets, including direct or indirect share ownership, as well as owners of their home and its contents. It is from this viewpoint that increasing numbers of people decide how they will organise their lives, and how they will vote.

Most people are now involved in the accumulation of capital assets in houses, life assurance policies, pension plans, unit trusts, investment trusts, building societies and bank deposits, quite apart from extensions in direct share ownership. Financial institutions compete to supply all these requirements from a myriad of premises in every high street – Britain actually looks different because of these changes.

Three important factors are fuelling this major movement in our society. Firstly, the majority of people are getting richer, up to half as rich again as they were at the end of the 1970s, depending on where they live in the country. Although much of this increase has been spent on consumption, some has gone into investing for the future in the form of a bigger mortgage or a bigger pension.

Secondly, we are beginning to see the important effect of property being moved from one generation to the next. Houses purchased thirty or forty years ago are being left to children who are already well advanced with the purchase of their own house, thus creating realisable capital funds for long-term investment or assisting grand-children in the purchase of a home. This process will become more and more important as time passes.

Thirdly, the property owning democracy feeds on itself by awarding itself key incentives, such as tax relief on mortgages and pensions, or the privatisation of nationalised industries and utilities. Pressures of economic expectations within the property owning democracy make it difficult for any political party to consider, for example, the reduction of mortgage tax relief, however great the evidence that it is regressive or that it has a distorting effect on a housing market already subject to exaggerated peaks and troughs.

Underlying the surface changes is the culture of the property owning democracy. For the vast majority of the population this means a vested interest in stability. There is an increased primacy of quantifiable financial criteria over other values. Some would say this had led to an increase in appetite and greed for acquisition and possession. Such a judgement is bound to be subjective, but throughout history it has been observed that wealthy people are often greedy people.

As property ownership spreads, so do the characteristics and preferences usually associated with the middle class. This has been called the 'bourgeoisification' of the working class – an expressive term if an ugly one. More and more people derive material proportions of their income from investments. This increases their sense of participation in society as it is and their willingness to conform to the *status quo*.

Home ownership

The foundations of the increase in property ownership lie in our emphasis on the desirability of owning our own homes. We give priority to home ownership as an expression of success, of 'getting on in life'. This emphasis is embedded deep in our attitudes and expressed in an advertising imagery of country cottages and leafy garden suburbs. The enormous popularity of council house sales shows that the desire to own one's home exists in all social classes. It is generally accepted as one of the first steps on the road to security and participation, even though this desire can lead to over-commitment.

Council house sales have simply accelerated and given expression to a movement which was already taking place, fed by a growing, if inaccurate, mythology about the inefficiency of public sector rented housing.[1] British working class life will never again conform to its previous stereotypes.

The proportion of owner occupation is now approaching two-thirds. The attraction of home ownership is likely to further increase as rents rise following derestriction and if the ability of local authorities and housing associations to offer subsidised rented accommodation is not dramatically enhanced. The logic of the free market is applied to the rented sector at the same time as the logic of self-help and electoral advantage is applied to mortgage tax relief.

The trends of post-industrialism are in tune with home ownership. The emphasis on housebuilding in the 1950s, in other words on production, has been replaced. The emphasis is now on consumption, on owning your own home – in spite of the problems of debt or homelessness. Increased home ownership and mortgage related debt has emphasized the importance of the housing market to the whole economy. Banks and building societies are involved in nationwide estate agency networks. Do-it-yourself has its own hypermarkets where vast consumer choice can be arrayed before the weekend home improver. Garden centres proliferate. The home is at the centre of a huge proportion of the economy, involving property, money and leisure, and plays an increasing part in people's personal aspirations.

There are signs that the prevailing pattern of separated compartments of home and work is beginning to change. The movement from an agricultural to an industrial society took people from the farm and the village to the factory and the town and later to the office and the suburb. Now the movement to a post-industrial society is taking people back to the village, with the increased possibility of working at or from home. Perhaps the future lies in the picturesque village, not rooted in the rhythm of the seasons and food production, but in the telephone system or satellite link connecting its work-points to the rest of the world. Here we can be part of the modern world, have a nice garden, leave the dirty city behind – compartmentalism takes a new turn.

This points up the effect that trends in home ownership have upon divisions in society. For some the rural idyll is inaccessible. This is often the case for young people brought up in a village where demand from outside, combined with planning restrictions and the end of council house building, takes a local home completely out of their reach. Long-term rises in house prices generally accentuate differences, for example, between those who already own their home and those who do not, between those who live in a prosperous area and those who do not, between those with employment and those without, and so on.

Ethical implications

Property, especially home ownership, gives people security in a changing world. In our property owning democracy that security is sought by increasing numbers of people. It is no longer the preserve of the wealthy minority. Rights to private property are as firmly established as they ever have been, and it would be very difficult for any political programme to be accepted which did not recognise that fact.

In a democracy where the majority have a material stake in the rights of property, an obvious ethical question arises. What will happen to the *minority*, whose relative poverty may well increase? As has happened in different ways in different types of society, property and power tend to end up in the same place. It is now possible to discern this pattern in western democracies, which are now, with the demise of state communism, the model of government for most of the world. In Britain this has ethnic implications, as it does in much of Europe and beyond. A major task lies ahead in enabling the one fifth or so minority to participate.

There is no guarantee that they will be able to. It is easier to safeguard the rights of property than to encourage the duties and obligations which may go with those rights. When the majority of the population have a vested interest in the status quo, represented above all by private property, the danger is that the minority will cease to find the ballot box a source of hope or helpful change.

Tawney opposed property where ownership and use were divorced. He distinguished betweeen property which has a function, and what he called 'Passive Property, or Property for Acquisition, for Exploitation, or for Power . . .'[2] He did not envisage a time when four-fifths of the population would be owning property which was a complex muddle of the two types, although he did recognise that property offers 'a kind of limited sovereignty'[3]. It does indeed and, having attained that level of control over their own lives, people will not willingly let it go. But where does proper self-interest end and unjustifiable selfishness begin when this is set against a background which includes relative poverty nationally and absolute poverty internationally?

There is another question. What happens to the souls of those who are acquiring the property, living in comfortable houses, secure from the poor and marginalised? In other words, most of us. Is it morally possible simultaneously both to seek to enhance our own security and to stand alongside the deprived? That is what most of us try to do, if we consider the subject at all. Is it possible for a market system to avoid an inordinate accumulation of property which ends up being, 'in effect, sovereignty over persons'[3]? Or, on the other hand, can we put behind us the days when property was identified with conflict, and agree with Brian Griffiths' view that social order is based upon the three pillars of private property, family and religion[4]?

It is also necessary to ask whether it is any longer appropriate to identify property and power in an unqualified way. The new generation of property is held on behalf of the investor by pension funds, unit trusts, banks, building societies and other mediating financial institutions – it is very diffuse. Only a minority retain immediate control and invest directly in shares, even after a sequence of privatisation offers. Owners are often in a vulnerable position, their property is handled by a small sector of society which has acquired financial expertise, and they are protected only by statutory regulation which can easily fall behind the latest developments. The Mirror Group pension fund scandal is a recent case in point.

Now that money is able to travel the world by electronic signal, much of the power of property has been ceded to those who control communications. Present institutions were not designed to deal with this situation, and the world of the property owning democracy may be more fragile than is often acknowledged, particularly without the imposition and enforcement of some form of international accountability.

Owners, trustees and stewards

The concept of trusteeship in the feudal societies of the Middle Ages was the precursor of the concept of stewardship which was developed by the Churches of the Reformation. It has been suggested that the word steward 'comes from Old English and reflects a practice of appointing particularly reliable workers to be wardens of the pig-sty: *sty-wards*.'[5] More conventionally, the Oxford English Dictionary points to the probability that the term is derived from 'stigweard' or 'stiweard', relating to 'stig', a house or hall, and 'weard', ward. In either case, a position of responsibility and trust is implicit.

To be a trustee was part of a person's position in Church and society – Christendom. In the post-reformation period this societal structure did not exist in the same way and so stewardship had to be introduced as part of the outworking of the individual's life of faith. Nevertheless, a vital connection between faith and life, a bastion against dualism, had been weakened. There was no longer an organic link. Ever since the Church has been struggling against the tide whenever it has called for the ethics of money, wealth and property to be taken seriously.

In practice, most people became owners, neither trustees nor stewards. A steward has to make value judgements which relate to God, a trustee has a duty in relation to society, but owners are on their own. So it is that the givenness of creation is undermined by both capitalist and marxist thought, both of which give prime attention to the ownership of property, particuarly the means of production.

People have come to be justified in their existence by productivity or appropriation, by doing, having and accumulating. They seek to justify themselves in these terms, not in being human, nor in their createdness, nor in how they use what they have been given.

Duchrow points to the formative role of Descartes' view of humanity as 'Lord and Owner of Nature'. 'Co-operation is replaced by operation pure and simple, by manipulation . . . objectifying science and technology. Supposedly "value free", it in fact absolutizes our dominion over nature . . . Humanity's stewardship is replaced by ownership; the accumulation of capital becomes the sign of election. The second idol is money.'[6] The result of this is unrestricted and variform exploitation of people and nature, together with the use of military force to defend domination and possession.

If Christians are to offer anything in particular to the world at large, they must find an organic link between faith and life. This needs to be more powerful than the dualisms and compartments which separate faith and life, idealism and realism, or worship and money.

This link is not likely to be provided by the superstructure of Christendom, with its attempted conflation of kingdom, Church and world. This is no longer an appropriate model in an age which has begun to come to terms with pluralism and has eschewed any partnership between imperialism and the mission of the Church.

It is no more likely to be provided by the astringency of individualistic puritanism. In practice this has been shown to carry an implicit dualism which identifies kingdom and Church and risks the exclusion of the world from the issues of faith. In the long run the individualism of puritanism has not provided the spiritual resources to prevent its ethical impulse being overwhelmed by the momentum of a growing money-based value system. Ironically, it fails to take original sin seriously enough, in so far as it is manifest in the structures of society and communal human life.

Any organic link between faith and life needs to renew or replace the concepts of trusteeship and stewardship in a way which is appropriate in a plural society and relevant to both the communal and the individual. It will need, most testingly, to connect the contemporary experience of ownership with the imperatives of Christian faith.

7. Charitable Giving

Roots of modern voluntarism

Charitable giving is as old and as hard to define as human civilisation itself, and it is not just the preserve of the Judeo-Christian tradition. The act of giving fulfils deep personal and social needs. Motives for charitable giving are diffuse and complex, and have been subject to critical analysis ever since the days of Aristotle, Cicero and Seneca. In our society, of course, the influence of Jewish and Christian thought in this area has been enormous, with examples running thoughout the scriptures and subsequent writings.

The Jewish tradition integrates the requirements of religion and society. It has a deuteronomic flavour[1], emphasizing that generosity will be rewarded and meanness punished.

By the Middle Ages the structures of Christendom – Church, education and welfare – were intertwined with and dependent upon charitable giving. Gifts and bequests were a means of institutional security for the Church and eternal security for each person within it.

With the Reformation this unitary structure began to be dismantled. In England, the state appropriated the accumulated wealth of the Church and the Church's virtual monopoly of social and educational functions could no longer be taken for granted. Acts of Parliament in 1545, 1597 and 1601 placed regulation under the authority of the state.

This ancient tradition underwent enormous expansion from the late eighteenth century onwards. A rapidly growing population migrated to the cities, which were expanding under the impetus of the industrial revolution. Once there, their lives were blighted by squalid living conditions. There were no state solutions to the consequent human problems and social misery – the option did not exist.

This provided the occasion for a new awakening of charitable activity, motivated and underwritten by evangelical zeal. The writings and campaigns of William Wilberforce, Hannah More and others galvanised upper and middle class people into a new sense of humanitarian obligation. Evangelicalism was liberal individualism with a caring, yet disciplined, human face. It proved to be a uniting force in the nation during a period of great social change.

Evangelicalism affirmed an individualistic creed wherein individual behaviour determined both spiritual progress and material success within the prevailing laissez-faire ethos. Puritanism took on a new lease of life, and required of the wealthy a restrained lifestyle combined with generosity in charitable giving. New charities proliferated, and competed with one another for the attentions of needy sinners, seeking redemption for society in the redemption of individuals through networks based in family and parish. Their success and survival depended upon public approval and support, and they thus became both an expression of evangelical sentiment and a buttress of economic liberalism.

The emphasis was on 'sanctity of family life, social pity and moral fervour.'[2] Parish, neighbourhood and family were paramount, and served by a vast number of local institutions across the country. The parochial ideal, expressed architecturally through the Gothic Revival, offered an antidote to the problems of nineteenth-century urban life by superimposing upon it the manageable image of the village community.

Charitable obligation was not just an expression of upper and middle class ethics. Values were shared across class differences. Together, working class charity and middle class philanthropy brought social stability. Engels remarked, in 'The Condition of the Working Class in England', that 'although the workers cannot really afford to give charity on the same scale as the middle class, they are nevertheless more charitable in every way.' Many charities received the bulk of their income from working class contributions, and particularly from the respectable working class which was often identified with Church or chapel.

The confidence which Victorians showed in voluntary activity as a solution to the vast problems of poverty and deprivation may seem strange to the contemporary mind, but their horizons were of the nature of things very local. Poverty was encountered locally, in all its horror. It was natural to think of local and neighbourhood remedies. This particularly applied to women, who were the backbone of much Victorian voluntarism. Mothers' meetings were a focus for a vast range of activity and fundraising. District visiting societies became established in many areas, and revealed even more distress.

Voluntarism produced innovation and advance during the nineteenth century, such as in the development of child welfare, where women's organisations were to the fore. The Ranyard Mission,

founded by Ellen Ranyard in 1857, set up the first body of
paid social workers in England. Mrs Ranyard's view was still
one of evangelical individualism, 'the source of distress was in
personal misfortune or moral failing, not the structure of
society.'[3] The surrounding environment was not discounted as an
influence, however, but was to be transformed by Christian principles into one in which the poor could take responsibility for their
own lives.

Such a policy, delivered with sincerity and kindness, did have an
effect, but it was not a match for the sheer scale of the problems of
urban deprivation. The moral reformation of the poor through self-
help was far too slow in coming to be of any use to many in the
extremity of suffering. Underlying this situation was the invidious
distinction between the 'deserving' and the 'undeserving' poor. The
'deserving' could hope for charitable help, the 'undeserving' would
have to go to the workhouse. Philanthropists often found this
distinction painfully inappropriate, but had to use it as their
activities were limited by available funds.

In time, in spite of their suspicion of the state, philanthropists
had to turn in that direction if they wanted their work to meet the
needs they could now discern. However ingenious, fundraising
could not finance the expansion they desired. As the century passed
a compromise evolved, whereby grants were made by the state, such
as those given to the National Society for school building, but
essential independence was retained. Throughout the Victorian
period belief was universally maintained in the superiority of charity
over state aid.

Twentieth-century philanthropy

As the nineteenth century drew to a close, new trends could be
discerned. Progressive philanthropists and other theorists were now
using social statistics, and drawing the conclusion that private
charity could not cope with the central issue of poverty. Fabian
socialism required a more comprehensive response to the social
conditions now being analysed in more detail. In her Minority
Report of the Royal Commission on the Poor Laws (1905–9),
Beatrice Webb called for an enhanced government role in dealing
with the great social problems of poverty and unemployment. The
Liberal legislation of 1905–11 began the long process of increasing

state welfare activity, consequently reducing the previously accepted strategic part played by voluntary charity.

The climate of opinion was changing, and the emphasis shifted from helping the poor to fighting poverty. Individualistic evangelical philanthropy may have delivered souls, but it had not thereby transformed society in the ways people now began to seek. The application of social science, it was felt, should eventually lead to the elimination of poverty altogether. Expectations rose.

Much charitable activity came to be seen as patronising and insensitive to social reality. The new orthodoxy called for an impersonal approach, legislation, government activity and state intervention.

Christian charity began a gentle decline, often outpaced by progressive advance in medicine or social service. For many people of goodwill, the individualistic and missionary cutting edge of Christian charity became increasingly inappropriate, and decreasingly relevant in the context of increasing state responsibility for welfare. New agencies, free of sectarian overtones, vied for attention in the area of contemporary social issues. Parochial horizons widened as mass media developed and as people were able to travel further afield.

Mothers' meetings gradually lost their purpose, and had to adapt to changed circumstances. The services they had provided now came from other sources. At the same time religious practice was in decline and the expectations and perceptions of women were being transformed. The only course for such organisations was to become part of the compartmentalised life of the Church, the various Christian women's organisations we have today. The Mothers' Union is still one of the largest voluntary organisations in Britain, with 173,000 members in 1990.

Service to the national community was sharpened by the twentieth century experiences of unemployment and two world wars. New charities continued to be established, usually with secular and social objects (Imperial Cancer Research Fund, Wellcome Foundation, Shelter), sometimes with international ones (Save the Children Fund, Oxfam). Activities were often undertaken in partnership with the state (The Women's Royal Voluntary Service, Citizens Advice Bureaux).

At the end of the Second World War, the vision for the future lay with the Beveridge Report, published in 1942. The Welfare State created a different environment within which charity now had to work. Many supporters of the Labour government felt that all charity was demeaning and that its days must be numbered.

All the same, Clement Attlee remarked that philanthropy was 'not confined to any one class in the community' and that 'we shall always have alongside the great range of public services, the voluntary services which humanize our national life and bring it down from the general to the particular.'[4] The Victorian roots ran deep, and were never completely dug up.

Modern charity

By the 1960s it looked as though the voluntary sector's role in welfare provison was firmly designated as subordinate to that of the state. Apparently, this role would continue to diminish as public services increased in scope and thoroughness. It now seems that this corporatist sunrise was a sunset.

The 1980s showed quite clearly that the decline of the voluntary tradition in Britain had been greatly exaggerated. More than that, in the popular consciousness, if not in reality, it had gone some way towards once again claiming ascendancy over political action or social change as a remedy for poverty and suffering.

The ideological landscape has also changed, a change emphasized by the increasingly evident limitations of public provision and expenditure. It is now more generally accepted that voluntary flexibility enables a rapid response to public perceptions of need in education, health, overseas aid and environmental issues. The disarray of formal political opposition, the shortcomings of adversarially oriented political parties and the rise of issue-based pressure groups contributed during the 1980s to a blurring of the edges between voluntary, charitable and political action, so that some voluntary groups are unable to obtain formal charitable status. Self-regulation, too, came with the rapid growth of the Institute of Charity Fundraising Managers.

Public policy has encouraged these trends, by restricting the areas deemed appropriate for state activity, by encouraging accountability in the voluntary sector and by adapting fiscal systems. Tax benefits became available to the elderly if they used the private or voluntary sector for health care. Charitable giving increasingly assists the provision of new services and equipment in the health service and some health authorities are appointing professional fundraisers to co-ordinate voluntary activity. In 1987 Great Ormond Street Hospital launched an appeal which aimed to net £42 million in charitable money.

Similarly, the hospice movement is largely financed by an enormous amount of local fundraising, the average support received from the NHS via the area health authorities being only 27%[5].

David Mellor, when Minister of State for Health, has said: 'Voluntary organisations are able to move much more quickly and imaginatively to meet particular demands. They also blaze important trails in changing the ways services are delivered.'[6] To support this, public money is used. It is estimated that public sector grants for voluntary organisations in the year 1989/90 were £0.8 billion from local authorities[7] and £2.4 billion from central government[8].

Gift Aid now allows tax to be reclaimed on single net donations of £400 or more. Payroll giving, advertised as 'tax-free, painless and heartwarming', has been introduced and expanded – after a slow but steady start the size of the maximum contribution has been regularly increased, and by April 1991 more than 278,000 people and 3,900 employers were participating[9]. These recent changes augment the long-standing private/public partnership expressed by tax concessions available for giving under a Deed of Covenant.

Giving by corporations to charity and the arts has similarly been encouraged by government as an expression of the increasing responsibility which is seen as one of the benefits of the free market. Margaret Thatcher, as Prime Minister, said 'This is what the Victorians did, so why not you lot?'[10] and the 1988 edition of Charity Trends detailed figures which showed giving by the corporate sector to charity to be around the £1 billion mark, although the real total is very difficult to establish. Support by companies for the voluntary sector also takes other forms, such as gifts in kind, sponsorship, secondment, joint promotions (for example, affinity cards), matched giving of staff donations, and various types of non-cash assistance.

Spotlight on Fundraising

The renewed emphasis on the consumer and the market economy has put the spotlight on fundraising, but in reality this has remained a constant leisure-time activity for the British people for many decades. Modern technology is applied to basic themes which would have been familiar a century ago. Charities have used much creative energy in raising money ever since Victorian times. Everyone is a potential contributor, young and old, rich and poor. Collection boxes, charity stalls, bazaars and jumble sales, fundraising entertainments, use of children as collectors, local branches, all can be traced back to the nineteenth century and sometimes beyond. Now they are all out there competing for attention in the market place.

As the differentials between rich and poor increase, the charity shop is well placed to meet the needs of both the poor, for cheap clothing, and the rich, for painless giving. Oxfam's income from its shops is at £17.8 million per annum the biggest single source of its funds; Imperial Cancer Research makes £7.2 million, Spastics Society £3.3 million, Barnardos £2.4 million, The Sue Ryder Foundation £1.9 million, Save the Children £1.4 million, and the British Red Cross and the Children's Society £0.9 million each.[11] Secondhand women's clothing dominates turnover, followed by menswear and craft goods, often produced with a self-help emphasis at home or overseas.

Charities have always played upon emotion by using children in their fundraising, and sponsorship is the contemporary manifestation of this moral pressure. Parents and neighbours find it much harder to say 'no' to a child engaged in 'good works' and encouraged by school, local or national charity and local or national media.

Perhaps one of the most striking examples of charitable activity in a market environment is the introduction of the affinity card – the charity sponsoring credit or charge card. Here competition is growing. The Girobank/Oxfam Visa Card involves Girobank donating £5 to Oxfam when the card is first used, and 0.25% of the value of subsequent purchases. Although the brochure headline proclaims 'Imagine you could help them every time you bought something', if this proportion is described as one-fourhundredth it does not sound so startling. The card offers kudos, being, in the brochure's own words, 'deliberately designed to stand out from ordinary credit cards.'

Victorian 'respectable entertainments' have come of age with the advent of the telethon, the latest manifestation of a 'compelling mix of benevolence and entertainment' which is 'deeply rooted in British community life.'[12] A succession of marathon programmes broadcast nationwide, including Live Aid, Sport Aid, BBC Children in Need, ITV Telethon and Comic Relief, have raised large sums of money for charity, sometimes in excess of £20 million a programme, and have simultaneously raised the public profile of charitable giving.

The red nose has become, in British culture, a symbol for our times: 'Mr Norman Fowler, the Employment Secretary, confused his Japanese hosts at a new training centre in Tyne and Wear by conducting the opening ceremony wearing a 50p red plastic nose.'[13] Very large numbers watch these programmes, with corresponding benefits to those participating as performers, producers or sponsors.

Telethons show the same benefits and drawbacks as any charitable fundraising – writ large in the language of mass entertainment. The juxtaposition of trivia and tragedy, such as the direct edit during Comic Relief, 10th March 1989, from Kylie Minogue to limbless children in Mozambique, can be seen as grotesquely inappropriate or as a stark statement about the human condition, depending on your point of view. The demands of media producers and consumers for strong emotional content cannot always be in harmony with the need for potential beneficiaries to be represented with dignity: 'They show us as excluded and different, which reinforces the status quo.'[14]

Comic Relief at least has made a valiant attempt to concentrate on what people can do instead of what they can't, and to present some sort of context rather than 'the needy' – what Ben Elton called 'a little bit of politics'. Agnostino Chirrime, Oxfam worker in Mozambique, told Billy Connolly and the British people, 'We don't need gifts, we need instruments of work.' Nevertheless, an underlying tension remains between this sort of sensitivity and the constant requirement for hysterical hype around the accumulation of the running total. 'A little bit of politics' can also run the risk of falling foul of charity law.

Similarly, events which have to hold their own in the market place tend to succumb to public prejudice about such things as administrative expenses, 'our expenses are sponsored, your money goes on projects', and charity beginning at home, 'it doesn't matter where you are in Britain, Comic Relief is working somewhere near you'. Corporate donors and sponsors require sycophancy and publicity as they hand over billboard size cheques, and often give with strings attached.

The pressure to raise money and to do better than the last telethon, can lead to images which are, like many traditional fundraising techniques, 'emotional, retrogressive, cruel and unreal',[15] with a tendency to emphasize the powerlessness rather than the humanity of the beneficiary. There is an underlying tension between the needs of the donor to be affirmed in terms of attitudes,

views and self-esteem, and those of the beneficiary to be treated as a
whole person rather than a good cause. Charitable organisations are
stretched in both these directions, being committed to supporters in
order to achieve regular income and, of course, to those whose needs
represent the charity's aims and objectives.

Virtues of charity and philanthropy

The deep urge to reach out in love to common humanity finds vital
expression in charitable and philanthropic activity. It is therefore of
great value to society, not only in terms of the primary objects
themselves, but also in terms of the way of life of those who are
active. Love of humanity is the key, and it does not always involve
a rich-to-poor direction – a beneficiary of the hospice movement
may well be wealthier than both volunteers and donors. The
continuity of charitable traditions, especially in Britain at the local
level of their nineteenth-century expression, is an expression of
mutuality, community and benevolence.

Philanthropy has been called a 'nursery school of democracy' [16].
It encourages a wide range of personally and socially beneficial
actions, whereby people can enhance both their own lives and the
lives of others. People grow into citizens, fulfilling duties as well as
enjoying rights.

Voluntary activity offers an arena to those excluded from society's
customary structures of power. Women were active in philanthropy
a generation or more before they sought political reform – many
nineteenth-century voluntary societies were both managed and
supported by women. The voluntary sector remains an important
channel both for those who need to receive and those who wish to
give.

In an age in which state welfare is no longer accepted as a final
solution to all problems, voluntarism is one again playing a strategic
part, and adding to it the role of watchdog for the powerless. This
latter role is taken up for those at home or overseas by organisations
as disparate as, for example, the National Association of Citizens
Advice Bureaux, the Child Poverty Action Group, Shelter, the
World Development Movement, Oxfam and Christian Aid. Pressure
is on from within charitable bodies to widen the definition of what
is appropriate activity to include issues such as human rights and
economic justice – but this can lead to problems as charities try to

stretch the compartment within which they are legally allowed to operate.

Across the political spectrum there is a move away from collectivism and centralism. Charitable activity is now accepted more unquestioningly than it has been for many decades. A 'gradualist welfare pluralism'[17] has developed, providing a variety of activities and structures by which services are delivered. The voluntary sector's capacity for flexibility, immediacy, innovation and experimentation make it increasingly attractive in complex modern society, particularly amongst minorities and deprived groups which are suspicious of authority.

In the modern world – international, local, plural, relative, fragmented – a voluntary response can be made to all sorts of need – social, developmental, ecological, medical, educational, creative and so on. Giving is in cash or kind by both companies and individuals. Large numbers of people are helped. Large numbers of people engage in activities which broaden their vision and help them grow. There is a lot of choice, people can identify with whichever charity or pressure group they feel they want to or ought to identify. Individualism and compassion, and sometimes conscience, march closely in step.

Drawbacks of Philanthropy

Many people would agree that philanthropic activity is more necessary than ever in an age of increasing prosperity, if society is not to become simply an arena of selfishness. However, there *are* questions which need to be asked, but which tend to be asked only very quietly when funds need to be raised. These questions relate to the donor, to the recipient and to society at large, local, national and international.

To ask questions about the donor immediately takes us into the area of motivation and thus onto dangerous ground – perhaps this is one reason why these questions are not asked as often as they should. It is much more agreeable to talk about charitable giving in terms of generosity, compassion and human mutuality than to examine in any detail the other side of the issue and risk sounding judgemental, sour, cynical and intolerantly rigorous.

Nevertheless, the negative side must be faced. Charitable giving can be a variety of things which are ultimately unhelpful to the donor. It can offer a salve for the conscience when the deeper need is for a radical appraisal of circumstances and way of life. Reinhold Niebuhr pointed out that '. . . philanthropy combines geniune pity with the display of power and . . . the latter element explains why the powerful are more inclined to be generous than to grant social justice.'[18] Giving can accommodate the retention of power by the donor by euphemistic use of accountability – 'people need to know how their money is being spent'.

Furthermore, the donation of amounts which are small and derisory relative to the wealth of the donor has to be greeted with unctuous thanks and praise for great generosity, whatever the truth of the matter. This applies to both individual and corporate donors. Often the requirement, spoken or unspoken, is for publicity or advertising to be given to the already powerful.

The consequences of this can be to ameliorate, or make more tolerable, injustice rather than eradicate it. Paradoxically this raises the possibility of charity perpetuating the problems it sets out to address, partly by affirming the powerful position of the donor.

Secondly, the problems for the recipient are as serious, and it is not necessary to be as scrupulous to identify them. Especially if you are not one of the more popular, fashionable or noticed causes, charitable giving is often plain inadequate and the strings attached can be unfortunate or inappropriate. Donors are not impartial. Efforts to make giving more personal, such as setting up a direct relationship with an individual needy child, can be much more difficult for the receiver than the giver.

The situation of the unfashionable or unnoticed recipient is unlikely to be improved as charities manoeuvre to make themselves more attractive in the 'giving marketplace'. It is humiliating to be subject to whim, prejudice and fashion. Popular prejudices may not be that wholesome. For the second Comic Relief fundraising campaign, arguably one of the more enlightened and aware, the proportion of the proceeds going to development and health care overseas was reduced from four-fifths to two-thirds.[19]

The plight of less noticed recipient groups can lead to unedifying recrimination and competition between charitable bodies. The success of the Wishing Well appeal for the childrens' hospital at Great Ormond Street was regarded with a complex variety of emotions, few of them positive, by those hoping to raise funds for less popular causes.

Thirdly, there are drawbacks, too, in terms of wider society. Giving implies relationship, a giver and a receiver. There is some truth behind the cynical view of overseas aid, which defines it as 'the means whereby the poor of rich countries give to the rich of poor countries'. This is a negative side of the tendency for the poor to be more generous than the rich. In terms of proportion of net income devoted to charity, the most generous households in the United Kingdom are the retired, those in the lowest quintile of net income, skilled and unskilled manual workers, and those living in Northern Ireland[20].

In any case, it is impossible to conclude that charitable giving is in any way sufficient for it to be seen as a serious attempt by society at large to help the poor or to contribute to an integrated and caring society. The 1989/90 Charity Household Survey[21] revealed that the average given per individual was £7.73 monthly, or 0.76% of average gross earnings. However, this average is heavily influenced by a few very large contributions, just 8% giving £20 or more, and 49% giving £1 or less. The median monthly giving, the mid-way point with half donating more and half less, was £1.28. The much-vaunted generosity of the British public is a fantasy brought into being by the genuine generosity of a few. Only a fifth of those who took part in the survey planned any part of their giving. There is also a case for saying that even these low figures and proportions may be overstated, for 36% of the giving defined as such by the survey was in fact some form of purchase made through a charity event, shop or catalogue.

Given these figures, it seems that the charitable giving of the British people is running between £3.4 billion and £5.0 billion per annum. In spite of reductions in direct taxation weighted in favour of those with higher incomes 'it is highly probable that the proportion of the population donating has declined and that the typical amount they give has decreased in real terms' (over the period 1987-90)[22].

When these facts are set aside total Government expenditure rising above £250 billion, over 60% of which is spent on health, education and social security, it is difficult to see the swing back to voluntarism as being as far-reaching in substance as it is often perceived to be. Perhaps the image we have of ourselves is out of touch with reality. If so, it is fed by Government policy, for voluntary activity is given a much higher profile than its income from fundraising and donations would allow – this only forms about one-seventh of total charitable receipts. There is a hidden public contribution to voluntary activity in terms of fees paid to charitable bodies operating in a variety of areas of education, health and welfare. The reality is not so much that there is a striking increase in charitable giving, but that public provision is increasingly being *delivered* by means of voluntary bodies which offer flexibility and cost-effectiveness – the so-called 'contract culture'.

This increasingly complex intertwining of voluntary and public sectors, 'gradualist welfare pluralism', carries with it a number of difficulties. Independence is qualified. Voluntary societies are able to do less innovative pump-priming than they would like as they spend more and more time competing to raise funds for existing commitments and as Government tries to withdraw from the post-war welfare consensus. This leaves charities with the alternatives either of colluding with what they see as the state's abdication of its proper responsibilities or of leaving their client groups without the services they need. It also leaves them vulnerable to changes of political policy and withdrawal of public sector support.

In view of this intricate relationship between public and private sectors, the incessant call upon charitable bodies to stay out of the political arena seems increasingly anomalous. The Chief Charity Commissioner has said: 'Charities have a responsibility to draw public attention either to factors which impede the fulfilment of their charitable objects or to knowledge, whether derived from research or from experience, that affects their objects and their beneficiaries. If they are working in circumstances adverse to their objects, they should seek to influence and encourage change in those circumstances if they can. But how far should they persist if the powers that be take no notice, and the circumstances remain the same? Not very far, in my view. They must get on with the job . . .'[23]

Once again, compartments are constructed between different areas of life with the result that voluntary bodies are required to take on growing responsibility whilst having inadequate power and freedom of action to address, as fully as may often be necessary, the issues thereby raised.

An example of this problem is the recent Charity Commissioners' report on the campaigning policy of Oxfam. This concluded that the charity had gone beyond the invisible line which marks the beginning of unacceptable political activity. However, at the same time the Charity Commissioners insisted that others must be cautious in drawing general conclusions from the ruling, so the overall situation is still confused.

One of the attractive features of charitable activity is that it offers choice and variety, together with perhaps greater sensitivity at the point of delivery than services which are publicly planned and thus tainted with the tarnish of bureaucracy. This is, at any rate, a common perception, but the distancing from planning processes means that reflection and analysis is less likely to be given a priority, which can result in duplication of effort and wasteful unnecessary competition. It is claimed by some that Great Ormond Street's Wishing Well Appeal siphoned off so much funding that 'it led to the authorities which serve Leeds to shelve plans to rationalise the city's paediatric services.'[24]

Justice – the unanswered question

Charles Gore, in commenting that 'the Church bore the strongest witness to the idea of property as a trust for the common good', noted that 'in no way is this more strikingly shown than in its identification of "charity" – that is, charity in the narrower sense of almsgiving – with justice.'[25] In the same work, Vernon Bartlett noted that even in later Old Testament times, after the exile, there was an increase of individualism in which justice 'dwindled' to mercy, and in which good is done to benefit the individual pious soul, rather than the commonalty[26].

St Ambrose saw almsgiving as an act of justice. Aquinas filled out that view, seeing it not only as an action which belongs to love and mercy in its spiritual character or intention, but also as a matter of obligation. Possessions, so far as they are superfluities, can in some sense be called upon by others who have serious need of them.[27]

Scott Holland applied the same criteria to nineteenth-century individualism and philanthropy. 'It was right to rate very highly the virtues of charity. But the very earnestness of the personal appeals made to the conscience of the rich on behalf of the poor was itself a witness to the absoluteness of their command over their property. It depended wholly on their goodwill whether they would respond, and the appeal to their generosity could never rise above the level of an emotional motive. This appeal to charity, whenever it is greatly in evidence, is a sure signal that things have gone wrong. It always means that the individual right is treated as absolute in itself, and has escaped out of its proper subordination to the demand of justice.'[28] The common good requires charity to be seen in context, and demands upon a person's 'private purse, which the general welfare renders expedient' are not invasions of personal wealth, nor drafts upon charity, but are 'acts of that identical justice' by which that person is qualified to be an owner.

In fact, the Church holds strongly that charity can never be a substitute or an alternative for justice. The Second Vatican Council made this point quite specifically. Duncan Forrester has said that 'love is the inwardness of justice, the clue to the real meaning of justice. Doing justice then becomes a way of loving, indeed the only way of loving that is possible when large numbers of people are in question and when we are dealing with groups and collectivities. Justice can be spoken of as love distributed, the way in which a community loves its members.'[29] Both love and justice are necessary and mutually supportive. Temple's comment still stands: 'It is axiomatic that Love should be the predominant Christian impulse, and that the primary form of Love in social organisation is Justice.'[30]

Duncan Forrester goes on to issue an important warning: 'Love in its Latin garb as "charity" has been devalued in modern usage by frequently being separated from justice so that it becomes grudging hand-outs to the "deserving poor" rather than giving a person that person's due. Such patronising charity degrades the recipient and salves, but does not challenge, the conscience of the giver.'[29]

The demands of justice set a perpetual question mark against all charitable activity, for charity can never be an adequate substitute for justice and ceases to be an expression of love and human mutuality when it crosses over the ambiguous and imperceptible line which marks the beginnings of paternalism. If justice is ignored, there are no criteria for judging where that line is, and charity risks damaging the integrity of human relationships.

A Compartment for the Conscience

The Chief Charity Commissioner's personal definition is that 'charity is best defined as an action or a gift that is of benefit to others'[31]. But any simple definition turns out to be deceptive and illusory. Does 'benefit to others' rule out benefit to self? What sort of benefit? What of motivation, especially mixed motivation? Whose needs are being met? What is the real relationship between donor and recipient? The whole area is complex and inimical to any attempt to make judgements.

Certainly it is possible to dismiss fairly quickly the claim made by rigorous exponents of free market philosophy that charity is the *only* morally legitimate way to fund welfare. The moral question is not so easily resolved, for questions of justice apply and the freedom of action of the potential recipient must be weighed in the balance as well as that of the donor. Humanity cannot be limited to the rights of private property. In any case, this is as utopian as any socialist dogma; the whole idea is quite impractical. In the real world, unfortunately, generosity is insufficient. People do not give more as they become more prosperous; if anything, the opposite is the case. 'A person's fate cannot be made to rest solely upon other people's spiritual condition.'[32]

In fact, the recent increase in the voluntary sector's activities has been to a large extent funded by public money in the form of fees or grants. Much proclaimed increases in private and corporate generosity, whilst perhaps being large relative to previous levels of giving, have been marginal, or even reductions, in terms of the growth in personal incomes and company profitability.

Furthermore, at times of economic downturn, charitable giving apparently falls back more than it rises during the up-stroke of the economic cycle. The well-being of the vulnerable is thus doubly susceptible in a market system which favours the wealthy, once through recession itself and once again through a reduction in charitable giving.

If one of the virtues of a free market is that people are free to spend their own money as they wish, if that freedom is increasing for more and more people in a property owning democracy, and if the choices for the consumer are of greater variety and flexibility, the question has to be asked – in practice, why is the preference for charity so little expressed? If, as some say, there has been an overemphasis on the virtues of individualism, stressing what the individual can do for society and undervaluing what society does for the individual, why is the individual not rising to the occasion with greater generosity?

Frank Prochaska makes the point that the history of voluntary activity over the last two centuries has been that of a 'nursery school of democracy'[16]. It gave people opportunities to take on responsibilities which would otherwise have been inaccessible to them, and to fulfil themselves as 'autonomous individuals'. But there seems to be a limitation. With increasing leisure, people will spend time more generously than they will spend money, with the result that voluntary activity has resources to ameliorate, but not to rectify, the underlying and growing divisions at all levels of society – local, national or international. There seems to be a limit to what can be done by a 'responsible society' of 'autonomous individuals'.

Nineteenth-century charitable activity was part of a total world view, a view which centred on the parish. Voluntary activity took place within that context and was an intrinsic part of it. Benevolence, self-help, material and spiritual welfare, all went together. Evangelicalism and philanthropy were hand-in-hand; the 'parochial ideal'[33] was central and embraced the whole of life. This emphasis on religion and the parish provided the corporate element in individualistic philanthropy. Later, it can be argued, 'the growth of government responsibility for welfare contributed to the devitalization of Christian charity and by implication Christianity itself . . . As the state's activity in the social sphere tended to divorce material from spiritual welfare, philanthropy became more a question of personal choice.'[34]

Charitable activity and giving now relies more than ever upon individual choice. It is no longer supported by the social and moral imperatives and peer group pressure of parochial Victorian society. Instead it occupies part of the leisure compartment of life. There it has to fight it out in competition with all that is available to the consumer in the form of things on which time and money can be spent.

Horizons provided by mass media extend far beyond the village, but do not necessarily provide the moral imperative for generosity and action. Ironically, but perhaps predictably, that part of the United Kingdom which is popularly regarded as the most parochial – Northern Ireland – is also more than twice as generous as the average in terms of donations as a percentage of income.[35]

Advertising and public relations were very important for charities in the nineteenth century. Approval had to be sought from potential donors and benefactors as part of fundraising. In the late twentieth century that is still the case, but it is set in the context of consumer pluralism, operating without any generally accepted moral consensus. Fundraising becomes increasingly shrill and competitive, fighting for donations out of a frustratingly static proportion of the national wealth, as charities are squeezed between growing needs and the decreasing moral responsiveness of an increasingly wealthy majority of the population.

It is in order to address this situation that the so-called Windsor Group of charities is undertaking a generic campaign to increase giving as such, to increase the size of the cake from which all fundraisers are seeking a larger slice. 'However, knowledge of, as distinct from speculations about, the springs of philanthropy is scarce indeed. Considerable importance must be attached to research in this area, the funding of which would be a significant indicator that government was truly concerned about the infrastructure of voluntary action.'[36]

Current trends in charitable giving and fundraising are thus connected with the wider trends in society. In a compartmentalised society, charitable giving is in danger of providing a compartment in which the motivation of conscience to help the poor and suffering can be contained as an activity separate from political action or wealth creation and distribution.

The value of charitable activity can only be enhanced if those taking part in it strive to break through these barriers. It is encouraging that many at the centre of national charities, especially those with an international or ecological dimension, are moving in this direction. However, the danger is that the charitable world can develop a clear tendency towards a fundraising orientated, no-deep-questions-asked culture. If this happens, those who pay the piper still have a very good chance of calling the tune.

8. An Emerging Pattern

The Ascendant Market

Undoubtedly the market economy has in recent years assumed an increasingly important position in views of society spreading right across the political spectrum. It is now generally admitted that the market is the most efficient way yet devised of delivering goods and services. However, although more and more people are making this admission, there are differing ways in which the market is regarded. It is perhaps possible to discern three centres of gravity – market as ideology, the social market and market as mechanism within a social context. It is useful to define these types, but in practice they tend to merge into one another.

For some the free market is in itself an ideology, laissez-faire capitalism, the principles of which have to be applied as fully as possible or, rather, not applied, since the general principle of non-interference prevails. The market is quite simply natural, the economic manifestation of natural selection. Any attempt to adjust or regulate it is unnatural and, in the long run, disastrous and doomed to failure. If constraint is applied to market forces, it will only be by constraining the freedom of the individual, which is the highest human value. This view is very attractive to utopians in flight from the failures of socialism, for they are able to avoid the possibility of human failure and further disappointment by proclaiming the new utopia of the free market.

Secondly, others take a related, but more qualified, view, which can be described as advocating a social market. Here the individual remains sovereign and choice paramount, but intervention in the market for socially useful purposes is permitted. The individual judges that usefulness, in relation to his or her own purposes, and expresses such judgement through available political processes. The free market place is qualified by the democratic market place, but still provides the overall framework. This view can become acceptable for Christians as it moves towards a position which allows intervention to address, for example, the problems of poverty or ecology. Social marketeers would, however, be reluctant to allow excessive regulation to attack inequality, as this would compromise the market system.

For some there is an unresolved tension in the social market position. On the one hand it acknowledges the existence of social values over and above the market, and thus permits regulation. On the other hand it gives the market primacy of position in the overall social framework.

For others the social market is simply a qualified competitive market – one in which there are limitations of property rights and an acknowledged role for public authorities in underwriting co-operating social institutions. It is this model of the social market which harmonises with Catholic social teaching, such as that derived from Aquinas on property, and achieves Christian and Social Democratic consensus in some European countries. In this case the market is in a symbiotic relationship with the social structures needed to sustain it.

A third view is to regard the market as a mechanism operating within society, distributing scarce resources. Again the market provides a framework for participation, but here it is subject to overall criteria set by or for the whole of society. The market operates within society to serve society, and can be set social purposes as well as individual ones. This view of the market would accommodate and even welcome manipulation of the market for ecological purposes, for example, or to promote family values, or to limit economic divisions, according to particular preference. Here the presumption is more towards social constraints on the market than with the social market model, but the boundary between the two positions is not clear.

The underlying issue, often inadequately understood, is the question of autonomy. The definitions differ in the way in which they handle the relationship of the market with matters such as social justice and personal freedom. The clearer the definition and the advocacy of the free market, the greater is the degree of autonomy accorded it. Arguments favouring differing views of the market proceed logically, but cannot be resolved because they proceed from differing premises concerning automony. The result is either bald assertion or ambiguous compromise.

The market economy has become the cornerstone of European political life, in spite of the difficulties of competing nationalisms and recession. Indeed, the renewal of the market's susceptibility to peaks and troughs may be part of its resurgence. Economic downturn and dislocation do not create a viable alternative to the market, although they do mean that there is additional credibility for intervention designed to serve longer-term objectives.

For many Christians the position of the market remains ambiguous. The tendency towards accumulation of wealth and thus towards economic divisions in society cannot be denied. It causes Brian Griffiths to point to the jubilee and sabbatical years in the Old Testament as 'part of the ideal'[1], although he does not attempt to move towards their application to modern conditions. Nevertheless, a market economy does work better than any tried alternative, and so seems to be necessary, even desirable, on practical grounds.

It is possible, for example, to say that the market as now understood offers a form of subsidiarity in the distribution of goods and services which should be welcomed *provided that* undue accumulation of wealth and power can be democratically reduced or controlled. Subsidiarity as a concept has a long history, notably in the Roman Catholic ethical tradition. It recognises the desirability of achieving a balance between the needs of the individual and of society, giving a place to various levels in between. It calls for the maximum amount of delegation and decentralisation compatible with justice and the common good. Authority is devolved to the lowest practicable level.

Such thinking, applied to the market system, is in harmony with the general move away from command economies and could be a source of criteria for decisions concerning regulation. The shape of the 'macro', large scale, economy could thus be seen to be determined to some extent by the decisions of consumers and the response of producers at the 'micro', small scale, level. The extent of this determination would be defined by the amount of regulation decided upon by democratic processes.

Part of the ambiguous nature of the market is its apparent requirement of a strange and unstable mixture of 'liberal' economics and 'conservative' social patterns. These pull in different directions and represent conflicting value systems. In contemporary circumstances, with an accelerating role for money and the consumer, we do not know if it is possible for the market to be managed as a method which can be appropriated and used to express Christian values in society. It may be that the divisive or ideological tendency will inevitably emerge in the long run.

We do not yet know whether consumer society, symbolised by the market, offers Christians a real opportunity to express their own values across the compartmentalism of post-enlightenment western culture for the benefit of all. It may be that it is incorrigibly and corrosively individualistic, divisive, corrupting and unsustainable. The recent victories of western capitalism over its erstwhile opponent do not necessarily remove its inherent problems.

In spite of not knowing these things, Christian must continue to live in the world as it is, simultaneously to affirm it as God's good creation and to announce the supremacy of God-centred values. The task before the Church is to undertake that involvement whilst seeking to avoid consumerist addiction or being in thrall to possessive individualism.

We never feel that growth in human moral capacity matches the pace of technological or economic change. There is for all humanity a resulting common experience of uncertainty.

The Church must in these circumstances become an expression of hope – it cannot stand by, bewailing the present and dreading the future. The paradoxes of money will not go away, and may well get worse. This must be honestly faced, which will mean constantly examining and reassessing the moral problems raised and fighting rigorously against restricting compartmentalism in all its forms.

An Underlying Moral Question

Oliver Cromwell sent the following famous despatch to Parliament: 'Be pleased to reform the abuses of all professions, and if there be any one that makes many poor to make a few rich, that suits not a Commonwealth.' Now the problem is different, more one of a democratically sustained status quo in which an increasingly wealthy majority presides over a system in which the poor minority remain stuck below the level of any effective 'trickle-down'.

Marx's revolutionary proletariat has failed to emerge. Instead, the majority benefit from the property owning democracy whilst a perpetual minority remain trapped on low incomes and living in bad housing, or no housing at all. This raises for the affluent majority a moral question which will not go away.

The danger is that, just as the poor minority can be accused by some of excessive dependency on state assistance, the affluent majority is itself suffering from its own dependency on consumption and accumulation. This dependency can require indirectly, by excessive demands and exaggerated differentials, the maintenance of a sector of relative poverty within national society. It may also contribute towards trading conditions which exacerbate absolute poverty at the international level.

The heavy priority often given to economics, and the acceptance which greets its constant occupation of the bottom line, signals the pre-eminence of money values in our society. Dependency takes the form of the assertion of economic rights, and a shift of values away from a sense of duty. This leads to fragmentation and loss of meaning in society. Tawney pointed out that 'duties, unlike rights, are relative to some end or purpose, for the sake of which they are imposed.' Rights are a point of division; they enable people to resist. Duties, however, are a principle of union; they lead people to co-operate.[2]

The perennial problem of inflation is our most prominent symptom of dependency. William Temple commented that only the first part of Wesley's dictum, 'Gain all you can, save all you can, give all you can', cannot be traced in the New Testament[3]. In contemporary economic culture this first part is the only one which is diligently observed by most. However, it inevitably tends to exert inflationary pressure if it is isolated from saving and giving, augmented by borrowing, and diverted towards spending. Attitudes and economic behaviour are interrelated, expectations and desires are enhanced by advertising and the whole atmosphere of society. Inflation and increasing levels of indebtedness is the result. Speed of circulation can, as readily as growth in money supply, be inflationary – especially in an electronic age.

For free market theorists the only answer to this is preaching and exhortation, attempting to influence economic behaviour, which in theory remains sovereign and free, by changing attitudes. 'In order to reduce the economic current, neo-liberals conclude in effect, it will be necessary to strengthen the *moral* circuits . . .'[4] But we have already insulated the economic circuits from the moral ones, to ensure that they work properly, and we do not have the equipment readily to hand to prevent them overloading.

Dualism and compartmentalism

Compartmentalism is a recurrent pattern in contemporary culture, and has been a recurrent theme throughout this discussion of contemporary economics and ethics. Lives are lived in separate compartments of homes, jobs, leisure activities. Our thinking, especially since the Englightenment, is done in categories – scientific, economic, philosophic, religious, literary and so on.

There is indeed value in the autonomy of some of these categories – the sound theology of the Christendom Group did not prevent them producing some bad economics – but bridges must at some stage be built between them if life is to be lived to the full. Theology, in particular, cannot exclude itself from any area of life without diminishing the God it serves, even if the alternative is the hard work required to master other disciplines. A bridge has to have firm ground on both sides.

Furthermore, the Church, particularly in the West, has tended towards dualistic patterns of thought, based upon a perceived division between spirit and matter and a tendency to identify these with good and evil respectively. Feminist theology has rightly pointed to the serious dangers of a simplistic identification of evil and the flesh.[5]

Ulrich Duchrow has remarked that Luther's thinking was an attempt to realistically face the tension between the kingdom of God and human evil. The aim was to draw out the vocation of each and every person to become a fellow worker with God, to become aligned with the ultimate purpose of creation.

These ideas incorporated the two kingdoms approach to social ethics. This became dangerous when mixed with a whole new set of dichotomies and dualisms unleashed by the enlightenment. '. . . the basic philosophical pattern into which Luther's ideas are being pressed . . . is the Cartesian divorce between the free self (ego) and "things" (matter), with an automatic, autonomous logic on both sides of the great divide.'[6] The end result is an inability to handle social evil, even if its expression is as obvious as in National Socialism.

Similarly, the idea is commonly held, in the Church as elsewhere, that economics is a completely autonomous discipline, permanently separate from other disciplines and existing in a sphere of its own. This is so in spite of the inability of pure, 'scientific' economics to handle adequately serious problems such as inflation, unemployment and world debt.

Whilst the autonomy of economics as a discipline does need recognition, it is important in addition to hold human and social factors within the frame of reference. The autonomous compartments containing economics (preoccupied with what works), ethics (preoccupied with what's right) and theology (preoccupied with God's place in it all) must at some point have their rough edges knocked off on the factors more adequately disclosed by the other disciplines. Again, the need to connect economic and moral circuits is apparent.

A person's individuality and place in society cannot be separated. Neither can private and public realms, but often the assumption is made that they can. The Church is not exempt. If faith is not connected with social reality, it can support or acquiesce in the unjust use of economic power.

In practice the Church has permitted issues of economics, wealth and money to be dealt with globally, structurally and publicly, but has failed adequately to connect these with personal faith and morals. The converse tends to be true of family and sexual ethics, which have a high profile in the area of personal faith. These therefore tend to be perceived to be matters which are of concern to the Church, to the exclusion of much that is at least of equal importance.

This is partly because, compounding dualism and compartmentalism, the Christian ethical stance on money and material wealth was worked out in the 'pre-industrial' period. The response to the development of modern capitalism either was negative or ended up in practice being permissive towards an autonomous economic sphere.

The development of more 'incarnational' strands of theology in the past hundred years has included a more positive attitude towards industrial activity, as exemplified by the work of industrial mission, and a growing interest in social ethics across denominations. However, much of this has not affected the majority of Christians. Connections simply are not made between such new thinking and the way Christians live in the world. As we approach the 'post-industrial' era, the work of building bridges betweeen these compartments still has to be done, particularly at the level of the local church.

This difficult task may require a reformulated incarnational theology, for it is likely that a strong emphasis on the incarnation is required to connect dualisms and compartments. The work done, for example by 'Lux Mundi' in 1889, to bring materialist forms of thought within the ambit of spirit and faith, needs its twentieth-century equivalent, one which will address the difficulties raised by the paradoxes, provisionalities and uncertainties of a quest for progress.

Late nineteenth-century theology focused on the incarnation as part of its response to evolutionary scientific and political theory. It tended to sanctify progress in the process. This is no longer tenable in a world which has experienced the holocaust and Hiroshima, and which faces possible ecological disaster and grotesque global poverty. New formulations are needed which stress redemption in balance with divine acceptance of humanity, and which offer an expression of redemptive truth to those who live and work in the market place of contemporary economic culture.

New Consumers

Market theory elevates consumer choice, and does so in a way which gives that consumer choice a moral absolution. The individual can remain indifferent to the larger problems of social and economic justice, because the individual has no responsibility for such matters. This underlines our natural tendency to develop an outlook which concentrates our quest for security on the 'home' compartment of life.

However, we all have to go outside sometimes, and matters such as the environment and transport cannot be entirely private – they are deeply communal. Security, therefore, cannot in the longer term be reconciled with social indifference, any more than can morality. If Christians are to work effectively in the context of contemporary economic realities, they must reverse acceptance of market amorality.

The need is to find an enhanced role for consumer choice, in promoting long-term social cohesion, justice and ecological sustainability, which can be integrated with its primary purpose of distributing scarce resources.

As economic change enhances the position of the consumer, ecological pressure is growing on patterns of consumption. This offers people connections between their personal patterns of expenditure and global issues which are often more visible than matters of justice. Perhaps self-interest dictates that a CFC aerosol seems more environmentally harmful than a jar of coffee seems unjust. In either case it is feasible to try to influence the situation by means of consumer choice, and thus to exercise duties as well as rights, to express mutuality in human relationships.

This fact can be recognised even by governments with a liberal market philosophy. Many countries, including Britain, have moved to make a large tax differential in favour of lead-free petrol as an encouragement to the responsible use of consumer power. By any definition this is intervention in the free market. Professor David Pearce's 1989 report to the Secretary for the Environment, 'Sustainable Development', advocated fiscal measures to penalise environmentally harmful activity. The fact that this report seemed to be shelved as the General Election approached raises important questions about the capacity of democracy to respond to issues of justice or the environment.

The power of the consumer is shown by the speed with which supermarket chains are adapting themselves to the green issues considered important by their customers. Increased space is given on their shelves to environmentally acceptable products and increased space in their advertising to their own environmental credentials. Producers are more and more aware that social awareness and responsiveness can enhance the brand loyalty shown by consumers.

It is too early to say which will be the stronger force, the enlightened self-interest of consumers or the inherent qualities of the market tending towards social division and personal indifference. Experience to date has shown that the market has tended to become an end in itself, even when people have a strong sense of using it as a means towards some other, more lofty, end. This does not mean that the task should not be attempted, but that it must be attempted both with discernment and with an awareness of the difficulties involved.

A new organisation was launched in 1989 to operate in this area, called 'New Consumer'. It aims to encourage people to become more aware of their power as consumers, and to educate and inform them so that they may use that power positively and effectively to serve the common good. It has already been involved in a variety of publishing and information initiatives. Partly funded by the Joseph Rowntree Charitable Trust, the initiative brings together people from a variety of backgrounds – foreign aid and development, human rights, ecology, ethical investment, intermediate technology and consumers' organisations. It sponsors a magazine, 'New Consumer', which is not the only one in its field; there is also 'Ethical Consumer', published by an independent research co-operative. Similar initiatives are gathering pace in many developed countries.

The 'new' or 'progressive' consumer is in an ambiguous position – by definition it is necessary to be relatively affluent to exercise these choices. It is not possible for the poor to take part in this way of influencing events, so it cannot be fully participatory. Loading the system by fiscal means will further emphasize the fact that money can purchase the ability to behave anti-socially. Both environmentally harmful behaviour *and* access to good environment become 'positional goods'.

Furthermore, we do not know whether more than a small active minority will exercise choice in favour of what will often be more expensive options. Strong motivation is required in order to be prepared to engage in the minutiae of assimilating the information required, to persevere on through a morass of often confusing and contradictory facts. The whole issue of information availability is a key issue in the development of consumer activity. Details are often not forthcoming voluntarily and increasingly sophisticated regulation of disclosure may be required.

In some ways the new consumer will need to be anti-consumption – concerned with sustainability. What is wasted has to be considered as important as what is used. 'This is another way of pointing to the necessity of consciously developing a service society (the drift is that way in any case). It is entirely congenial to Christian ways of thinking, which hold that we should live in a community of giving and receiving. . .'[7]

Christians are amongst those in the vanguard of 'New Consumer', seeing hope in the consumer model if it can be redeemed from its means, the market, becoming ends. In many ways the division economists make between consumers and producers is a false one. All of us produce and consume at the same time. As producers we are often tempted to treat as uneconomic things for which we have to pay through taxation. Transport, environment, education, health and social services all come in this category. As consumers, however, we call for all these common goods to be valued and given greater priority. The shift in the post-industrial market from production to consumption perceptions *may* possibly be its redeeming factor.

Paul Ekins points out that no satisfactory means have ever been found to express social or environmental factors in a way which is quantifiable and would enable them to be incorporated into macro-economic or monetary systems, but that this does not apply to the micro-economic level of personal consumer choice. Individuals, however, can make their own choices, can opt for communal benefit, without or prior to converting social factors into some monetary scale or equivalent. Furthermore, he claims positive benefit, rather than just the minimalising of bad effects. 'By locating consumption in a circular process which feeds back into the productive part of the economic cycle, rather than treating it as at the end of a linear chain of events, consumer choices can be seen to have real wealth creating, value adding, potential.'[8]

Whereas 'the poor are always with us', we are increasingly aware that a damaged environment might not be. At the end of the nineteenth century the fight against poverty and social deprivation moved from individual to corporate action in order to address the sheer size of the problem. At the end of the twentieth century we are confronted by worldwide crises of poverty and environmental damage; these are on an unprecedented scale. Can it in any way be true that consumer decisions are useful in such circumstances?

Are not even more wide-ranging corporate actions needed? Of course they are, and of course relationship is more than economic transaction. But if economic transactions undermine or oppose relationship, and run counter to justice, corporate action can be undermined – as developing countries have found in the face of the patterns of world trade.

Such doubts are real and must be faced, but the 'new consumer' and 'ethical investor' movements, particularly if organised, can provide a symbolic lead and a training ground for the rest of society. This is the cutting edge of present day voluntarism. There is here a potential bridge between business realism and social idealism, an opportunity to draw the market towards making a positive contribution to its own social context.

The multiplicity of pressure groups working on these priorities may well contain the early stages of a new generation of action – one which harnesses both the individual and the corporate, and which gives modes of expression to the multiplicity of values at work in a plural society.

9. Issues before the Church

Questions and guidelines

The demand before the Church is to strengthen the 'moral circuits' in the face of the uncertainties of economic change. However, it will not be sufficient to resort to preaching and exhortation and otherwise to leave things as they are. The underlying problem of compartmentalism means that exhortation largely fails because the 'moral circuits' are not adequately connected to, in particular, the economic circuits. A strategy needs to be developed and implemented in order to improve the connections.

An integrated approach to money is required in which theological reflection, individual responsibility and corporate action are all included and are all related to the worship of God. 'Without God we would wander around eternally insecure and ultimately despairing and bored in the sphere of our freedom and of our decisions, because everything we might choose would be finally finite and ever replaceable by something else and would therefore remain indistinguishable.'[1]

In a plural and relativised society it is important to emphasize and clarify the God-relatedness and worship-centredness of a Christian approach. This must happen in service to the world, not in retreat from it. A worship centre of gravity can then pull on other areas of life both through the Church and through the lives of Christians in the world.

The Church needs to break down the rigidity of some of its own compartments. Then worship and theology can be, firstly, related to the reality of the economically changing world, and, secondly, allowed to inform ethical choices at all levels (not just some), individual, ecclesial, commercial, social, national and international. Clarity of thinking and purpose is required in order to ensure that, for example, questions such as ethical consuming and investing, which can be addressed more easily in the first instance on the individual level, are addressed on the other levels as well.

So, having reflected upon the trends in contemporary economic life, five main questions or guidelines are here provisionally identified for Christians and the Church. These give interrelated priorities which could, if acted upon, serve as a countervailing pressure against undue compartmentalism in general and evasion of money issues in particular. These priorities overlap and resonate with each other, as is to be expected from the overall direction of my argument.

1. *Facing money issues*

The Church must face up to the issue of money in three areas, in society, in its own corporate life and in the lives of its members. The characteristics of our economic culture already described – the high profile of money, the dominance of the market, the growing importance of the consumer, the paradoxical effects of debt and credit, the entrenching of property ownership, the imperfect but none-the-less moral response of charitable giving – add up to a total with profound spiritual implications.

These matters are the Church's business. Nothing less than the integrity and credibility of the Church is at stake in dealing with them. The task, made harder by compartmentalism and presently often avoided, calls for clarity, honesty, discernment and objectivity within a cross-disciplinary approach.

Connections need to be made across these three areas, of society, Church and individual Christians. The world of money interacts with political life, social life, family life, personal life in a multiplicity of ways. It forms a linkage, often unrecognised, between the compartments of life which are often kept separate. Decisions made about money represent people's values. The corporate stewardship of the institutional Church speaks as loudly as any formal pronouncements, perhaps louder if hypocrisy is suspected.

In western society, operating largely in the Cartesian tradition 'in which our understanding of ourselves and the world has to be built outwards from the private data of consciousness'[2], money can provide a connecting network linking outwards from 'my money' towards some of the greatest problems facing the human race. The Church fails adequately to point this out and so misses an enormous opportunity to speak to the human condition as it presents itself in the modern world.

In the past, religion, together with the ethics built upon religious foundations, has had an enormous influence upon conduct. This is not the case in contemporary economic culture, and both religion and economics are devalued thereby. A vacuum remains, stubbornly unfilled by any ideological or political system, leaving a quest for meaning which the Church should be equipping itself to answer.

Facing money issues must form an integral part of the preparation for, and carrying out of, this task.

2. *Balancing idealism and realism*

A balance should be sought between idealism and realism, leading to the formulation of practical criteria for handling money and wealth. This needs to go further than saying 'On the one hand . . .' and 'On the other hand . . .' Instead it should attempt an accommodation between the two. At present idealism is often identified with theology and realism with economics and financial management, a situation which approaches dangerously near to dualism. Achieving a proper, connected balance is therefore a key factor in bridging compartments and facing money issues.

Solely utopian solutions are inadequate. There is a difference between meaning well and doing well. Nevertheless, moral perfectionism must form part of Christian debate on social issues, and consequently the balance between idealism and realism will always be unstable and provisional. Judgements will always need to be reassessed in the light of events; there will be ambiguities, uncertainties, balances to be struck. A paradoxical and nuanced approach is required which recognises opposites in creative tension, affirms the value of each, and moves towards making a theology which can help to establish feasible criteria.

In the sphere of economic activity the Church is often in danger of moving too easily and quickly to the idealistic resolution of the argument, proposing solutions which call for changes in behaviour and eschew the need to hammer out hard economics. This may be because those whose task it is to define the position of the Church tend not to be as vulnerable to the exigencies of money realities as those who have to make a living in the market place. The Church provides secure employment and accommodation. This is not a good position from which to pass judgement upon others' search for financial security, or consumer dependency and greed, or susceptibility to the power of money, or indebtedness.

Similarly, the Church must come to terms with the market as a reality to be managed and steered towards right ends. It cannot simply be ignored as a separate mechanism which just exists with no particular moral implications. Neither can it be condemned out of hand as an ideology in direct opposition to Christian morality, for its capacity to devolve decisions, to provide a means towards subsidiarity in economic life, is positive. This should if possible be developed towards full participation, at the same time as limitations, voluntary, regulatory or fiscal, on the deleterious effects of the market are specified and tested.

Again, compartments must be linked. The Church must be rigorous in applying the same standards in the specifics of its own situation which it seeks to apply on the more abstract plane of its wider pronouncements. A suspicion exists, already noted in considering the Church's performance in adjusting to economic change, that the Church keeps money as a moral issue safely tucked away in the sphere of political economy, away from the challenge of personal faith to individual and ecclesial ways of life. This, too, will be examined further in the next section.

3.   A Third Kingdom?

Thirdly, the Church should consider seeing its own role in the context of 'three kingdoms' – the kingdom of God, a kingdom of the world, and a kingdom of the Church. This would acknowledge the need to develop beyond the 'two kingdoms' way of thinking about God and the world. This strand of theology 'can go disastrously wrong unless the two kingdoms are seen as intentioned with one another, intimately related, distinctive, but not to be pushed into separate compartments.'[3]

A serious danger of the 'two kingdoms' approach is that the emphasis on the distinction between the kingdoms of God and of the world offers Christians the temptation to identify themselves and the Church with the former. To succumb to this temptation undervalues the seriousness with which Augustine and Luther took the spiritual implications of what was going on in the world. It flatters the Church, and in so doing confuses intention with performance and ignores human sinfulness as a fact of life inside the Church as well as outside it.

Ronald Preston has noted the assumption 'that the Church stands in an independent principled position apart from the causes and struggles which divide humanity. There is no recognition that it has a keen nose for its own self-interest as an institution, and therefore no exploration of how this happens and how it might be modified. We know that for centuries churches identified themselves with the Kingdom of God in the New Testament. Modern biblical scholarship makes this no longer possible, but the convenient habit of thought remains.'[4]

The paradigm is the kingdom of God, where God is God 'without interruption, diminution or distortion,'[5] and Christians must work to bring the other kingdoms more closely into harmony with that paradigm. However, to identify the kingdom of God fully with either the Church or the world leads to a distortion of the gospel.

Identification with the Church ultimately requires that the gospel itself be conformed to what the Church actually is. Identification with the world means going beyond using a system of social analysis and adopting the ideological stance proposed by that analysis. Both are utopian and ignore the reality of fallible human nature, and thus the reason why thinking in terms of 'two kingdoms' arose in the first place.

In many ways it would be easier, in the face of these difficulties, to dispense with any concept of 'two kingdoms' altogether and leave it at that. Unfortunately the concept, in its abused form, is so influential and so descriptive of existing dualism and compartmentalism, that a corrective *is* required.

The idea of 'two kingdoms' remains of importance in the thought patterns of Christians and the institutional structures of the Church. This is so because the coming of the kingdom of God has priority in the proclamation of Jesus and in the prayer of his followers. Difficulties immediately arise because this kingdom is in some way both a present reality and practically unattainable – hence a second kingdom has often been accepted as an expression of this duality of truth.

A 'third kingdom' is therefore suggested here as a modification of this approach aimed at both avoiding dualism and expressing the reality of human experience, whilst allowing plenty of room to explore an old problem – the relationship between Christ and human culture. This accepts the fact of the two kingdoms, as a perception which reflects in many ways the existing situation and present experience of reality, but takes it forward in an attempt to transcend the problems of dualism.

Interplay of 'three kingdoms' – of God, the world and the Church – allows eschatology to be present and future, and to have a means, in the Church, of realisation and movement from one to the other. It extends, through service rather than domination, the territory which can be claimed for God in the compartmentalised modern world, by presenting an intermediary role for the Church. It encourages the Church to judge itself by the same criteria which it uses to judge the world, and provides a pattern and framework within which the Church can empty itself in service of the world.

This will assist in defining what the Church should express in its structures. It will allow judgement of those structures to be both faithful and realistic. It will encourage the Church to be more aware of itself as existing to serve the world, and more aware of itself as implicated in and part of the structures of the world.

In a period of confusion for the Church as it adjusts to pluralism and relativism a 'third kingdom' creates a clear space for the Church from which it can relate to both the kingdom of God and the world – a space within which to think and pray and worship and be, to realise eschatology in daily life, to hold faithfulness together with realism and to place the present moment on God's timetable.[6]

This space or linking structure is needed to provide a means to connect compartments and to avoid the twin dangers of privatising the kingdom of God or politicising it, in the sense of identifying it with any particular social programme. The role of the Church is properly affirmed without claiming for it any utopian perfection.

The Church is not the kingdom of God, it is the body of Christ. Therefore it proclaims and announces the kingdom, and ultimately it suffers and is sacrificed and laid down for the kingdom. Only by losing itself can the Church become the kingdom of God, but it does contain that potential, and along with it the vocation, separating it from the world, to call and serve the world towards the same destiny.

4.   Owners called by God

Attention must be given to reformulating some of the theological concepts which have traditionally been used in the area of money, wealth and ownership. Theologically themes such as trusteeship, stewardship and dominion need to be reworked in the light of the ecological crisis, the shift in perception away from production and towards consumption, and contemporary patterns of ownership. None of these concepts readily applies, for instance, to the contemporary use of credit financing. None speaks directly to the modern person's apprehension of economic reality.

James Lovelock has expressed his dislike of the term stewardship, claiming that human dominion is dangerous however it is dressed up. Perhaps it is more honest to speak of ownership, and face this danger head on. A concept of ownership, having direct application to that which we can control or over which we can have some influence, may be more meaningful for most people. It may be that we need less stewardship of the environment and more sensitivity towards it.

The changed context affects the shape and usefulness of guidelines formed. The role now given to the consumer cannot be accommodated by the post-reformation stewardship tradition with its emphasis on thrift, work ethic, saving and investment. A reformulated concept is needed which can break down barriers – one that can avoid being compromised by the excessive individuality which has a vested interest in retaining and strengthening compartments. This will be difficult to achieve because people now relate much more readily to the concept of ownership, and this has itself a strong pull towards individualism and compartmentalism.

All the same, it may be that private property can be newly understood as having a potentially positive impact on the common good. This might be thought of as being analogous to the idea of the self in the Christian tradition: the acceptance that there is a proper place for love of self as something which is both a prior requirement of and necessary for love of others.

The need is to enhance the sense, already present in the verb 'to own', of acknowledging something in relation to one's self, of confessing its connections and implications. In this way the element of 'being responsible for' or 'being responsive to the meaning of' can be strengthened in our concept of ownership. Owning means owning up.

In the context so far described, therefore, our new formulation should: derive from and be subordinate to the kingdom of God; be relevant to both the communal and the individual, and actively make connections between them; be realistically capable of expression in the world; be actually expressed in the structures of the Church; be able to express the role of the Church in the world; be spiritually sustaining and sustainable; and express subsidiarity, philanthropy and voluntarism.

It may be necessary to develop what could be called a 'just wealth' tradition. In the same way as the just war tradition is based upon a strong Christian presumption against war, this would be based upon a presumption against economic injustice. Criteria would then need to be developed for deviating from the basic presumption, giving conditions and parameters for the accumulation of wealth and setting limits to the toleration of inequality. These could be reflected upon and adjusted in the light of developing experience. Issues such as debt and credit, qualifications of absolute rights of property, the place of charitable giving in economic relationships, consumer duties and rights, and division and injustice in market economies could all be addressed from this angle.

At present the only criterion on offer seems to be an expression of neo-puritan asceticism, but this is solely individually-based. It does not have that corporate expression which is necessary for viability in a plural society and is in danger of being lost amongst a plethora of burgeoning individual preferences. Our reformulation, on the other hand, would be a practical example of the interplay of a 'three kingdoms' approach, the Church serving the kingdom by providing a forum with the world.

It would be a messy business, still involving the need to encourage flawed humanity to act in ways which are beneficial to the common good. Motivations such as economic selfishness could not be eliminated, but would need to be harnessed. However, in practice the alternative is to retain compartmentalism and dualism, and thus to fail in mission to the world.

This new structure of thought for owners called by God would be set within the united interplay of three distinct kingdoms, God, world and Church. It could enable what the Church says about money, and what it does when managing its own affairs, to be reconciled in a way which could offer realistic criteria to Christians. An ethical approach to investment is an example of an area in which this would be beneficial.

In this reformulated pattern, individuals would be nurtured by and act as representatives of the communal. They would respond to their God-given individuality and personality by acting thankfully as representatives of the communal, of Church or world or both. They would thus form an interconnecting linkage across fragmented modern life and across the three kingdoms themselves.

5. *Pastoral implications of money*

The wide-ranging and disparate pastoral implications of money should be the subject of much more study and reflection. How people handle money relates to how the Church cares for people. As security is sought in home ownership and investment, supported by high levels of borrowing, the Church should examine how ultimate values and meanings can be offered and ultimate realities faced. It should consider how ecclesiologies and relationships within the Church are affected by its own handling of money. In the Church of England, for example, this would involve forming a view on whether its handling of money is appropriate for its role within the nation.

Very importantly, too, the Church needs to consider the effect on authority in the Church if subsidiarity becomes a presumption of its attitude to wealth. What would happen if it expressed in its own structures the importance it gives to the essential nature of personal responsibility? In these circumstances it will be necessary to be alert to the danger, already inherent in charitable giving, that whoever pays wins the debate about spending priorities. Nevertheless, God needs and requires the free co-operation of human beings, and cannot and will not gain the divine purposes without that free co-operation.

There is no way of knowing if it will be possible to develop a spirituality for the Church and a pastoral relationship with society which can give a sense of meaning to an owning, accumulating and consuming culture. It remains to be seen whether property for self can be improved, adapted, or induced to include property for others, whether a thought pattern can be encouraged which suggests that owners are called by God. It may be possible to develop the role of the consumer ethically as it is enhanced economically. However the poor overall response to increased affluence in terms of charitable giving indicates that words, preaching and exhortation, will not be enough.

As a pastoral priority, therefore, the Church must practise what it preaches, both individually and corporately. It must reflect upon the dualism in its own handling of money and wealth. This will be the subject of Part Two. In the meantime, this examination of the part played by money in contemporary culture has provided an indication of the directions in which it will be necessary to explore.

Money and the Church

10. Introduction

In examining economics and Christian ethics several important questions have been raised. These questions cannot just be addressed to the world at large. If the Church is to ask them of others with integrity it must, as a matter of priority, ask them of itself in its own corporate life and in the lives of its members. This will be the task of this second part.

'Worship expresses what we cannot say for ourselves, and very rarely put into practice.'[1] There is mystery in the life and worship of the Church, and some things are beyond definition. Nevertheless, the challenge to put the life of worship and prayer into practice, into tangible shape, remains constantly before us. Prayer cannot be used 'as an escalator to bypass the complexities of human living'[2], for the incarnation shows us a God passionately concerned to redeem human living and to bring it to fulfilment.

This passion, re-enacted in the eucharist, is at the very heart of Christian worship, and it provides the vision for the living out of Christian lives in the world – a vision which must be shot through with thankfulness. Life and worship in constant dialogue is the life-blood of any Christian pilgrimage. We must constantly seek ways of making the Christian vision real in day-to-day living, of expressing the thankfulness of worship in our behaviour.

For the Christian, making the vision real means allowing oneself to be questioned by the person of Christ, a person who in his very being announces the reconciliation of the spiritual and the material, of the ideal and the real, and who makes whole the fragmentation of human life. This questioning cannot be limited by false barriers which cut off worship and theology from the prosaic realities of life. It is an inter-rogation which allows no segmentation into 'them' and 'us'. Christians must ask themselves the same questions which they ask the world, before they ask them of the world and as they ask them of the world.

It is not, therefore, surprising to find a symmetry between the pressures placed by money upon society at large and upon the Church itself. Both inhabit the same world of economic circum-stances and money preoccupations. For both the signs of the times are the same.

So we return to the questions raised in Part One, and now set them alongside the practice of the Church. Firstly, in a general way whilst surveying the overall background of the ways that Christians and the Church have handled wealth and money. Secondly, in a more specific and contemporary way, whilst examining, with the Church of England particularly in mind, three specific areas of 'ecclesiastical economics'.

These specific areas to a large extent form a parallel with the three examples of economic change described in Part One. They are (1) the ownership of land and property by the institutional Church, (2) the funding of the structured mission and ministry of the Church, and (3) voluntary giving in, through and for the Church. In all three contemporary economic reality impinges closely upon the Church.

Furthermore, they are matters which show a high profile in the life of the Church and the Church's life in the nation. They give scope for comparison between individual and corporate handling of money and wealth. It is interesting that many of the elements in an individual's Christian responsibility for money were dealt with in Part One. The actions of individual Christians in the world are a vital part of witness to the gospel.

To these areas we bring from our consideration of economics and ethics the five crucial questions already defined, and put them to the Church. In itself, this process should at least begin to make some connections, bridging those gaps between compartments which have been so noticeable:

(1) Are money issues honestly faced?

Is the high profile of money in society taken seriously in the life of the Church? Are matters such as the influence of the market, the place of the consumer and the ownership of property recognised as being very important in people's lives and taken into account when social pronouncements are made? Are the motivations and relationships of charitable giving properly thought through, and related to attitudes to Christian giving?

If these questions are faced, the issue of money might form a network which bridges the compartments of life, a linkage connecting economic and religious culture, enabling an interplay of life and worship.

(2) Are idealism and realism held in balance?

Is income generation balanced with distribution, practical finance with justice, social imperatives with pastoral facts? These questions are as important in the life of the Church as they are in society at large. Is the balance openly arrived at, or is tension avoided by thinking of the idealism in one context, for example the Board of Social Responsibility, and the realism in another, for example the Board of Finance?

If the latter course is taken, avoiding tension, an opportunity to make connections is lost, doors have been closed. For the Church, money as a moral issue cannot be tucked away in the sphere of political economy, it must also and at the same time impinge upon how the Church and Christians themselves make decisions about property and finance. Grace is costly, and hypocrisy is of its nature often much nearer than we think.

(3) Is the 'Third Kingdom' active?

Is the undue separation which can be the product of the 'two kingdoms' approach avoided? Is the Church, the 'third kingdom', actively seeking to proclaim the gospel by serving both the kingdom of God and the world? Is there self-critical reflection in the Church on its own relation to the world's structures, particularly as expressed in the handling of money?

Such reflection is needed to provide Christians with an eschatology which is both for the present and for the future, which offers a kingdom which in some way comes on earth as in heaven and which relates to practical experience of life in the world, including the Church itself.

(4) Are owners called by God?

Is there a search for a theological concept which will speak to the contemporary property owner of the things of God, in the way that trusteeship spoke to the medieval catholic and stewardship to the puritan and the evangelical? Does this take shape in the actions of Christians or the Church, acknowledging the power of money, the power expressed though wealth, and relating it to a sense of living vocationally?

Realistic criteria and symbols are needed so that the insights of Christian faith can be brought to bear upon people's lives. Nowhere is this more important than in the area of money, often left aside in spite of its day-to-day potential as an arena for practical ethics. If it is possible to define 'just wealth', it must be necessary for the

Church to do so as a matter of urgency. If it is not possible, the implications are enormous, given the prevailing attitudes towards property held by Christians and non-Christians alike.

(5) Are we aware of the pastoral implications of money?

Is thought, care and attention given to the effect of money matters on Christians and on society at large? At the corporate level this means an attempt to match ecclesiology and theology with practice. Does the way the Church is funded correspond with it being universal, denominational or sectarian? Is Christian freedom and responsibility represented by a commitment to subsidiarity?

At the individual level this means an attempt to infuse inhabitants of consumer society with a sense of meaning and purpose. Is there an ethical direction to people's lives as expressed by the way they handle money? Does a general lack of connection between the life of faith and the way that Christians handle their money indicate that for many being part of the Church is a leisure activity? Do pronouncements on politial economy lack credibility if connections are not made with the ways of life followed by individual Christians?

What is the real authority in our lives? In fact Jesus refuses to answer for us the questions which we should answer ourselves. He does not resolve the question of authority, but responds enigmatically to throw us back upon the resources given to us – an example, perhaps, of subsidiarity in action. In questions of money and the handling of wealth it is impossible to avoid some of the hardest questions which faith asks of life. 'Saying yes means saying no'[3], and all the trade-offs need to be understood clearly and discussed frankly, not least in the Church itself.

11. Background to Ecclesiastical Economics

Before looking more closely at our three detailed examples and the five questions to be set alongside them, I will give an overview of some of the main ingredients in the Christian attitude to money and in the Church's own economic culture. Some of the patterns revealed have a long history.

A perennial conundrum

Money is the subject which shows most clearly the difficulty of drawing codes for living in simplistic fashion from the Bible. Those who desire to proclaim the Bible as a literal source of direct authority often stop short of taking on board the full implications of Jesus' strictures on wealth. Instead they find in the Old Testament guidance more congenial to their circumstances – the decalogue or the tithe. Fortunately for the literalists, the Bible contains the stories of many wealthy patriarchs, as well as that of the announcement of the kingdom of God and the good news of Jesus Christ.

The tension between the radical demands of Jesus and the practical demands of daily life surfaced early in the life of the Church. Early Christian attitudes towards wealth, therefore, contain conflicting ingredients[1]. There were experiments with forms of ancient communism and abandonment of wealth. The poor were thought to be more pious than the rich. Continued acquisition of riches after conversion was thought by the fathers to be sinful. Simplicity of life and spiritual detachment from wealth was encouraged.

At the same time, however, there was a high view of almsgiving, which implies approval of wealth. Clement of Alexandria's theology gave wealth a positive part to play in the salvation of its possessor, provided it was used aright[2]. In fact, the control of wealth was left alone, abandonment was never the norm, and primitive communism was never formally imposed, even at Jerusalem.

This divergence may well express the social make-up of the Church, as well as the beginnings of its insitutional life. As expectations of an imminent coming of the kingdom of God receded, maintenance of long-term structures and welfare apparatus became more important. Simultaneously, so did the social significance of rich members. A lapse could be very worrying, and rich laity inevitably held a higher profile in society at large which made them vulnerable to persecution. 'If the fathers, at one moment, say that private property has no foundation in God's will and, at another, ascribe phenomenal merit to the correct disposition of it, there lies between these seeming contradictions the necessity of the church's officers to keep the rich under control, and yet to keep them attached to the church.'[3]

No defined Christian doctrine of property came out of the New Testament or the early Church. This was so *in spite of* there being a radical criticism of riches, a call for detachment from this world's goods, an attempt to conquer the barriers between rich and poor, and an eschatological sense of urgency. It is possible to see in this the emergence of the institutional life of the Church as an increasingly formative influence. This required a dual tradition which included statements, on the one hand, of principle and, on the other, of accommodation and compromise.

Institutional dualism

This institutional dualism has been a recurrent theme in the history of the Church. Throughout the centuries property has been accumulated, clergy have been paid, strategies devised to increase giving (one of which, the sale of indulgences, provided great moral force for Luther's denunciations). Repeatedly, however, this has been renounced or denounced, and poverty-as-virtue proclaimed – the asceticism of the hermits and early monastics, the attempts to renew and restore monasticism throughout the Middle Ages, the mendicant orders, various radical reformers. In prison towards the end of his life, Dietrich Bonhoeffer came to this latter view: 'The church is the church only when it exists for others. To make a start, it should give away all its property to those in need.'[4]

This stark view, from the prison cell, was perhaps prefigured in Bonhoeffer's first major theological work, in which he developed the notion of the Church as an interpersonal community. 'The community is constituted by the complete self-forgetfulness of love. The relationship between I and thou is no longer essentially a demanding but a giving one.'[5] What is at question is the very nature of the Church as defined objectively by its own actions, over and against the, perhaps more subjective, definitions of its own pronouncements. Bonhoeffer takes to its logical conclusion the need for the Church to witness to the self-giving love of God.

Nevertheless, the structures of the institutional Church remain – buildings, property, investments, giving, stipends, salaries, pensions. These cannot be swept away without abandoning many trusts and responsiblities. However, it is a constant challenge to ensure that the institution serves its primary purpose, proclaiming the gospel, rather than its own continuation or proliferation as an end in itself. The Church is not exempt from the tendency of any institution to develop a self-perpetuating life of its own.

J. P. Wogaman points out that Barth speaks, in Church Dogmatics, of 'creation as the external basis of the covenant' and of 'the covenant as the internal basis of creation' and that this 'affirms the value of the natural and also locates moral value in the specifics of the created world.'[6] If this internal/external concept is adapted it can perhaps provide a useful basis for understanding and handling the dangerous dualism which can be engendered by the institutional manifestation of the Church. Seeing the Church as the external manifestation of the gospel and the gospel as the internal basis of the Church might be a way of differentiating, without dividing, the medium and the message, and at the same time calling the institution to fidelity. Another mediating concept is Bonhoeffer's 'penultimate', which can only be understood in relation to the ultimate, which cannot be separated from the ultimate, and yet is not the ultimate. 'The coming of grace is the ultimate. But we must speak of the preparing of the way . . .'[7]

Decline and pluralism

It is not possible to consider the Church's attitude to money and the handling of wealth without looking at its general state of mind and being. Ronald Preston has remarked that 'the churches as institutions find themselves with the apparatus of a Christendom structure but without the means to support it . . .'[8] There is an obvious connection between money and a growing sense, felt by many, of living in a post-Christian culture. Here the Church forms a subculture and no longer exercises a formative influence, yet struggles to maintain long held beliefs about its own identity.

Whilst Church affiliation in Great Britain in 1986 ran at 85%, weekly Church attendance was only 14%[9]. It is likely that such nominalism may die out in a generation, the children of nominal

Christians being more likely to be non-Christians than otherwise. As the Church grows in many parts of the world, it seems to decline in the European culture from which it spread outwards in the post-Reformation period. Many local churches and congregations are too small to be self-supporting, and require external subsidy of some sort if they are to continue.

The evidence is not conclusive. Some commentators see the decline as being largely confined to nominal Christians, whose real value and relevance to the life and witness of the Church is limited. But mainstream churchgoing gently falls, and seems to have been so doing for the best part of a century. Meanwhile house churches and those offering greater certainties grow. The overall picture shows a trend towards sects (rather than churches), often suburban and middle-class. These tend to withdraw from the social arena into the private, perhaps searching for perfection away from the complexities of modern economic life.

Recent research in Toronto by R. W. Bibby shows a reduction in the areas of life over which religion has significant input. 'The 20%-25% whom he styles as active Anglicans exhibit 'compartmentalised commitment': their religious faith is having decreasing impact on social, economic and political values. The other 75%-80%, the inactive Anglicans, have moved from 'commitment to consumption': they select what they want from the beliefs, practices and professional services of the church in a highly selective, consumer-like fashion. In the light of this thesis, Bibby identifies the challenge facing Anglicanism today as its response to these 'market realities' of compartmentalisation and consumption.'[10] Similar research has not taken place in Britain, but the likelihood is that the pattern would be similar.

Twentieth-century western humanity, including many Christians, no longer looks with confidence towards traditional sources of moral guidance. Bible, Church, law, social structure, custom – all seem relative, fallible and provisional, leaving the individual to choose from amongst a plurality of options. In such circumstances any moral message becomes simultaneously both more important and less easy to hear or understand. The temptation of the certainties of a dualistic private religion may therefore be very strong.

Lesslie Newbigin, influenced by the work of Alasdair MacIntyre,[11] points to the dualism of modern western culture, where religion operates in a private sphere of values and science in a public sphere of facts. This dualism flourishes in the context of a society of atomistic individuals. Here private choice is sovereign, particularly so in areas such as morality and religion. In spite of his disclaimers, Newbigin comes close to requiring the faithful, as the logical conclusion of his argument, to reject the scientific world view in its entirety in order to overcome this dualism and the resulting relativism and reductionist individualism. MacIntyre regards the situation, of an emotivist culture where moral objectivity is a lost possibility, as being as serious for civilisation as the dark ages, calling for the modern equivalent of monasticism as a necessary response.

The arguments presented in these books are complex and sophisticated, and still being developed. Nevertheless, the requirement to choose is not without its own problems. If one side of the dualism is rejected (rather than an attempt made to assimilate it into the whole, to overcome the dualism itself) in the end this may reinforce the dualism which is a major constituent part of the problem. The danger is that in rejecting dualism and the post-enlightenment world-view, we in fact affirm dualism in its oldest manifestation – the rejection of the world and the flesh – and give it in to unorthodoxy in the effort to be orthodox. Nevertheless, the problem is a serious one and the dualism diagnosed by Newbigin is integral to much of our contemporary thinking and acting.

The Church is caught, to some extent hoist by its own petard. It has helped mould attitudes throughout the post-Reformation period. However, now that it wishes to move away from the resulting individualism and relativism and recover a more communal approach, it cannot, because society at large has retained the attitudes of individualism. In such circumstances Christians cannot abandon ship without some concern for the fate of the other passengers. Difficult as it may be, we have to work through individualism towards the communal. Notions of the common good have to be incorporated into the life of the individual, without rejecting the positive things which have been brought to society by the enhanced sense of the importance of the individual implicit in post-Enlightenment western thought.

Integrity and authenticity

Compartmentalism affects the life of the Church, reflecting the situation in the wider world. Parish ministry, sector ministry, theological reflection, the laity in the world – all lose in as much as they are cut off from each other. 'If there is a growing gulf between academic theologians and the clergy, then there is also a gulf between the claims of church theologians about their churches and the empirical realities to which they refer.'[12] Throughout the Church there is a need to relate theory and practice much more rigorously, and thus to claim integrity and authenticity.

Robin Gill identifies as a compensatory symptom of decline the need felt by Church synods and assemblies to pronounce on social issues[13]. Church members are very varied in their attitudes and behaviour, and often at odds with an 'official' line which may well have been reached at some distance from pastoral realities. 'It is distinctly easier to moralize in theory than it is in practice when the minister must continue to be a face-to-face pastor to the individuals concerned.'[14] The Church 'line' on politial economy often operates unduly independently of the way of life adopted by many Church members. Credibility is lost as a result. In practice, theological contentions must be tested in the life of the worshipping community itself. A recent study indentified as a problem: 'The tendency of clergy to ignore their congregation when they address society, rather than to speak with and through their congregation as representatives of society . . .'[15]

If there is a danger of social pronouncement operating too independently of personal witness and worship, there is a similar and linked danger of it operating independently of the Church's corporate handling of money and property. Both are important issues which must be faced if the message is to be credible and matched by Christian action.

In spite of the decline of the mainstream Churches, the view that this is the result of the long-term secularisation of western society is at least an oversimplification, at most wrong. Now the view is gaining ground that society is more pluralist than secular. Levels of church-going in western countries vary enormously. Interest in religious belief and the supernatural remains, even where Church attendance is low, although it may manifest in strange ways. Many talk of a search for meaning and identity in society. Green issues provide a focus for new forms of spirituality and ethics. People desperately try to define the 'New Age' so that they can decide whether it is a good thing or not. New democracies in the east struggle with old nationalisms and religious loyalties alongside a new market orthodoxy.

If the elevation of choice is matched by the elevation of conscience, there is the potential for a more mature spirituality to emerge. This is not negated, in practice it may be strengthened, by the inevitable self-interest of a growing sense of ecological urgency.

David Marquand, also influenced by Alasdair MacIntyre's analysis, points out that 'reductionist individualism' has two modes for living in society. One is the 'command mode', found in state security and centralised planning, and the other is the 'exchange mode', exemplified by the free market, its institutions and transactions. However, this shows a deficient view of human nature, which has other needs – a 'preceptoral' or learning mode is also required.[16] Concepts such as double loop learning, hermeneutical circles, mutual education leading to change, imply a common good which is not opposed to the individual, but necessary for the individual. The search for meaning and identity is, in fact, strongly communal.

Will the Church be of use in this search for meaning? Much depends on the level of integrity and authenticity which can be attained, and this relates very closely to issues of wealth and money-handling. For it is here that the pressure is on – buildings to run, people to pay, not so many in the congregation to give, inflation only fitfully kept at bay. It is here that society's prevailing 'economic determinism' will pull towards maximum return on investment, towards an uninhibited run with the markets. But it is here, too, that the ability, or otherwise, of the Church to practise what it preaches will be most obvious. Poor witness here will mean less to offer to a searching society, for the first thing the searchers will find will be a lack of authenticity and integrity.

Social profile of the Church

The social dimension is also relevant. Many in the Church, especially those active in its structures and positive about the need for a prophetic role on social and political issues, are embarrassed by its middle class image. They long to see a deeper identification with the poor.

Others do not see this as a problem, they see an active commitment to a Christian way of life as finding expression in middle class virtues and values. Lives are transformed for the better and it is natural for this to have a material and social expression.

Commentators do seem to agree that the middle class weighting is real. The Church is most successful in middle class areas, and in other areas its membership is disproportionately middle class. Middle class churchgoing can often involve choosing a congregation where the social profile and style of worship are congenial.

Neville Black reaches similar conclusions from his research into the housing tenure of inner city congregations: 'I draw three simple conclusions; that the Church of England is becoming increasingly a "property-owning community"; that it attracts a considerably higher proportion of owner occupiers than the communities in which it is set; and these features are more prevalent in the urban priority areas.'[17] He goes on to comment: 'My hunch is that property ownership for first-time buyers takes on the significance of an "initiation rite" whereby one leaves the community and culture of origin to be baptised or "encultured" in a new set of values, beliefs and aspirations, which has at their focus "property ownership"'.

So, it is hardly surprising to find, churchgoers are members of the property-owning democracy, too. In fact, they are better at it than many. They are not set apart from this characteristic of society at large, they have it in more pronounced form. The effect of this on attitudes cannot be quantified. The likelihood is that both attitudes and way of life are mutually reinforced.

Interestingly, there is one group of churchgoers in the Church of England, at least, which does not conform to this pattern. The stipendiary clergy almost always have good quality accommodation provided for them – for convincing pastoral reasons. This ensures a certain freedom and security from which to minister. However, it may in some cases lead to a lack of understanding of or identification with the need felt by the laity to establish their own form of security, through home ownership in particular. If, as is sometimes claimed, the clergy line up further to the left than the laity, this fact may be relevant.

Important questions applied

So the important questions which have been identified from the contemporary economic and ethical context are set alongside today's Church. This is the necessary first stage in any attempt to build a bridge between compartments of life which are normally kept separate:

(1)   Are money issues honestly faced?

Although the Church takes the high profile of money in society very seriously, it does not adequately or apparently recognise the import-ance of the fact that Christians themselves are active in the market place as consumers and as owners of property. Some claim that consumerism is addictive. If so, Christian consumers have to work out to what extent their lives are out of control, have to identify precisely from their own experience just where the addictive elements lie. If the Church, as it often seems to, takes upon itself the role of conscience to the nation, it must pay more attention to the economic activity of its members and use it positively to strengthen the use of praxis in its theology. This can only enhance its credibility and add moral force to its pronouncements.

Feeling perhaps cornered or threatened by prevailing pluralism and relativism, many Christians are attracted towards increasing doctrinal conservatism and biblical literalism. This search for certainty is in danger of building up, rather than breaking down, the barriers between the life of faith and life in the real world outside. Application of stark and over-simple principles in relation to money, taking little account of people's actual circumstances, can call out a small number *from* the world. It will not address the need of the majority to relate Christian principles to living *in* the world.

(2) Are idealism and realism held in balance?

The ideal Church of the poor and the real Church of the increasingly affluent are held in balance only by the failure to think as both, as the same Church, at the same time. The Church meets in small groups to talk of development, peace and justice; it meets in councils and synods to talk of institutional finance; it sits at the dining table to work out personal household budgets. Rarely do these strands come together.

The difficulty felt by the early Church in preaching the gospel to the rich *and* keeping them in the Church remains. It may be more important than ever. This situation is itself prey to compartmentalism and leads to a tendency for idealism and realism to diverge, rather than be held in balance. Giving strategies are a prime example of this and will be looked at later. There are few instances of any mediating concepts, such as Barth's 'internal/external' or Bonhoeffer's 'penultimate', being used in practice or expressed in Church structures.

(3) Is the 'Third Kingdom' active?

The Church's calling to serve both the kingdom of God and the world is heard, and activity results. This will always be imperfect, for it is, again using Bonhoeffer's term, 'penultimate'. However, institutional dualism always threatens this diaconal call, always stresses survival before vocation and means before ends. Kingdom of God principles are proclaimed to the world, but often without reflection and appraisal of the accommodation and compromise in the kingdom of the Church.

In the face of numerical decline, the Church clings to old and tired views of its own identity and of the kingdom of God. These were formed out of Christendom (the kingdom of God will come by conflating Church and world) or its reformation aftermath (it will come when every individual is coverted into the Church). A new mediating model or concept is required which more effectively counters the dualism of modern western culture. This needs to express the interplay which exists between Church and world and the challenge which the kingdom of God places before both of them.

(4) Are owners called by God?

There is little evidence of a search for a symbolic or metaphorical concept which can speak to contemporary property owners of the things of God. 'Stewardship' excites few and in the Church itself carries overtones of institutional misuse as fundraising. It needs redeeming or replacing. At present, inside or outside the Church, owners are not aware of being called by anyone. God is provident, but everything is owned by someone – the connection has still to be made and the implications taught.

The implications of the compartmentalised and consumerised commitment described in Bibby's study[10] are important in this context. The security-mindedness of property ownership is the dominant culture in the Church, yet there are few signs of the Church working with its members towards a deep consideration of how this relates to their own vocation and response to God.

(5) Are we aware of the pastoral implications of money?

Some individuals in the Church may be aware of the pastoral implications of money, but signs of an open and general awareness are limited. People are aware that some are poor and some (in fact, many) are rich. They are aware that social problems result, but not so much that pastoral problems for the Church may result, just as they did for the early Church as it tried simultaneously both to contain and guide the rich. The pastoral implications of baptism policy and marriage discipline are exhaustively debated, but the ethical discipline required in handling money and wealth, and its pastoral implications, is a rare subject. Perhaps the pastoral implication is that if we talked seriously about money, people might leave. So we don't.

The need is to find ways of working through individualism towards the communal and the common good. There is no legitimate reason why the Church itself should not offer a lead to society. In economic life there are developments towards this, such as the 'new consumer' and the 'ethical investor', but there are few signs in the Church that any strategies are being formed to encourage Christians in this direction, either individually or corporately. In fact, the main impression is one of resistance to change, especially in trying to bring practice into line with theory.

It is difficult to pronounce to the world when the Church is shy of making clear statements to its own members about money and does not really work out what it needs to do when those members show signs of being 'consumers' of religion, having the last word on what the product should be like. Teaching about money might be the place to start on the task, identified above, of speaking with and through the congregation as representatives of society. Eventually it will be necessary to relate money to modern society's search for meaning, and nothing is to be gained by delay.

12. Land and Property Ownership

Historical summary

The contemporary financial affairs of the Church of England cannot be understood without a brief summary of the historical process which formed them.

The medieval parish priest's income came from three main local sources. Firstly, land or glebe, given over the years by benefactors and applied by the priest to provide some form of annual income. Secondly, the tithe, theoretically a tenth of the produce of the land. Thirdly, fees and offerings for masses. Some of this came to an end with the Reformation – monastic lands were taken for the crown, as were the 'first fruits and tenths'.

Some benefices were left in a very difficult situation, and little was done about this until the time of Queen Anne, when the crown returned some of the monies. Queen Anne's Bounty was the first of several attempts to reduce the inequality of wealth distribution across the Church, it was designed to enhance the position of those benefices most in need. Later, in 1836, the Ecclesiastical Commisioners were established to reform and redistribute Church revenues and to provide stability in clergy income.

The nineteenth century was a time of expansion. Churches were built to serve the growing urban populations of industrialising Britain. Particular benefices received the attention of benefactors. The resources of poorer glebe land were often reinvested to provide improved income, so that the Ecclesiastical Commissioners and Queen Anne's Bounty each held an investment portfolio for each benefice, from which the clergy were paid their stipends.

This meant that some benefices were very much better off than others. In 1948 the Church Commissioners were formed from an amalgamation of the Ecclesiastical Commissioners and Queen Anne's Bounty, and thereafter a single investment fund was created from all the separate benefice funds. Effective investment policies increased income, but stipends were frozen at 1951 levels, so that clergy income could be augmented on a discretionary basis via Diocesan Stipends Funds. Gradually inequalities were reduced, and moves were made to standardise the criteria used in the calculation of stipend augmentation. In 1972 the General Synod appointed the Church Commissioners as Central Stipends Authority.

Further rationalisation took place in 1976 through the Endowments and Glebe Measure. Benefice glebe became diocesan glebe, available for augmentation. Management improved. This did not diminish disparities between dioceses, on the contrary, it progressively increased them.[1] Following two papers on historic resources[2] moves have been made to correct the imbalance.

Wider economic events in the 1970s and 1980s had their effect on the Church. Inflation took off and for a time left clergy stipends behind. Many industrial and urban areas went into decline leaving as residue a Victorian ecclesiastical infrastructure. Demographic trends left the church with an increasing bill for pensions. The consensus in society at large towards fairness affected the Church's targets for stipends and pensions. Then the recession of the early 1990s badly affected income from investments. Pressure has steadily grown for more realistic giving in the parishes.

The Church's property

In terms of area the Church of England is one of the four largest landowners in England, along with the Forestry Comission, the Ministry of Defence and the National Trust. The Church Commissioners are the largest landowners of farms in England, and their December 1990 Balance Sheet[3] shows property valued at £1,708 million. A large quantity of land is also held by dioceses and parishes in a multiplicity of forms, notably diocesan Glebe Committees and by voluntary societies. It would not be possible to quantify the land occupied by church buildings, parsonages and church schools.

All these corporate manifestations of the Church of England also own investments, in the case of the Church Commissioners, £942 million worth in December 1990[3]. The Church Commissioners alone therefore control well over £2½ billion worth of assets. To this must be added the investments held by the many and various other levels of Church life.

The Church has a great deal of property. By and large it is inherited wealth. This wealth takes two forms. Firstly, there is property which is held for use in the Church's ministry, over fifteen thousand church buildings, housing for clergy, halls, administrative accommodation and so on. This produces little in the way of income, but requires considerable resources for maintenance.

Secondly, there are investments of various types of property and Stock Exchange securities. Much of this is in the hands of the

Church Commissioners, producing considerable income, £164 million in 1990. 'We provide about 48% of the stipends costs of the serving clergy, much of their housing costs and almost all their pension costs. We also provide substantial capital sums for housing serving and retired clergy.'[4]

An underlying principle can be discerned. The property of the Church is held in trust for present and future generations. This is totally in harmony with the tradition of charity law in Britain, with its stress on the autonomy of economic decision making. A multiplicity of trusts passes on the generosity and giving of earlier generations. In the Church this is emphasized by a sense of its history as an institution called to carry eternal verities though the turmoil of human affairs.

The broad range of property owned means that the Church is economically closely integrated with the society in which it is set. 'Just as the Commissioners' resources support the Church's ministry throughout the length and breadth of the country, so do their investments give the Church an involvement in virtually every aspect of our national economy and in virtually every county.'[5]

Investment policy

Although much Church property does not fall under the responsibility of the Charity Commissioners – for example, the Church Commissioners are responsible directly to Parliament – the general atmosphere is very much that which is set by the tradition of English charity law. That is to say, each charity or trust must order its affairs so as to apply funds as fully as possible to its own charitable aims and objectives. If assets have to be sold, they must in general go to the highest bidder, and if trustees use any criteria other than financial advancement they risk personal liability for the shortfall. The investment policy of charitable trustees can give weight to ethical criteria, but not to the detriment of the financial interests of beneficiaries.

This principle has given rise to much discussion, especially in the light of the recent high profile of ethical investment. Trustees may well be required to take action on behalf of their charity which they would be unwilling to take for their own benefit. 'In determining where the best interests of the charity lie charity trustees must try to be objective and not to allow their personal, moral or religious principle to influence their decisions.'[6]

The ruling in the High Court in 1991, in the Bishop of Oxford's case seeking to establish the Church Commissioners' duty to follow a stricter ethical investment policy, did acknowledge that it would be permissible for charity trustees to abstain from investing in concerns obviously running counter to their objectives. However, it reckoned the likelihood of this being a practical issue as rare, and remarked that trustees should not see investing as a way of 'making moral statements at the expense of their charity.'[7]

The Church Commissioners interpret their own duties and aims as follows, casting the clergy of the Church of England in the role of main beneficiaries: 'The Commissioners' primary aim in the management of their assets must be to produce the best total return. An ever-increasing flow of income is needed to maintain the Commisioners' current share of the cost of clergy pensions, stipends and housing. Future growth in capital is vital to underpin support for tomorrow's clergy.'[8]

Current income has to be weighed against the need for long term capital security and growth. Property owned is a mix of agricultural, residential, industrial, offices and shops. Some commercial property is owned in the United States. Similarly Stock Exchange securities are a mix of UK and overseas equities and convertibles, and fixed interest stocks. The amount of the assets involved means that it is prudent for the Commissioners to pursue a policy of diversification – a wide spread of investments of different types both in the UK and overseas.

The Commissioners give a carefully worded and qualified assent to the importance of ethical issues in investment. 'While financial responsibilities must be of primary importance given the Commissioners' position as trustees they also continue to take into account social and ethical issues in investment decisions. Investments are not made in companies whose main business is in armaments, gambling, alcohol, tobacco and newspapers. These are categories which the Commissioners believe might cause distress to a significant body of Christian opinion . . . Investments are not made in any South African company, or in any company where more than a small part of the business is in South Africa. The Commissioners also seek to ensure that where they invest in any company with a small stake in South Africa it follows enlightened employment and social policies. While there is no evidence that these restrictions on the type of company in which the Commissioners are prepared to invest have damaged financial performance over the years, any extension of the restrictions could easily have such an effect.'[8]

Other Church of England bodies take a similar line. For example, the Central Board of Finance Investment Fund, a sort of unit trust for parishes, operates a policy on ethical matters after liaison with the Church Commissioners' Investments Department.

So the investment criteria are mixed – financial considerations are primary, but within that context and subject to that proviso ethical matters are taken into account.

For example, one of the Church Commissioners' major investments in recent years has been the large combined shopping and leisure complex near Gateshead, the MetroCentre. In their 1988 report the Commissioners were able to record its financial success: '. . . by the year's end over 98% of the total retail space of 1.5 million square feet was occupied. Trade expanded rapidly with the number of cars and coaches visiting the Centre some 35% higher than in the previous year. It had 16 million visitors while the estimated turnover of all the shops was over £350 million. It is now an established success and should bring the Commissioners considerable financial benefits in the years ahead.'[9] However, the Commissioners are also able to present this investment, along with a similar development at St Enoch's Centre, Glasgow, as an example of investment in a depressed urban area in harmony with the Church's concern for Urban Priority Areas.

The issues involved in such a large undertaking as the MetroCentre are varied and complex. Some in the Church tend to question the imprimateur that is seen to be given to unbridled consumerism and its attendant debt problems, to deplore the creative energy poured into leisure and shopping activities, to regret the contrast with surrounding depression, and to fear the effect on nearby town centres and the closure of local businesses. Is the Church here standing with the affluent over against the poor? Are not any new jobs created trivial, low-paid and part-time, a poor substitute for the skilled workers made redundant from real jobs in heavy industry or shipbuilding?

Others point to the much-needed boost given by the development to the morale and economic activity of a depressed area – bringing competition which raises standards in the area. New retail employers have been brought in. Expectations have risen. People actually like the MetroCentre and go to it in droves – why should the Church stand aloof and judging?

In the category of residential property, ethical and financial considerations can also pull in different directions. Much of the Church Commissioners' residential property comprises three estates in London. On the Hyde Park Estate the policy is to make long lease sales as property becomes vacant. On the Maida Vale Estate property is upgraded for sale. Sales from these two estates, even during the difficult year 1990, reached £28.3 million[10]. In both these cases financial criteria rule out policies which might be of greater benefit to sitting tenants or the wider community suffering great housing shortage and cost of housing inflation in central London.

However, the Commissioners feel able to operate a different approach for the 1,595 rented units on the Octavia Hill Estates, which 'are good examples of affordable housing in inner city areas.'[10] On this estate a network of on-site housing managers maintains good communication with tenants, and vacant tenancies are offered to relatives.

In rural areas the Church can often have a high profile as a landowner, via the diocese or the Church Commissioners, as well as being part of a local community which can be feeling deprived of employment, housing and transport, or that its environment is in jeopardy. In legal terms these roles have to be separated, but it is difficult to expect this separation to be understood locally. The Archbishops' Commission on Rural Areas reported that the Church seems to some to be 'rich, grasping and unheeding of local views'.

In making decisions about the sale of Church land for housing there is bound to be a tension between the need to generate income, the need to provide affordable housing, and the need to affirm the local environment. So conflicts arise whereby plans for low cost housing are objected to by a prosperous PCC, or are legally found to be not permitted.

Environmental issues loom larger. In 1989 the Church Commissioners received unwelcome publicity as they planned to extend some gravel workings in Kent for the fourth time in eighteen years[11]. Local objectors complained about damage to the local community and environment, and said that they had been assured that the third extension would be the last, but the Commissioners argued their primary duty to maximise income for the sake of their beneficiaries, the clergy.

Lengthy debates have in recent years centred around the Church Commissioners' refusal to disinvest totally from any company with South African involvement. Political change may now have taken some of the steam out of this issue, but the principles remain important. The Commissioners' policy, as stated above, has been not to invest directly in South Africa, nor to invest in any company with more than a small part of its business in South Africa. They have argued that to disinvest further would narrow investment options and so be financially imprudent, and is thus outside their powers.

Conventional arguments such as these are challenged by those who point out, for example, that 'the performance of stocks on the Financial Times actuaries (FTA) All-Share Index *without* interests in South Africa was slightly better than the Index as a whole over the past five years.'[12] EIRIS (Ethical Investment Research Service) does not suggest here that ethical judgements are bound to bring financial rewards, but that the cost of ethical choice can be very small, if it exists at all. On both sides the arguments are hypothetical and it is difficult to see them being resolved within the present legal framework.

Although the basic position of the Church Commissioners and the Central Board of Finance Investment Fund on South Africa has been broadly stated in this way, detailed examination of the policy reveals inconsistencies. For example, a small proportion of a large company can represent a larger investment than a large proportion of a small company whilst remaining within the criteria. Shell does less than two per cent of its (strategically vital) business in South Africa, but comes first by value in the Church Commissioners' Stock Exchange investments as at 31st December 1990, over £21 million.[13] Similarly, it is difficult to see that indirect investments, which are undertaken, are ethically preferable to direct investments, which are avoided. In both these examples, it is easier to see that the criteria used fits with financial prudence than with ethical principle, in which case it is disingenuous for the policy to be presented as if the ethical priority is definitive.

Strengths and benefits

Given the power and influence of money in our society, the wealth and property of the institutions of the Church of England provide an enormous repository of strength and security. Thus the Church is able to provide, in the terms of The Ecclesiastical Commissioners Act 1840, 'for the cure of souls in parishes where . . . assistance is most required in such manner as shall . . . be deemed most conducive to the efficiency of the established church.'[14]

The Church Commissioners have taken this objective into the context of post-war Britain. They have steadily built up the capital wealth of the Church and maximised the income available for the support of the clergy, mainly for pensions, stipends and housing. Encouraged by General Synod, they have used their powers to bring more equity to the comparative financial positions of dioceses and benefices.[15] The Commissioners themselves report the targeting of less wealthy dioceses for additional allocations for stipends and both capital and revenue housing outgoings.[16]

The security of this capital wealth has enabled the Commissioners to respond to the changing needs of stipendiary clergy. In 1988 an interest free car loan scheme was introduced, replacing a variety of diocesan schemes, and the initial take up of around 200 a month showed that this met a real need. In 1990 stipends were adjusted to as far as possible ensure that clergy and their spouses would be no worse off following the introduction of the community charge. Funds are also available to make grants for church building in areas of new housing.

The Church Commissioners have thus carried out the purpose for which they were established in 1948: 'to promote the more efficient and economical administration of the resources of the Church of England.'[17] Over a period, the situation has been transformed, clergy income has been made more equitable and the Church enabled to meet its obligations towards those who work for it. The importance of effective management has been shown – in the nineteenth century much land was controlled by the clergy and a great deal of it stood unused or derelict, a poor witness. Now the Commissioners have a reputation for effective and productive invest- ment in all areas of their activity. They are proud of their record and say so in their annual reports.[18]

It is right for the Church to participate actively in the economic life of the society in which it is set and from which it draws its income. There is a positive side, affirming wealth creation and positive responsible share ownership, to the participation of Church institutions in the life of the City, a place which Christians can often look upon with some disdain as a hot-bed of greed and acquisitiveness.

The handling of wealth by the Church Commissioners and by diocesan authorities demonstrates a sense of the historicity of the

Church, of the need to pass on what has been given, of holding
security received on trust for future generations, and of participation
in economic life.

Problems and drawbacks

Many claim that the accumulation of wealth by the Church is more
of a drawback than an advantage. It is a process which has the
danger of identifying the Church more with the powerful than with
the poor, distancing it further and further from the priorities of the
gospel. Decision making can thus be compromised, and confusing
signals given to society at large. Church people can be insulated
from the challenge of realistic giving, settling into a state of
dependency upon their corporate inherited wealth, and grace can be
cheapened in the effort to make it accessible.

For example, the tied parsonage, whilst providing (hopefully)
every stipendiary cleric with suitable living and working accommodation, is also an influence which separates and protects the culture
of the Church from the surrounding realities which face the local
population. The congregation need take no responsibility and can
take for granted the fact that housing will be provided. Clergy are
released from the mortgage treadmill, on the one hand, and denied,
on the other, the opportunity to participate in the financial benefits
of home ownership in an era of overall long-term rises in prices.

Problems as well as benefits arise, too, out of the trusteeship of
the Church's property. The Church Commissioners claim they must
show undivided loyalty as trustees to their beneficiaries, the clergy.
This is an even narrower definition of trusteeship than that of a
charitable body or trust, where some sort of public purpose or
object exists which can sometimes be argued to have an overriding
importance over financial benefit in certain circumstances, perhaps
opening to trustees the possibility of differing from their financial
advisers.

In every case, as Michael Bourke points out, 'the property is held
on a Trust for the benefit of a quite specific religious or ecclesiastical
purpose, as defined by law. The legal principles involved are the
same as for any charitable trust: first, that the assets of one charity
may not be used for the benefit of another, however worthy, . . .
and secondly that the Trustees are obliged to maximize the value of
the assets.'[19] Thus when glebe land is sold it must be sold for as

much as possible and the money must be allocated to the payment of stipends.

Very serious problems arise because of this. Financial management can pull against social responsibility, and legal arguments have to be deployed by the Church to defend its position. These legal arguments may well run counter to the Church's theological position. 'So the archdeacon, while hopefully clarifying popular misconceptions about "church land", secretly suspects that the people are less *theologically* confused than the Church itself.'[19] Means have taken priority over ends, and the position is defended by a legal compartmentalism which is very much to the Church's monetary advantage. The arguments of Reinhold Niebuhr in 'Moral Man and Immoral Society' are enshrined in law, compelling the Church to adopt for its own advantage courses of action which for individual Christians would be regarded as wrong. 'I often ask myself what we are doing when we open Board meetings with prayer; for once we have solemnly invoked the guidance of God, an autonomous business ethic seems to take over, and the "culture of the institution" seems secular rather than Christian.'[20]

In this way the accountability of the Church is divided up amongst various bodies and institutions which are legally obliged to conduct their affairs with autonomous self-interest – Church Commissioners, Central Board of Finance, Diocesan Boards of Finance, PCCs, multitudes of local trusts, and so on. All these bodies can be in danger of delegating ethical responsibility to the planning system and legal constraint, because for each body such responsibility is legally defined as being subsidiary to material economic gain.

Similarly, the Church as a whole can hide from its ultimate obligations behind convenient legal barriers. 'Everyone knows that the Church Commissioners are not the Church. This is an investment, not an act of worship.'[21] The concept of trusteeship in English church and charity law reinforces institutional dualism and compartmentalism, and gives legal sanction to actions which may well be theologically and ethically dubious.

The larger the institution, the more likely it is that it will be run by establishment figures who will not challenge the autonomy of the business ethic, and who will bring down the shutters on any attempt to bridge compartments and reconcile financial policy with theology. The Church Commissioners have been called 'a microcosm of the British Establishment'[22]. They are responsible to Parliament. They report to a government minister for home affairs. Questions in the

Commons are taken by a government back-bencher who is also a Commissioner. They preserve a great deal of autonomy by means of their own interpretation of narrow terms of reference. The First Church Estates Commissioner has said: 'The Church Commissioners have to live in two worlds, the world of the Church and the world of business because we have a job to do for the Church.'[23] The legal constraints are dualism in action. In fact the views on either side of this barrier are not integrated, and the life and witness of the Church is impoverished as a result.

An emphasis on financial prudence as a priority makes it difficult for the Church's institutions to engage in experiment and innovation in investment – a more positive version of ethical investment, which tends very often to be a negative concept defined by which investments are *not* made. This militates against unproved investment in inner cities or less developed countries, and against taking seriously longer term ecological and environmental considerations when they might be more expensive in the short term.

The sheer size of the Church Commissioners' operation, which is brought to bear as an argument against stronger ethical criteria, conversely gives the Church an opportunity to participate in, lead and influence the market. At present this opportunity is lost and Church affairs are market-led in one compartment whilst the market is politely regretted in another.

Important questions applied

How does the Church's handling of the land and property which it owns measure against the important questions which have been identified? Not surprisingly, there is considerable overlap between some of these questions as important issues repeatedly come to the surface.

(1) Are money issues honestly faced?

The involvement of the Church, and notably the Church Commissioners, with the economic life of the nation is positive, but this involvement is not taken up and owned as such by the Church at large. The sheer size of Church property ownership needs to be acknowledged, and this ownership needs itself to be owned corporately. No Church member fails to benefit in some way from the property corporately held, yet somehow it is 'theirs' not 'ours'. It is set apart, deemed useful in terms of accumulating capital and gathering income but not seen as an important link with the world of money which plays such an important part in people's lives. Rather like the engine room of an ocean liner, in contrast with the clean lines and well appointed comfort of the structure above, it is not familiar to the travellers.

Although there are many people in the Church who wish to face up to the challenges raised by money, corporately the church is content to rest protected from hard economic facts by its inherited wealth, and from hard ethical ones by the traditions of English trust and charity law. So neither economics nor ethics in practice is debated as vigorously as it needs to be.

The legal shelter from ethical problems applies at national level to the Church Commissioners, but the issue is the same in microcosm for local Church-based charities and trusts. As an established Church the Church of England should not, if necessary, be afraid to initiate a public debate on legislative changes to rectify this.

(2) Are idealism and realism held in balance?

Both idealism and realism are present, but they are only held in balance by being held separately. Much of the Church's handling of its wealth and property is highly realistic and competent. There is also much idealism at work, expressed by arguments for economic justice and ecological concern. But, aside from the very real progress made in the direction of greater equity between dioceses and benefices (very much a 'world of the Church' matter), these two things have little dialogue or contact with one another. The Church Commissioners' investment policy for commercial property shows them to be very realistic about retail and consumer trends, but this sits uncomfortably, for example, with the Church's protests about Sunday trading. Such tensions and conflicting claims remain unresolved. So does the natural tendency for the more powerful in the Church to argue for realism and the less powerful to espouse idealism.

Again, the separation set up by legal structures is important. Charity and trust law, in safeguarding a proper continuity of purpose, tends to make a compartment for the conscience. It holds idealism within defined limits, restricting the application of theological and ethical principle in the real situation of the Church. The debate over the MetroCentre provides an example. Both ends of the argument carry weight; the Church cannot isolate itself from economic life, nor should it ignore the serious ethical questions which arise when such an investment is made. Better witness might have come from a balance or mixture of ethical and financial factors and the public emergence of criteria which could then have resulted. This would have been a much more challenging task, but one which would have been commensurate with the moral requirements of the Church's economic position.

(3)   Is the 'Third Kingdom' active?

The 'third kingdom', the Church, is severly constrained in serving the kingdoms of God and the world by the compartmentalising of the Church's handling of its property. There is a damaging dualism at work if the Church just keeps its money in the kingdom of the world and its soul in the kingdom of God. Views on both sides of the divide can be two-dimensional, and debate on the development of policy, a key 'third kingdom' activity, is impoverished. Legal compartmentalism, insisting upon maximum financial returns, forces decisions which can be contrary to basic aims and underlying objectives.

It is important to note here that there is a real duality, a real divergence, between the kingdom of God and the world. Economic realities are part of creation and as such have their place under God. The concept of 'three kingdoms' allows due autonomy to economic, social or political reality, whilst providing a structure to relate this to the ultimate Christian paradigm – the kingdom of God. In this structure the mediating or bridge role belongs to the Church, the body of Christ, in service, in sacrifice, in proclamation, in communion, with and for the world.

An example of an area in which the Church does not adequately respond to its role as 'third kingdom', by offering 'penultimate' patterns or demonstrating the 'internal/external' principle, is that of positive ethical investment, of engagement in experimental or innovative economic activity. This might particularly be relevant to offer models of hope in combating social problems such as debt, homelessness or unemployment. Housing schemes, credit unions, craft workshops and the like are promoted, but locally and sporadically rather than institutionally or strategically.

(4)   Are owners called by God?

The Church is an owner writ large. It needs to show in its own life that owners are called by God, that handling of material wealth is an aspect of Christian vocation in a material world dominated by money culture. This is a prerequisite to the development of a body of teaching and criteria to guide individual and institutional owners of property in their responsibilities. Neither hand-wringing on one side nor unbridled profiteering on the other do anything at all to express a sense of call in or to the world, corporate or individual.

At present, the Church is in danger of being left behind when it should be giving a lead on questions of ethical investment, which is an important positive element in the new consumerism. In the trend to the progressive consumer and investor, social responsibility *via* the market rather than *contra* the market can be enhanced. In this the Church should lead and encourage, but it cannot credibly do so without setting an example. The Church's wealth is powerful, its policy decisions are more than symbolic, but compartmentalism requires that this power be disregarded just where it might be so useful.

Some dioceses and housing associations are working through a legal minefield in an effort to obtain use of Church land for low cost housing. Nevertheless, it is difficult to achieve anything on any great scale, or on a scale commensurate with the property owned or the potential for leadership and innovation. It may be that the legal and ecclesiastical energies thus employed might be better spent in working towards changing the legal framework and dualistic culture. The Church cannot proclaim God's call to other owners until it has responded to that call itself.

(5)   Are we aware of the pastoral implications of money?

Society at large is much quicker to discern hypocrisy at work than to understand the fine legal arguments concerning the constraints of charity law. This has implications for public perceptions of the integrity of the Church and thus for its ministry and mission. What happens if the Church often seems to say one thing, but to do another? What happens pastorally in a village up in arms over Church Commissioners' gravel workings or a sale of glebe which disregards environmental considerations or the need for low-cost housing? What will be the situation in hearts and minds in ten or twenty years time? Will it all be forgotten, or will attitudes to the Church be permanently scarred?

There is a growing awareness of the deleterious effect of bad decision making on the group at the wrong end of the decision – but this tends to be limited to those who have to deal with the problem locally. As Michael Bourke has said[19], then the Archdeacon is hauled in to explain why it can't be any different.

If a determination grew to see that in due course it *could* be different, the Church might begin to move towards taking a creative leading role in the market place. This would be a position appropriate to its pastoral relationships with people making their way in the world, with local communities struggling for a fair deal, and with financial institutions which have enormous influence on the way lives are led.

13. Responsibility for Funding

The Church's structures

The Church of England, with its roots in the parochial system, has a great deal of structure to maintain. Its land, buildings, clergy and other staff make it a large organisation in any terms. Church electoral rolls are much more accurate than they used to be, and the latest available figures (1989) indicate over 1.6 million members[1]. There is a church building for approximately every hundred of those members – 16,425 in 1990 – and a full-time stipendiary cleric for approximately every hundred and fifty – 10,300 in 1990[2]. There are, in addition, non-ordained staff members and administrative buildings at parish, diocesan and national levels.

The costs involved in maintaining such a structure are considerable. Church buildings are notoriously difficult to keep in good order, and are often far larger than appropriate for the present size of the worshipping congregation. Their architectural qualities often mean that necessary work is very expensive if it is to be done properly. In many cases the local population has a considerable emotional attachment to a building which it uses rarely, but is glad to know is there.

Great responsibility is also involved towards those who work for the Church full-time, and their families. Much progress has been made since the war in improving the Church's performance of these obligations, notably in respect of clergy stipends, pensions and housing. Between them these items account for about 85% of the Church Commissioners' expenditure. Only 28% or so is recouped from diocesan income and giving in the parishes, or about half the sum spent on stipends. The dependence of the living Church upon its inherited wealth is heavy. The present structure could not be maintained without the contribution of the Commissioners. The steady work which has been undertaken towards proper working conditions, housing or pensions would not have been possible.

In addition to the parochial ministry and its support structures considerable work is done by sector ministries run by various General and Diocesan Synod Boards and by the various well-established Church-based voluntary and missionary societies such as the Mothers' Union, Children's Society, Church Housing Association, Church Army, Church Missionary Society and United Society for the Propagation of the Gospel. In many such organisations income from investments, together with current giving, pays for the present workload.

Much more detail could be added, but the basic picture would remain. Very few parishes 'pay their way' in any real sense. Living Church members are heavily subsidised and sheltered from the financial realities of their present commitments by property ownership and income from investments. However, this situation is to some extent being eroded by a variety of pressures, notably inflation, demographic trends and numerical decline.

The perennial problem of inflation has undermined the capacity for investment income to be applied so that stipends and pensions keep in pace or proportion with national average income. In 1980 the General Synod approved the objective of increasing clergy pensions to a level of two-thirds of the national minimum stipend for the previous year, and this was achieved in 1985[3]. Demographic trends point, as in society as a whole, towards a smaller working population paying for a larger retired population. It is the declared policy of the Church Commissioners to move towards a situation where current giving in the parishes can fully pay for clergy stipends, leaving them free to apply their resources towards pensions and housing.

Gradual, but steady, numerical decline over many decades has reduced the numbers of committed Church members willing or able to share this responsibility (see figure 1). In these overall circumstances the pressure on the local Church to take on more financial responsibility steadily increases, and there is no obvious reason why this should not be the case. Church members have not had to bear the real cost of ministry for centuries, however, and so the subject of money is a constant cause of stress.

Pressure on the local Church

Approximately a half share of stipend costs is reclaimed from parishes via the dioceses by means of the 'quota' or 'parish share'. This share is steadily increasing, especially when wider economic problems such as inflation or recession exert pressure. Therefore quotas are likely to grow at a faster rate than retail prices for the forseeable future, being subject to both inflation and this increasing proportion. Quota payments consequently form a large and increasing part of the expenditure of any Church of England parish.

Figure   1
MEMBERSHIP
Church of England (excluding Europe)

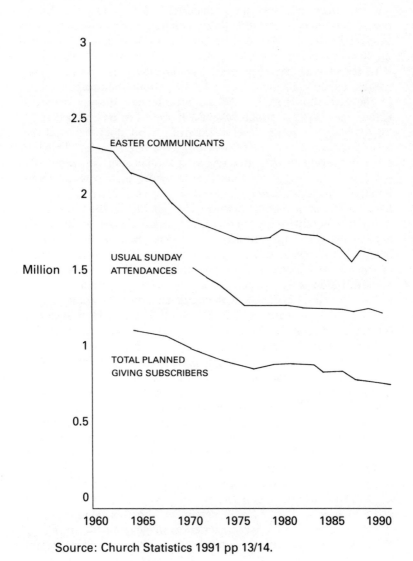

Source: Church Statistics 1991 pp 13/14.

The other major responsibility at local level is the maintenance, insurance and repair of the church building. In some places this is an enormous burden compared with the number of people who are trying to look after it – a load which can be out of all proportion to the normal running expenditure attributable to worship and ministry. For many parishes this problem is a dominating one. Large restoration projects to distinguished buildings can receive help from English Heritage, representing some input from the wider community, but these are subject to stringent conditions.

In recent years much progress has been made in the reimbursement of expenses incurred by the clergy, an important responsibility of the local Church. 'In 1970 an incumbent's average expenses amounted to £209 of which he could expect to be reimbursed 35%: by 1987/88 the average level of expenses stood at £1,365, and the incumbent could expect 83.5% of this to be reimbursed.'[4] This is a great improvement, but still reveals a serious shortfall, especially when it is noted that for some clergy 'where their parishes faced financial difficulties they felt obliged to keep their claimed expenses low. This figure is masked in the figures obtained in the survey.'[5]

Another notable responsibility for the local Church is the motor expenses of the clergy and Church workers; these can be considerable, particularly in dispersed rural multi-parish benefices. Such expenses are reclaimed on a mileage basis, but the user is responsible for acquisition of the vehicle, often a considerable outlay and one not usually borne by people with comparable duties in commerce or industry. Until recently car loan schemes have been run by dioceses, but these have now been replaced by an interest free central scheme run by the Church Commissioners.

Parishes in the Church of England are also looked to by a variety of missionary societies to give towards the work of the Church overseas. However, this has been falling behind inflation for many years. Although the proportion of parish income given outside parish and diocese has remained fairly constant, less than half of this now goes to the Church overseas compared with more than two-thirds in 1960[6]. Missionary societies, looking to the parishes for steady and reliable support, have felt squeezed by the growing and competitive demands of quota, aid and development agencies, Church Urban Fund, and parish running expenses.

The influence of economic determinism – 'there is no money' – is therefore a reality of Church as well as of government spending. PCCs feel themselves to be hemmed in by money constraints, preoccupied by the question 'What can we afford?' when forming policy, or even unable to form policy at all and just living from one demand to the next. A PCC which wishes to expand its activities or to give more away will often feel constrained, on the one hand, by inadequate giving by Church members, and, on the other, by the demands of maintaining Church structures as expressed by diocesan quota or their own building. They feel trapped by circumstances, and Church life is one of constant struggle. In many cases the pressure for funding is constant, and a recent survey showed that 95% of people believe that raising money for the Church is among the clergy's main duties.[7]

Allocating responsibility

The assessment of parish contributions to diocesan quota, in view of the great shortage of money generally felt at PCC level, is the source of constant debate in PCCs and deanery and diocesan Synods. In recent years assessment based on actual PCC income has tended to be replaced by a variety of systems which attempt to assess potential. There is little or no uniformity between dioceses.

An actual income system of allocation takes parochial income for the most recent year, or an average of recent years, and makes allowances for certain categories of expenditure. It has the advantages of simplicity and of being, by definition, actual. However, it is open to criticism for being unfair to the parishes where the giving is most generous and unduly protective of parishes which do not or will not face the challenges of direct giving.

Potential income systems attempt greater equity, but are more complex and therefore both more difficult to understand and more open to manipulation, for example by restricting electoral roll membership. Assessment can be based on one or more of a variety of considerations, such as: electoral roll membership, average Sunday attendance, Christmas and Easter attendance, annual communicants, planned giving contributors, local socio-economic circumstances, parish population, parliamentary electors, local property values, or parochial staff costs. A diocese can make such an apportionment on a parish or a deanery basis; if the latter, the deanery must then allocate the amount between parishes.

One of the most sophisticated systems of allocation by potential has been developed by the Diocese of Portsmouth. It is seen by its designers as the Church making a response in its own structures to the increasing disparity of income and wealth in society at large, and thus giving credence to its own calls for social justice. Indicators from the 1981 census, chosen for their ability to discriminate most clearly between parishes, were used to show 'state of economic health', 'type and quality of housing', and 'level of employment'. As a consequence the factor in the apportionment calculation designed to reflect ability to give was set on a five point scale of 0.6 to 1.2 – a larger range than is usually possible – based on five clusters of parishes.[8]

The results have been described as being: '(a) to narrow the extreme range of variability in Quota targets, expressed in terms of the sum per head of average Sunday attendance (ASA), per year. Whereas under the previous system parish targets might vary from £33 per head of ASA to £140 per head, in the first year of . . . the new system they ranged from £40 per head ASA to £95 per head ASA.' and: '(b) to redistribute the liability to pay. In the first year of operation, some parishes in Cluster 1 (poorest), previously required to pay £140 per head ASA, had their liability reduced to between £40 and £50. Parishes in Cluster 5 (wealthiest) previously required to pay only around £50 per head ASA, had their liability raised to around £95.'[9] This is possible because the largest cluster of parishes was the most affluent, 36 parishes compared with 11 and 6 parishes respectively in the two poorest clusters.

Compared with the previous system, because their circumstances have been taken into account and the targets are seen to be fair and reasonable, there is greater moral obligation on poorer parishes to meet quota targets. 'Wealthier parishes have had to acknowledge more fully the gulf that separates them from their less affluent neighbours.'[9]

It is probably too early to say what the long-term response of such wealthier parishes may be, or how long statistics based on the 1981 Census will be valid. In any such system it is difficult to take into account factors such as symmetry of the Church congregation with the local population, social mobility, or proportions of the population who are non-Anglican or adherents of other faiths.

A totally different potential system has been adopted in the Diocese of St Edmundsbury and Ipswich, as a replacement for a much more complex system which was in practice very difficult for the participants to understand, agree upon or trust. Quota is apportioned to deaneries quite simply according to the number of clergy. A special ministerial needs allowance is used to make adjustments for special factors. The deaneries usually use the same basis, making any necessary local adjustments between parishes. In a heavily rural diocese decision-making about quota on this relatively local level, in a way which makes clear the largest item of expenditure, introduces some reality into discussions about allocation of clergy and pastoral reorganisation.

These two examples show the two polarities between which methods of quota assessment are ranged. On the one hand, the Portsmouth system is designed to incorporate redistributive justice, emphasizing solidarity and sharing amongst parishes in a diocese. It is an attempt to be fair according to widely differing socio-economic circumstances, but it does this at the price of considerable complexity, although once the factors are set up, they can be used for as long as is deemed appropriate.

On the other hand, the St Edmundsbury and Ipswich approach, with its staff costs basis, offers nothing in the way of social equity, but instead relates quota to expenditure in a very direct and simple way. This calls for more lay responsibility and participation and gives a greater degree of subsidiarity in an important area of decision-making.

All quota systems are voluntary, and many dioceses are troubled by material levels of under-payment. However, they are all designed to give a clear signal of what is expected, and the moral pressure to pay is high – it is often felt to be some form of 'Church Tax'. There is in fact no compulsion, but it is well known that the allocation of clergy can be used as a measure of last resort in persistently recalcitrant cases. In this context, potential systems of quota apportionment offer a low level of coercion designed to give encouragement to those who give attention to the matter of direct giving, by making sure they are not immediately penalised for their efforts. There is as yet no evidence to show, however, that any one method is more effective than any other in encouraging direct giving.

Strengths and weaknesses

In many ways the allocation of funding responsibility across the range of the Church's structures reveals both strengths and weaknesses – positive and negative points often arise simultaneously.

The merits and demerits of the parochial system are constantly discussed: a complex and expensive structure is in place which covers the whole country, providing places of worship, facilities for rites of passage and pastoral care without boundaries. Without this network and presence the construction of a report such as 'Faith in the City' would have carried much less weight. The statistics of numerical decline and financial difficulty tell us that it will become increasingly difficult to maintain this infrastructure. The argument on the other side is just as powerful, that to dismantle it would simply be a recipe for further decline. In any case, the emotional commitment of Church members to local Church and parish is so strong that the issue is hardly a live one. Nevertheless such an institution is vulnerable to inflation, demographic trends and any further numerical decline.

So, given the benefits and tenacious will to survive of the parish, it is inevitable that the Church should be moving towards a position designed to encourage more and more parishes to pay their way, so that historic resources can be directed towards poorer areas or new work. However, this task has only just begun – in 1990 the cost of the stipendiary ministry was £131.6 million, but only £42.7 million of this came from giving. No contribution at all was made by parishes towards the Church Commissioners' expenditure on pensions and housing, a total of £68.9 million[10]. Parishes still remain very dependent upon the inherited wealth of the Church; they pay less than a quarter of the real cost of the stipendiary ministry.

There have been steadily increasing efforts to achieve greater equity in the sharing of financial responsibility across the Church, at both diocesan and parish level. This is partly in order to create an atmosphere in which moral pressure to pay the quota can be legitimately exerted. However, the situation is not uniform, because dioceses adopt differing methods in allocating funding responsibility to parishes. This disparity in methods underlines the fact that, although assessment by potential is fairer than by actual income, it is still not ideal. As the Portsmouth study has revealed, there is a shortage of information and much complexity involved in applying it.

One inequity which the Church has not addressed is the very haphazard way in which the burdens of buildings fall upon parishes. This can involve huge sums of money. The building may or may not have been soundly designed and built, or well looked after by earlier generations. Endowments, a fabric fund or a recent legacy may or may not be available. A grant from English Heritage may or may not be forthcoming. The building may or may not be interesting or distinguished enough to attract support for a fundraising campaign. Church buildings remain a lottery as far as their financial implications are concerned.

Although there is no room for complacency, the Church has made good ground in more adequately meeting its obligations as an employer in terms of housing and paying stipendiary clergy, reimbursing their expenses of office and providing an adequate pension. It is noteworthy, though, that much of this has had to be sorted out centrally. Where responsibility lies locally, as in the case of expenses, a material number of clergy are still in an invidious position. This situation is partly redeemed, again centrally, by the Church Commissioners' interest free car loan scheme.

Anglican voluntary and missionary societies are an important part of the life and witness of the Church. Their independence of the Church's institutional structures gives them a freedom and a flexibility which is vital for the effectiveness of their work. However, this very independence also makes them vulnerable as the calls on parochial monies increase. 1992 sees several of the Church's most important missionary agencies running considerable deficits and having to make stark choices about work undertaken at home and overseas.

Overall, the picture which emerges is one in which the problem of money exerts great pressure upon the acknowledged mainstay of the Church of England – the parish. It is a picture of an enormous amount of energy being used to find enough money to keep going; of a parish culture often dispiritingly dominated by finance and buildings; and of a disproportionate amount of weight being borne by a few, with only a small number of people in each parish taking their giving at all seriously.

Important questions applied

How do the ways in which the Church allocates the responsibility for funding its work measure up against the five important questions already identified?

(1) Are money issues honestly faced?

Members of the Church of England have begun to face issues raised by the need to find the money to fund the work of the Church, but the process is very long and slow and is undertaken most reluctantly. Often the issue is subtly avoided by endless and inappropriate wrangling about expenditure or accountability: this is apparently an effort to face realities, but in fact enables the Church to sidestep some of the important elements in the situation, notably low levels of giving.

Similarly, a 'them' and 'us' attitude can prevail, in which the source of the problem is identified as being something to do with 'them', some other part of the Church which is not meeting its responsibilities. The parishes blame synod spending, the synods blame the recalcitrance of the parishes, the clergy deplore lay inaction, the laity claim the clergy are out of touch. In fact, 'we' are usually someone else's 'they'. The result is that 'I' have avoided serious reflection on my own part in the situation.

The parishes are in the forefront, but in very many cases the issue of money is dealt with warily or with embarrassment, and parish clergy often prefer not to address it at all. The underlying problem of poor giving is a difficult one for many parochial clergy to handle because of the suspicion and sensitivity surrounding it. Even a relatively prosaic matter such as the reimbursement of expenses of office is still not dealt with properly in at least one in five parishes. In many parishes and other Church bodies and voluntary societies, those who are active bear a disproportionate part of the costs of ministry by means of poor pay or conditions of service and of expenses not claimed or reimbursed. Often this is unacknowledged or unquestioned.

(2) Are idealism and realism held in balance?

On the face of it the movement towards potential apportionment of quota payments is one which is both realistic and idealistic. It is idealistic because it attempts an equitable distribution according to the differing circumstances of parishes. It is realistic because that very quest for fairness is designed to reinforce the voluntary quota system with moral force which will encourage corporate feeling and therefore payment. In fact, however, a little probing reveals that this quest for equity is largely illusory, and the case that it encourages payment is unproven.

Firstly, the dependency on investment income is the same for rich and poor alike, to all intents and purposes all parishes are heavily subsidised in this way. Secondly, the expenditure liability represented by Church buildings is totally ignored. Thirdly, poten-tial systems are complex and difficult to understand, fulfil their aims only imperfectly and are therefore unlikely to carry the moral force ascribed to them. Fourthly, any allocation system is unrelated to the real pressure point – decisions about individual giving often made in an atmosphere of unhealthy secrecy.

In these circumstances it is simply unrealistic to expect to achieve the ideal of equity, however desirable that aim might be. This is not to say that what is undertaken should not be as fair as possible, but it is to say that the quest for a system that is so fair that all will gladly give within it is quite illusory and often a waste of time. The danger is that, in so concentrating on the ideal of equitably sharing out a quarter of the cost of the stipendiary ministry, we ignore the real, much bigger, problems of excessive dependency on inherited wealth for the other three-quarters and the total absence of any attempt to share the burden of buildings.

Perhaps it would be better to change the emphasis and to move away from equity towards greater subsidiarity and responsibility at parish level as far as stipendiary ministry costs are concerned. This would introduce some important realism into the lives of many local Churches, and pre-empt many of the avoidance tactics which are used at present to avoid money talk. At the same time, responsibility for buildings *might* be more effectively and equitably moved away from the local level, allowing burdens to be shared over a wider area.

(3) Is the 'Third Kingdom' active?

A parish Church is well-placed geographically to be a centre of activity for the 'third kingdom' in its relationship of interchange with the kingdoms of God and of the world. Its members are active in the world, in paid and voluntary work, in homes, offices, shops and factories, in leisure pursuits.

Sadly, this key unit of Church life is often more involved in its own fight for survival than in relating to the world, or helping its members to do so. Energy is directed towards the maintenance of what happens in the building on Sundays, not on discovering how that affects the rest of the week.

(4) Are owners called by God?

Unfortunately, the responsibility of managing money and property is not adequately put before Church members. In particular, there is little or no sense of ownership of the assets of the Church Commissioners, even though these are almost entirely used to subsidise parish life.

Clergy pay, housing and pensions are dealt with centrally. Little responsibility is called for from Church members, and it is no surprise that little is forthcoming. Individual giving – and corporate outward giving to charities, aid agencies and missionary societies – remains stubbornly low even in times of increased affluence and lower taxation.

(5)   Are we aware of the pastoral implications of money?

This lack of realism and responsibility about money at parish level has pastoral implications for the relationship between clergy and laity, for the development of commitment and for the building of bridges between the compartments of Church life and life in the world. Many Church people would simply prefer the problem to go away, and often try to behave as if it has. Church life is then in danger of taking on the features of a protective cocoon, rather than being a way to deal with reality.

A problem is posed, however, by any attempt to change the situation, because many people would be wary of giving PCCs responsibility for the pay and conditions of clergy, especially those who do not yet even pay expenses properly! This could perhaps be handled by using a system of central administration and then invoicing parishes for the service they receive, subsidising in appropriate cases after discussion at deanery and diocesan level.

14.   Voluntary Giving

The giving problem

It soon becomes apparent in any enquiry that many of the Church's sums about money do not add up because the level of giving is too low. The figures are difficult to analyse, but the most optimistic view of giving by Church members (that is, direct giving by individuals through the Church and missionary societies) is that it is around 2% of income for Church attenders[1]. In fact, it is not really known what the income of Church members is – it may well be higher than in the population at large.

Figure 2 shows that the Church's real income from giving has remained remarkably static over the past thirty years, having dipped seriously in real terms during the middle and late seventies, presumably due to a mixture of numerical decline and high levels of inflation.

The overall picture (shown in figures 1 and 2) is of fewer giving more in order to stand still, but not so much more as to reflect increased affluence. There are some indications that the boom of the late 1980s was much less influential on levels of giving than the subsequent slump. The problem remains. It is generally accepted, too, that in almost every parish current levels of giving are maintained by a small proportion of active Church members. The giving of the majority of Church members must still be reckoned to be inordinately low.

Christian Stewardship

Since the 1950s in particular the question of giving has been inextricably tied up with the work of the 'Christian Stewardship' movement in the Church.[2] Initially the pressure which drew out this response was financial. Many attempts to deal with this issue have been adaptations of fundraising methods developed in the United States. However, although fundraising is not reprehensible or wrong in itself, it does not provide an adequate structure for Christians to consider, reflect and decide upon their Christian stewardship of money. So the search soon began for definitions and methods which would establish theological credentials for the concept.

In 1958 the Lambeth Conference defined Christian stewardship

Figure   2
GIVING in real terms of 1989
Church of England (excluding Europe)

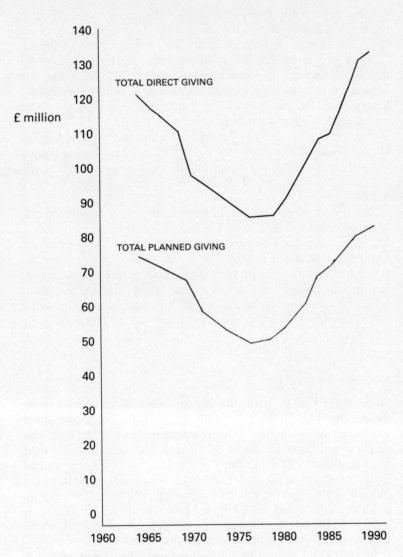

Source: Church Statistics 1991 pp 14/15.

as 'the regarding of ourselves – our time, our talents and our money – as a trust from God to be utilized in his service.' In 1980 the British Council of Churches' Stewardship Committee came up with: 'Christian Stewardship may therefore be defined as the response which the Church and men and women are called to make to God for all that he has given to us and done for us, above all in Jesus Christ. In this response we worship God with praise and thankfulness; we look on the universe as God's creation; we treat the earth and its resources as God's provision for the needs of all mankind; we regard our lives, our powers and our possessions as gifts from God to be enjoyed and used in His service; and we seek to be stewards of the Gospel and to share in Christ's mission to the world.'[3]

It is hardly possible to argue with these broad definitions. The same BCC committee saw the pressing need for these principles to be exercised at every level of Church life in view of the pressures on deployment of paid servants, readjustment of congregations, use of buildings, allocation of income between maintenance and ministry, and raising members' giving.[4]

This is where we come to the unresolved conflict at the heart of the 'Christian Stewardship' movement in the Church. This is the tension between theological principle and sociological fact, between ethical imperative and institutional need. The theological and ethical approach is exemplified by the definitions given above, but the sociological and institutional often has greater gravitational pull in the Church. 'In the language of sociology Christian Stewardship is a movement within the churches as institutions. It is a social reality and has a social function.'[5] Everyone knows that the function is to increase levels of giving.

The result is that 'Christian Stewardship' has been felt by many to be a subtle and devious method of fundraising engaged in by the Church, notable only for its inability to talk straight about money. 'Tell us what you want!' the target group mutters despairingly.

'Stewardship is not difficult.' But people 'have a hunch that this is not what the church is really talking about, for the church is not using its discovery to illuminate the Christian's relationship to the world, which is the logic of teaching about stewardship, but is rather on its own behalf making a bid for the Christian's money, time and talents – especially money. However visionary and religious its language, the church has been essentially seeking its own ends.'[6]

The shadow of sophistry did not seem to be far away. For many of those involved in the movement it seemed that any attempt to build or present a theology of Christian giving was hamstrung by the demands of the institution for its own survival.

A recent survey reports that 'in its widest aspect, the practice of Christian Stewardship is a response to God that should know no bounds, yet in most of the supporting literature submitted with completed questionnaires this broader understanding was eclipsed by a parish's more immediate needs.'[7] Similarly: 'The format of many time and talents pledge cards/leaflets . . . indicate(s) that God's stewards are intent on being kept busy servicing the church . . .'[8]

In the Church of England a network of diocesan advisers, largely set up in the 1960s, continues to exhort and encourage the practice of 'Christian Stewardship', using a variety of methods. Originally stewardship advisers were usually attached to Diocesan Boards of Finance and centrally this is still the case, but they are now often responsible to other diocesan boards or committees – because of the ambiguities of purpose (theological principle or institutional need) under which they work. Whether this alteration has brought about any real or convincing change in the culture, or people's perceptions of it, is doubtful.

Some advisers respond to the ambiguity by openly adopting a funding approach which stresses institutional needs, and aims to be as effective as possible within those bounds. Others give precedence to wider issues of stewardship, stressing environmental and developmental issues. On a much smaller scale, the Anglican Stewardship Association works mainly with individual parishes and deliberately attempts to avoid centring discussion either on institutional need or on broad issues which effectively avoid an open discussion of money.

To encourage the others

Along with, or through, the diocesan stewardship network, the Church of England has in recent years adopted a variety of methods aimed at encouraging improved giving by the person in the pew. This is itself a comment on the difficulty encountered in trying to communicate the ambiguous message of 'Christian Stewardship'.

The shift towards allocation of responsibility for quota payments by means of potential, rather than actual, income is in the end a means of exerting moral pressure to increase giving. It is a gentle form of coercion, paradoxically set within a totally voluntary system.

Although non-payment cannot be forbidden, it is quite rightly not condoned by diocesan authorities and can come to be the dominant consideration in dealing with a particular parish.

In 1982 the General Synod, prompted by the Joint Liaison Committee, called for a standard of giving of 5% of net disposable income. Obviously, if this standard was accepted, the finances of the Church would be transformed. There would be a lot more money in the common purse, but this has not been the case. If this standard is criticised for being excessively orientated towards the Church in an inward-looking way, it is usually said that the hope is that a further 5% will be given towards other charitable, missionary or voluntary ends. There seems to be little reason why people should find this easier to accept than the tithe, or one-tenth, the biblical authority for which is constantly debated.

The espousal of such a standard of giving is very problematic, because regular and systematic giving is in the end a matter of personal, ethical decision. For the institutional Church to claim that decision for itself is hard to justify. The decision remains the responsibility of individuals and families, whatever is said. A standard cannot really relate to anyone in particular, because each person has their own circumstances, income, wealth, relationship with others in society, and need to express gratitude and generosity.

A particular standard will leave the wealthy unchallenged and risk placing an unnecessary burden of guilt upon the less well off. 5% is almost certainly too low for a highly paid executive or professional person, and almost certainly too high for someone on a low income supporting a family.

Unfortunately, the suspicion lurks that standards of giving are not really standards at all, but targets – and behind them lies institutional requirement, averaging out, multiplying up, raising the sights enough to allow for a shortfall and still get by. There is no objection to institutional requirement, but there is to subterfuge.

Criticism has often been levelled because the Church has been more concerned to find the money for maintenance than for mission. To counter this, parishes have been encouraged to strengthen their stewardship by drawing up a 'budget of opportunity', to meet expenditure not only on current activities, but also on proposed new work. This can be a genuine attempt to raise the level of vision within the Church, but in the end the emphasis remains, counter-productively if subtly, upon the needs of the institutional Church. The message becomes: 'Here is our prospectus, buy your share in it.' This is hardly an adequate theology of grace, and indeed much established 'Christian Stewardship' in our parishes has a distinctly Pelagian flavour to it. The call going out is all too often 'We must save ourselves!' and all too rarely is the focus on the givingness of God.

Overall, there was some increase in giving during the 1980s, but much less than would truly reflect increasing affluence augmented by lower rates of direct taxation. Such increase as there was has been probably more attributable to quota pressure and publicity – pressure from the administrative hierarchy – than to a materially growing commitment to standards of giving, budgets of opportunity or any other exhortations. There is always some effect when people's attention is drawn, but deep or radical changes in attitude are few and far between.

Creating the Church Urban Fund

The Church Urban Fund was set up in 1987 in response to one of the main recommendations of the Archbishop's Commission on Urban Priority Areas in their report 'Faith in the City'[9]. The income needed for its work was estimated to be £4 million a year – £1 million to come from a capital fund, £1 million from the Church Commissioners, £½ million from linking projects with corporate and trust supporters, and £1½ million from local sources.[10] A national appeal was launched in April 1988 to raise £18 million to set up the necessary capital fund.

This was 'to be a widely based appeal which, while rooted in and organised by the Church, will go well beyond those who are regular churchgoers.'[11] Each diocese was given a target figure and asked 'to establish for the period of the campaign a fundraising team centred on two Diocesan Campaign Coordinators, to stimulate, encourage and organise fundraising within the Church and in the wider community in the area of the diocese.'[11] The target figure was designed to be fair, taking into account the relative prosperity and strength of Church life in different areas.

Some dioceses partnered their appeal with a local one. By early 1992 the target was reached, those dioceses which had exceeded their fundraising targets having compensated for those falling short.

In terms of fundraising, the Church Urban Fund is a great success, and is considering raising its sights so that it can offer grants to a greater number of projects in Urban Priority Areas. In this way, the Church of England is more able to carry out its role as national Church and, in particular, to serve those living in deprived urban areas. Nevertheless, there are some deeper questions which may need to be asked.

It is important to consider why the fund was necessary in the first place – the specific targeting of resources to UPAs, set against a background of the Church being aware that, for decades at least, its ministry was weakest in such areas. Both stewardship of resources and of the gospel itself had been lacking. To some extent, therefore, the Church Urban Fund corrects an injustice by means of an appeal to charity. The aim should be that such an exercise does not become necessary again, that the basic imbalance in the life of the Church be corrected. Theological reflection on the whole exercise, the fundraising as well as the spending, will be needed to ensure that this is the case.

The fact that it has been necessary to adopt a fundraising approach means that the Fund has been subject to the various difficulties associated with charitable giving. It was soon found that money from business had to be attached to a specific project, and fundraisers in several dioceses have felt a need to identify the Fund particularly with local needs. A somewhat paternalistic, or 'top-down', Anglican approach has been apparent, which is ironic for an exercise designed to promote participation, ecumenism, empowerment and local leadership in deprived areas.

There are also fears that the fundraising for the Church Urban Fund has had a detrimental effect on the income from donations of some Anglican missionary and voluntary societies. In August 1989 the Honorary Treasurers of the United Society for the Propagation of the Gospel wrote to the PCC Treasurers of all their supporting parishes: 'We know you have been asked to give to the Church Urban Fund, and to aid organisations and other charities. Yet we, as the mission arm of the church, need to ask you to continue – and we hope increase – your faithfull support of USPG.' Fundraising is an increasingly competitive business.

Underneath this is, yet again, the old tension between stewardship and fundraising, between theological principle and practical reality, between giving of one's own resources and seeking resources from others. The stewardship case is that the Church Urban Fund is part of the stewardship of the whole Church and should therefore be funded primarily by the Church itself, particularly by Christians in more prosperous areas, rather by feeding the myth of the begging

Church. The fundraising case is that it is desirable for the whole nation to be involved in the task. Fundraising involves the whole community in the effort, and provides a practical connection with the Church for those not normally involved in its life and worship.

In may places the result of this has been some confusion. The chairman of one diocesan CUF committee has, for example, written: 'We are not asking for a donation to the Church Urban Fund. We are asking parishes to lead a fundraising crusade to enable their Christian brethren in deprived inner cities to lead in the process of providing succour and help to communities caught up in the spiral of slums, violence, drugs, poverty, disease and unemployment. For any Christian to turn his back on this need, is an abnegation of all Christian teaching.'[12] At the same time as parishes are told they should ask others for money, rather than provide it themselves, they are told that the work is a gospel imperative for Christians. In our confusion, we are in danger of claiming that it is a principle of Christianity that our work should be funded by others.

Motivation

The question of motivation is a vital part of any discussion of giving. Why do, or should, people give? There are, of course, a variety of reasons. These motivations usually overlap and intertwine, and can be very emotional, making this an area inimical to empirical research.

Often, then, people are motivated to give because an object of *pity* or compassion is set before them, and an emotional response is made. This is an important source of giving to aid agencies at the time of a major disaster.

Then there is *altruism*, taking into account the interests of others, perhaps a less emotional response. Mature human beings and developed relationships cannot exist without concern for others. Giving, together with receiving (and knowing which is appropriate when), is part of this.

This motivation does not exclude the possibility of giving out of *self-interest*, precisely because of the mutuality of giving and receiving in relationship, or out of *guilt*. It is quite possible to give generously, for example to an environmental organisation, for these reasons. Giving can thus enhance our self-image and self-esteem.

Giving can also be a product of *commitment* to an ideology or particular cause or group – contributions to political parties and pressure groups can often be motivated in this way. Such commitment is often encouraged by imitation of others, voluntary experience, or religious or other peer group identification.

There is, perhaps, a particular need to give to realise our longing for *justice* and *solidarity* in a divided society or world. For Christians, this can help to provide a basis of credibility for any prayers we may utter for the common good. Giving as response to what has been given to us is part of the Judeo-Christian tradition of covenant relationship with God and with one another.

For some Christians, therefore, giving is also an expression of, and flows out from, *worship* and *thanksgiving*. It is a symbol and sign of an inner attitude and posture towards life arising out of an awareness of God's own giving and generosity.

Others lay more emphasis on the importance of *obedience* and *duty*. Giving is necessary because it is part of the teachings of the Bible and Christian tradition, and for the same reasons the tithe is the correct way to follow the instruction. This is probably the reason why direct giving can be very much higher in a Church where the authority of scripture is both taught and linked to giving. Alternatively, the tithe is seen as a useful guideline, but it is regarded as much more important to obey the overall thrust of the New Testament[13].

Finally, giving can be motivated by a sense of *obligation* or *responsibility*, or even of embarrassment arising out of the social circumstances of the exchange. Most of us have put money in a tin quite simply because it was much easier than not doing so. It is difficult, however, to see for most people how such giving could ever be generous or considered.

Obviously, not all motivation is of equal value, and motives are usually, if not always, mixed. Reinhold Niebuhr makes the following comment on philanthropy by the powerful, saying that the attitude of a person of power is at best 'one of philanthropic generosity toward those who possess less power and privilege. His philanthropy is a perfect illustration of the curious compound of the brutal and the moral which we find in all human behaviour; for his generosity is at once a display of his power and an expression of his pity.'[14]

In these circumstances the Church has the difficult task of encouraging the best of motives without being judgemental and holier-than-thou about their very mixed nature. It is right to be concerned with motivation, but we should also be aware that motivation on its own is not enough. In the real world intelligently good actions are necessary.

Strengths and weaknesses

The institutional life of the Church is an inevitable expression of its being in the world. So is the money pressure upon it and the consequent need to consider funding. This does not need apology, but it does require the Church to spend some time reflecting upon its actions and relating them to its principles.

Notwithstanding three or more decades of stewardship teaching, the reality of 'budgets of opportunity' and the Church Urban Fund shows that a basic fundraising approach remains pre-eminent in the Church. Perhaps it was ever so. Perhaps it remains, in practial terms, impossible to move away from fundraising in the near future – but, if this is the case, it must surely be important to develop criteria and guidelines for fundraising which provide integrity and ensure that the Church does not ask for money from others which it should be providing itself. A hierarchy of values is called for – gospel, ethics of money, fundraising – to provide that integrity. At the moment there can often be just confusion and ill thought-out short-term expendiency.

In spite of this there has been some improvement in giving in recent years. It is not possible to say to which reasons this increase can be attributed – the work of the Christian Stewardship movement; pressure from above expressed in terms of allocations of quota or clergy; espousal of standards of giving; greater awareness of an inflationary economic background; increased commitment by some in the face of numerical decline and erosion of fringe membership. All may have had some influence.

Nevertheless, the improvement has not been overwhelming, and hardly vindicates the optimism of the First Church Estates Commissioner, writing in 1985: 'We believe that if Church people are told the facts openly and fully they respond.'[15]

The Rt Hon Michael Alison MP, the Second Church Estates Commissioner, took a different line in February 1990 when answering questions in the House of Commons about the follow-up report 'Living Faith in the City'. 'Church of England leaders were advised in the Commons yesterday to be more circumspect in urging others – notably the Government – to be more charitable until they could raise extra money from the parish plate. Michael Alison . . . said the weakness of the church's report was "its failure to comment on the very modest level of giving" in parish collections. Barely £2 a week on average was given by worshippers, "scarcely more than they spend on newspapers each week" . . . it lay ill for churchmen to be so vigorous in calling for government spending on the inner cities when parish giving was so modest.'[16] The force of this argument is undeniable; integrity and credibility are at stake. If the Church is as middle class as it appears, appealing to home owners and the better off, then it is clear that giving by Church members should be much higher.

A major weakness must surely be the strong tendency to use the urgency of insitutional needs as the primary motivation to encourage giving, when other motives such as altruism, worship and thanksgiving have much greater resonance with the Christian faith. Budgets of opportunity, standards of giving, subtle quota coercion, most literature and methods at parish or diocesan level – all operate with institutional needs at or very near the surface.

The sociological purpose of Christian Stewardship in the parishes swamps the theological and ethical purpose of stewardship itself. The message of the need to keep the institution going is much more audible than consideration of overall purpose, or why the institution should exist in the first place. This is not to say that funding is unimportant, nor that discussion of it should be suppressed. It is important and should be discussed – but in the context of theological debate and within a hierarchy of values which ensures congruence between different levels of the discussion. Otherwise, against an overall background of dualism and compartmentalism, fundamental misunderstandings and misinterpretations can arise.

The Church rightly exists as a human institution, and as such it must be funded. How that is to be done is important to its integrity. This is not to deny, but to affirm, that the Church as institution has a legitimate self-interest in its own continuing existence in order to be able to carry out its purposes in the world. The Church's task in the world is affirmed by struggling to ensure that as far as possible its means are in harmony with its ends, that a genuine dialectic takes place between the sociological realities and the theological aspirations.

The problem is that although the teaching may be right, if the methods are not they speak much louder than the teaching. Methods and message should be in harmony, but often they are not. The priority is to teach about a Christian attitude to money and material possessions. This loses the clarity of presentation it needs when it is confused by accompanying discouraging and justificatory pie-charts, or block diagrams of financial gloom, which are in fact subsidiary to the main issue.

The provision in the Church of England of a network of diocesan stewardship advisers has raised its own difficulties. However well the theological or ethical issues are approached, in the end a funding priority becomes apparent. This is often interpreted as a problem which arises because what is being discussed is 'too much about money', and so the problem of dualism again becomes evident. A diocesan adviser comes under pressure to handle this in one of two ways, both of which avoid the issue. The first is to tell people how much is required in order to meet the needs of the Church – an, in this context, inappropriate fundraising approach. The second is to concentrate on the many, varied and valid aspects of stewardship which can be presented without concentrating on money implications. Concern spills over into mission, ministry, ecology and justice, but ineffectually because the cutting edge, provided by the discomfiting subject of money, has gone.

Compartmentalism is reinforced by this state of affairs, and so people in the parishes of the Church of England find it difficult to handle any real talk about the stewardship of money. 'By not facing the issue of responsible ownership we have trivialized religion.'[17] For too long this subject has been fenced off behind the main motivation for broaching the subject – meeting the financial needs of the institutional Church. Money given to the Church is put into a separate compartment of life and the reasons for giving it are kept under control, defined and limited. No serious challenge is offered to prevailing patterns of acquiring, owning and spending.

Only some of the motivations for giving are thus encouraged to enter into the equation, and they are largely those which can be recognised from the long philanthropic tradition of appeal to urgent need. The Church ends up competing on this ground with other charitable and voluntary bodies in the giving market place. There is nothing wrong with such motivation, but for Christians it must be incomplete – altruism, solidarity, worship and thanksgiving must be added so that Christian lives can develop and grow. These can allow increasing generosity to replace competing for voluntary giving, and accountability *by* the giver to become as important as accountability *to* the giver. Whether these additional motivations can be encouraged by appeal to institutional need is surely open to doubt.

At present differing motivations symbolise the difference between the personal compartment of the individual Christian and the corporate compartment of life in the Church. In the corporate compartment we are challenged by altruism and solidarity, it is a world still steeped in welfarism: quota is assessed according to solidarity and commitment, justice and equity. In the individual compartment we are exhorted by all techniques available to harness the voluntary impulse, it is an appeal to the atomic individual: giving is encouraged by reference to need.

In the corporate arena money talk is sociological, motivated by funding requirements, but method and argument aims to be theological and ethical. In the private arena money talk focuses on charity, rather than justice, for motivation, and relies on methods which stress funding needs.

Important questions applied

The problematic issue of giving needs also to be held alongside the five questions which are put before the Church by a consideration of economics and ethics in modern society.

(1) Are money issues honestly faced?

The record on giving in the Church indicates that the answer to this question must be 'no'. The ethical and theological arguments of stewardship need to be more than exhortations, they need to inform the structures, to affect what is actually done, so that the structures harmonize with the principles proclaimed. Unfortunately giving in Church is often not for others, but for ourselves, keeping our own show going. It is therefore not giving at all, but paying dues. Even on this level it falls short.

The purpose of the Church as an institution should be a criterion in judging how finance is to be handled and funding raised. However, an unwillingness to face deeper issues about money, such as those identified earlier in this study, has led to a tendency to treat the subordinate aim as primary. Lack of coherence and credibility is the result, at whichever level of Church life we find talk of 'Christian Stewardship'.

So 'Christian Stewardship' is debated *ad nauseam* at the insti-

tutional level, where discussion is undermined because what is
secondary dominates what is primary and the real issues are
therefore not faced. It is justified at the theological level, where real
issues can be faced, but are rarely communicated because the
structures only fitfully resonate with the theology. It is diluted at
the pastoral level, where there is fear of the challenge in case it
should upset anybody. It is abused at the parochial level, where it is
kept under control, within safe boundaries, by being interpreted as
a funding exercise. It is misunderstood at the individual level, where
it is regarded as an exercise within the Church compartment, and
not as a vital point of connection between faith and life. It is avoided
at the personal level, where there is comfort and security to be lost
and therefore plenty of reason to connive at the general blunting
and evasion of the subject.

Many Christians equate stewardship with free will offering envel-
opes and deeds of covenant. If this is the case after thirty years it
must at least be asked whether 'Christian Stewardship' has not
outlived its usefulness.

The emphasis on funding needs also helps to avoid issues in
another way. It is all too simple and straightforward to answer the
call 'Tell us what you need!' without giving sufficient attention to
the concealed presumptions implied in it. These are, firstly, that
'them' and 'us' are real and incontrovertibly part of how relationships within the Church are perceived and structured and, secondly,
that this is as deep as any discussion about money is going to be
allowed to go.

Even regular churchgoers think of the Church as 'them' rather than
'us', and thus define themselves as consumers of religion. Throughout
the Church an emphasis on funding leads us into this area – at every
level a financial discussion reveals that it is someone else's fault.
Parishes say that those who give are giving as much as they possibly
can, and that the problem lies with other people who give little or
nothing although they live in some style. Dioceses say that people in
parishes still do not give realistically. Both parishes and dioceses
complain about the expenditure and expectations of General Synod
and its boards. It is definitely 'them' who are the problem, not 'us'.

(2) Are idealism and realism held in balance?

The difficulty remains of keeping the affluent within the Church
whilst continuing to preach the gospel. In today's Church this

expresses itself in a divergence between idealism and realism in giving and funding strategies. For example, the fundraising for the Church Urban Fund (as fundraising inevitably will) operates nearer the realism pole, whereas the spending by the Fund is active much nearer the idealism end of the scale. The long term effect of the Fund on the Church as a whole, the possibility that it will result in real change and the danger that it might simply provide a succession of useful palliatives, depends to some extent upon whether we manage to replace this separation with a balance or properly thought out mixture.

A sociological and a theological approach should therefore be co-ordinated. Giving cannot be looked at in isolation from the other issues raised here by a consideration of money in the world and the Church. Inevitably, any practical model will seem inadequate in comparison with the gospel itself, but that does not diminish the importance of the task of building bridges between areas of concern which are more comfortably kept apart.

In such an approach, for example, criteria for fundraising could be developed within the hierarchy of values already discussed – gospel, money ethics, fundraising – remembering that it is not possible to move from the first level to the third without thinking, praying and teaching about the second. Such criteria might usefully state that fundraising for maintenance of public worship and pastoral care of Church members cannot fall within the criteria, being properly part of the responsibility of Church members themselves. However, it could be valid to fundraise publicly in partnership with others to achieve some end beneficial to society at large. Here the criteria would need to draw on the concept of 'three kingdoms', recognizing both the autonomy and the interconnectedness of kingdom, Church and world.

(3) Is the 'Third Kingdom' active?

Is the Church expending itself in answering the call to connect the kingdoms of God and of the world? Here, the Church Urban Fund can be said to represent a move in the right direction, but one where advance and change could falter if funding cannot in due course be brought into harmony with underlying aims and objectives. There is already some concern about the provision of long-term financial resources for initiatives supported by the Fund.

The present pattern is that 'two kingdoms' attitudes prevail, represented by the dualism between funding/realism and spending/ idealism. A 'three kingdoms' approach is called for to break this down, perhaps by means of mediating concepts such as the 'internal/ external' or the 'penultimate' already mentioned.

Here, too, 'Christian Stewardship' has allowed itself to become part of the problem. In this narrow sense 'Stewardship' has been used to peg out the boundaries between the life of the Church and the life of the world, instead of undertaking its real task, which is making connections between them. It has become a means to a very limited end, shrinking into 'the envelope scheme' and 'covenants'. It often therefore fails to address the big questions about what Christians do with their money. Funding becomes the end-product, instead of being part of an overall challenge to redirection, and as such manages to provide shelter from the sharper implications of the tensions between faith and money.

(4) Are owners called by God?

How is the altruism necessary for a proper response to the generosity of God to be enhanced in and developed by Christians? At the end of the twentieth century it is necessary to consider how owners, and consumers, are to become more aware of the element of vocation which exists in every part of every human life.

Obviously, there is a call involved in bringing the Church Urban Fund, or the needs of the local Church, to people's attention. However, this tends to be a segmented call; it does not impinge strongly upon the whole of life, but upon a part, often a small part, set aside for charity. Maurice Coombs suggests: 'A Christian theology of stewardship accepts that the world, its means of production distribution and exhange, belong to the human race. But the human race has been purchased by Jesus of Nazareth and Jesus of Nazareth has given it back to God. A valid theology of stewardship will build from that premise and seek to work out how at trinity of ownership is exercised.'[18]

The issue of responsible ownership must be faced otherwise the Church's claim to relevance will be more and more eroded. It will raise some much more disturbing questions than do many of the present efforts to encourage giving through the Church. It will dig deep.

(5)   Are we aware of the pastoral implications of money?

A study of some of the effects of the Church's efforts to improve giving shows that the pastoral implications of money need to be considered much more than at present.

Any fundraiser will advise against trying to motivate people to give by focusing on maintenance expenditure, yet for the Church this remains a common initial communication: 'It costs £x a minute to keep this cathedral going, will you help?' It is difficult to repeatedly put such statements before people without having some effect on their attitudes. What is the long term pastoral effect of nagging?

Pastoral relationships are affected. In rural areas, where small communities are under great pressure, the gentle coercion surrounding the quota (however justified), together with divergence of financial interest between parish and diocese leads to misunderstanding and ill-feeling towards other parts of the Church. This encourages an unhealthy parochialism.

Standards of giving can place a false burden on some and offer an unjustified complacency to others. An average does not apply to anyone, and its application to any number of particular cases may be pastorally inappropriate for any number of reasons.

Similarly, by concentrating on funding needs and presenting a balanced set of books as the end product, stewardship tends to become synonymous with stinginess and not spending becomes as valid a response as more giving. Motivation matters.

So what is to become of 'Christian Stewardship'? Some now consider it to be a wasted catalyst, held in suburban captivity. It can allow comfortable Christians to be more successful at being inward-looking when it should provoke them to serious reflection. If this is so, the pastoral implications are serious. If a decision to give is not about proper and thankful use of money under God, it may well be about paying a subscription.

15. An Emerging Pattern

The Church Compartment

For many Christians the life of the Church is kept in a separate compartment. The 'spiritual' life is a leisure activity, usually very local, and tends not to affect the way that life is lived in the 'real' world. Unfortunately, the Church itself must be partly held responsible for creating this exaggerated boundary. Members are urged towards the moral values of the kingdom of God, without being brought to engage in the task of working out a strategy of change for themselves, the Church or society at large. Christians end up with an ideal vision which remains detached from the harsh realities of life, especially economic life.

The issue of money plays a large part, much larger than many would wish to admit, in defining the shape and contents of this compartment. 'If you asked most people in this diocese what their major concern for the Church of England is right now they wouldn't say women priests, gay clergy or any of the other issues which dominate the pages of the *Church Times*. Their answer would be "keeping going, raising the share, paying our way". . . in the rural and industrial West Midlands most Anglican church life on the ground is a struggle. People don't feel ready to have their horizons broadened.'[1] In this atmosphere much activity aimed at encouraging Christians to engage more fully in the world is likely to be doomed to failure.

The pressures of contemporary life therefore tend to be inadequately acknowledged and addressed by the preaching, teaching and learning of the local Church. Conversely, Christian principles are not challenged as they should be by exposure to the pressures and signs of the times. In Church, as well as in society, we avoid challenge and disturbance by means of compartmentalism. The price for this comfort is high. That much longed for relevance is more elusive than ever. Instead, there is a 'dreadful ghetto-ising of the churches'[2]. Money represents a dominant force in society. Evasive and defensive thinking about it is therefore a very large blockage stopping the way out of the ghetto.

The secrecy which is often required to surround the details of people's giving in the local Church provides a striking example of these forces at work. This insistence may well be because people are ashamed of how much they give, but at a deeper level the secrecy can be said to secure the boundary between faith and life at a point where there is the possibility of it being breached.

The issue of deeds of covenant also shows the Church very near a neo-Lutheran two kingdoms approach in dealing with issues of money. Ulrich Duchrow points out that a legitimate use of Luther's thought involves the sacred in taking up a critical stance towards the secular, but that 'the misuse of Luther's views is connected at its core with an illegitmate accommodation to existing power relationships . . .'[3] In our terms this means that in return for tax repayments the Church is subtly expected to play its part by strengthening the moral circuits when required – '. . . politicians can claim no special authority in strengthening individual moral standards. That authority rests firmly with the Church.'[4]

In the end the Christian faith cannot be contained within the compartments often used to tame it. A Christian is a Christian whether at home, or at Church, or in the world; whether dealing with the household budget, the Church's common purse, or national and international economics.

The divisions between these compartments can assist us in self-deception. Often, the connections between them are more direct than we find comfortable and in need of more emphasis than we allow. Undeniably it must be recognised that each area of life has its own culture which Christians must seek to interpret and understand, but they must endeavour to remain followers of Christ as they do so.

John Paul II wrote, following the Second Vatican Council, that this split between faith and daily life deserves to be counted among the more serious errors of our age. The Church's ministry in the world is most profoundly affected by the question of money, its mission limited by the inability to use money positively as a bridging network between compartments of life. A potential connection, which could encourage more participation by Church members, is being missed. Instead, difficult money issues are shuffled off into the compartment where they are least challenging.

Consumer Christianity

Bishop John Taylor has pointed out the tension which exists for the Church and its task in the world: how to relate a theologically unchanging God to sociologically changing circumstances in both

Church and world?[5] But in the Church's task the sociological is at least as important as the theological. 'It is in practice not in theory that you realize the breakthrough truth.'[6]

We have to come to terms with the fact that the shape of contemporary Christianity is to some extent formed by the prevailing consumer ethos of the surrounding society. Church membership is part of a web of attitudes and relationships which also includes home ownership, social class and status, getting on in the world, the quest for emotional and financial security.

R. W. Bibby's research in Toronto has shown a reduction in the areas of life over which religion has significant input, and discerned a shift in attitude away from commitment and towards consumption. At the end of the twentieth century the challenge before the Church is largely one of facing the 'market realities' of compartmentalism and consumption.

Again, the subject of money illustrates this consumer thought pattern; even regular churchgoers tend to think of the Church as 'them' rather than 'us'. Divisions appear between those who pay for the work of the Church and those who do the work of the Church, and between those who pay for the work of the Church and those they would like to pay more for the work of the Church.

The question of accountability is raised, rightly, but in such a way that God's providence is perhaps insufficiently acknowledged by a consumer religion where 'they' are accountable to 'us', or the other way round. This accountability of wealth becomes dominant, rather than 'we' together being dependent upon and accountable to God, to the world, to the poor – the accountability of justice. If the Church is held accountable by the consumers of religion, rather than aware of its existence being *for non-members*, the effect can be seriously limiting.

This is an area where a distinction can be drawn between stewardship and fundraising motivations for giving. In the former, the emphasis is on relationship with God and one another, on showing responsibility in property ownership to God and one another. 'We' are accountable to God. In the latter, the emphasis is on persuasion, on persuading 'them' to support 'us'. Inevitably, 'we' tend to become primarily accountable to 'them'. This may well enhance and emphasize the power of the wealthy in the community – a problem since the earliest days of the Church – and brings with it the possibility that the Church will concentrate on comforting the comfortable, rather than the outcast and despised. Tensions therefore exist, and questions should be raised, for many growing and numerically successful Churches.

In this context, is the Christian group or individual the steward? What is the role of the corporate? Many Christians feel that the corporate stewardship of wealth by the Church leaves much to be desired and decide that they will redirect or direct their own outward giving independently, at least in part. This may be right in some circumstances (Christians must be active in the world) and is certainly understandable, but it is surely ironic that these Christians are themselves exemplifying an individualistic consumer and personal choice culture which many of them would deplore. They are caught in the dualistic offside trap, creating a self-fulfilling prophecy.

This trap exists for all of us. When the report 'Living Faith in the City' says: 'What is now needed are closer links between the Church generally – and the Church of England in particular – and the modern structures of secular society, at both national and local level'[7] it is quite right. But it must not be overlooked that for many people the modern structures of secular society are atomised and consumerist. How will the Church relate, adjust, assimilate and use these structures? Will the handling of money and wealth play an appropriate part in these processes?

Urban Fundraising Reflections

During the 1980s the Archbishops' Commission on Urban Priority Areas was a formative factor in the public perceptions and self-image of the Church. Although the report 'Faith in the City' was not above criticism, it was generally welcomed as a timely contribution to debate and a powerful challenge to both Church and nation.

By the early 1990s, the Church Urban Fund had largely taken over this mantle. Much has been achieved, but at the price of a subtle shift in emphasis. The fund has inevitably dealt with the provision of projects, rather than with the matters raised in the original report which relate to the profile of the whole Church, and has done so by means of an enormous fundraising campaign. Of its nature this has been much more 'top-down' than can be entirely in tune with ACUPA's 'bottom-up' approach. A new structure has been created, supplying an important service, but not addressing the problems of power and relationships within the Church. These remain.

The £18 million needed to create the fund could, in fact, have been provided entirely from historic resources – the aim is after all to correct an historical imbalance – without costing any more than two years' expenditure on the Church Commissioners' initial commitment to pay the clergy poll tax. The dangers of reinforcing compartments, inappropriate attitudes and patronising relationships by means of a fundraising struggle could then have been avoided. Furthermore, the nurturing of partnership across boundaries could then have concentrated entirely upon strategies such as active business participation, inter-Church skills transfers, ecumenical initiatives and use of workplace resources.

As it is, new money has been raised and a new structure created in order to undertake a shift in resources towards more just distribution within the Church. Existing institutions and patterns of relationship have not been affected, with minor exceptions, other than by a large scale fundraising effort. The effect has thus been compartmentalised in the manner of any charitable giving. A 'compartment for the conscience' has been created, but inadequate fundamental change has been made. Without such change, the continuing funding of projects is called into question. It may then become necessary to go through the whole process again, or to make the fund a permanent part of Church life. This would undermine its originating purpose.

Inclusive or exclusive?

The handling of money issues in the Church has implications for its character. Is it to be a Church, communal and inclusive, with a blurred and ambiguous boundary, or a sect, associational and exclusive, with a very clear idea of who is in and who is out? Local and parish Churches vary in their position on this spectrum. Rural Churches tend to be more communal and inclusive, whilst suburban, urban and Churches with a strong style tend to be more associational, gathered or exclusive.

It does seem that giving is higher, and a 'purist' view of the stewardship of money more appropriate and tenable, where the Church has a stronger identity and a clearer boundary with the world. Gathered Churches, often criticised for being sectarian and exclusive in their approach, can be more definite in the expectations made of their members. This particularly applies to Churches with an evangelical tradition, where teaching of the tithe combines effectively with a conservative view of biblical authority. These are the more 'successful' Churches in financial terms – do they point the way for the whole Church? They would certainly claim that a more inclusive view of the Church has the weakness of leaning towards what Bonhoeffer: called 'cheap grace'.

It is obviously easy for consumer religion to tend towards 'cheap grace'. But it is also the case that a religion which espouses certainty in an uncertain age has consumer appeal. Both may be, in their own way, an over-simplification. Grace must not be made cheap, but it must always be made accessible if the Church is to be the Church[8]. Definition must not lead to the creation of a barrier.

In this context the signals made to those on the boundary between churchgoers and non-churchgoers, the so-called fringe, are very important. What are the effects of a Christian Stewardship project on people at the edge of Church life? This depends very much upon the coherence and the clarity of the methods and teaching used. An undue emphasis on funding will tend to reduce Christian giving to the character of a subscription, to paying for what you get, whereas an emphasis on personal freedom and responsibility can provide real growth in both spiritual and material terms. Either way, there is great scope for misunderstanding given the diffidence and embarrassment surrounding money and the Church's record of confusion on the subject.

Perhaps, like John Tiller, the whole Church will be 'driven to regard the Church as having certainly a communal approach to its mission, but requiring an associational basis of membership in order to fulfil it.'[9] In other words, whilst the Church must see its ministry as being to the whole world, to the whole of society, it will not have the resources for that task without a strong sense of its own identity as a community of faith which makes demands of its members. The ideal cannot be pursued other than from the reality of a firm base in worship and commitment.

16. Facing Questions and Guidelines

How do our five questions and guidelines relate to the overall patterns and trends shown in the handling of money by Christians and the Church?

1.   *Facing money issues*

The Church seems to live in a vicious circle of embarrassment about money, and the question of Christian giving remains one of the most difficult, controversial and recalcitrant of ecclesiastical subjects. So often it is discussed without conviction, diffidently, apologetically, ineffectively. The focus usually lingers on maintaining the status quo, so horizons remain static and people are not challenged to apply their faith to their money across the whole of life. Because people do not apply their faith to their money (the two things are left in separate compartments) a double standard prevails and they do not share in the money costs of Christian ministry, therefore funding pressure on the Church increases. The circle is completed with yet another discouraging discussion about how to keep going . . . and so it goes on.

Much effort goes into cordoning off the subject of money, rather than facing up to it. This must be a major contributory factor in the low level of giving. In practice much of the energy used in encouraging giving is counter-productive because it strengthens the boundary between faith and money, built as it is on motivation via institutional financial requirement rather than via the application of Christian discipleship to life in the world. The sensitive area is entered at the shallowest point, and the depths are rarely investigated. Christian giving, 'The Stewardship', ends up just meaning an envelope scheme.

The problem is often expressed, the boundary often constructed, in 'them' and 'us' terms. The Church's property belongs to 'them', not 'us', so we don't have to apply ourselves to how the money is invested – just as long as the income is enough to protect us from the reality of having to pay for the cost of running the Church ourselves. 'They' spend too much, 'they' don't give enough, and that is the source of the difficulty – let us not examine our own lack of generosity. But no amount of burbling about accountability or synodical participation can hide the basic underlying truths.

A cordon around money is also a cordon around the Church's relationship with society. It means, for example, that there is an inadequate owning of, taking responsibility for, the Church Commissioners' massive stake in macro-economic life. It means, too, that the connections are not made at the micro-economic level of the owning and consuming of individual Christians. The 'three kingdoms' approach advocated in this study would be a way of establishing such connections whilst acknowledging the proper autonomy of economic life, that money and wealth have to be dealt with on their own terms.

2.   *Are idealism and realism held in balance?*

Affluence has always been a problem for the Church, providing as it does an obvious contradiction to the demands of the gospel. However, what was once an accommodation to be reached with an influential minority is now, in western society, a conundrum affecting the majority of Church members. The early Church struggled to preach the gospel to the rich at the same time as it retained them, and their wealth, for the work of the Church. This task now confronts the Church in respect of a much larger proportion of people claiming Christian allegiance.

One way of dealing with this problem, observable throughout the examples described in this second part as in the first, is compartmentalism: allowing idealism and realism to diverge into different areas of Church life; considering a 'bias to the poor' on one hand whilst planning fundraising strategies targeted at the affluent on the other; espousing ethical investment in General Synod and Board of Social Responsibility meetings and a strong City-oriented culture at the Church Commissioners; criticising riches and wealth from the vantage-point of an extremely wealthy institution; and so on.

This phenomenon is particularly noticeable in the divergence between the theological notion of stewardship and the sociologial manifestation of Christian Stewardship in the life of the Church. The concept of stewardship should in theory act to expand the vision of Christians. Within this the stewardship of money can serve as a catalyst for spiritual growth and an opportunity to sanctify and redeem human experience, because money touches every area of life.

However, in practice Christian Stewardship is often restricted to just one area, the maintenance of parish life. Potential is undermined by presenting to people what is in fact a survival kit for the Church compartment of life and telling them it is discipleship. It is difficult not to agree with the Bishop of Blackburn when he says that during many Stewardship projects in parishes a game is being played[1], in which a realistic response is made behind an idealistic facade.

Stewardship is in two minds, one sociological and one theological. Compartmentalised attitudes to money mean that it is exceedingly difficult to draw these strands together, as they must be if the Church is to be true to itself. Common reactions to the present situation propose the abandonment of idealism, 'it is better to be realistic and admit it than to put up a facade of idealism', or of realism, 'we must maintain the principles of Christian Stewardship and eschew anything that smacks of fundraising'. But the real need is to accommodate both idealism and realism in the equation, and this will mean using both stewardship principle and fundraising technique – the aim being to discern which is appropriate when.

3.   A 'Third Kingdom'?

The Church's attitude to wealth has always and inevitably been one of compromise, apart from a small number of notable exceptions. However, compromise can all too easily become conformity with the world, rather than a bridge between the world and the values of the kingdom of God. True compromise involves the stretching and pain of creative tension, the acknowledgement that every answer is provisional. It must be distinguished from the false, but subtle and beguiling, compromise of compartmentalism, which opts for a quiet life.

A 'third kingdom' perception is thus extremely important in looking at the Church's handling of wealth, providing a means of avoiding undue separation between the worlds of faith and money. At the same time the distinctiveness of each area is recognised: the possibility of the kingdom of God; the autonomy of economic reality, practicality and finitude; the vocation of the Church as a ground of interplay between these two and as servant of them. This vocation needs to comprise witness against two-dimensional postures on either or both sides of the dualism between faith/idealism and money/realism. In particular this can be done by the Church applying to its own institutional life the remedies and recommendations it lays before the world, leading towards the building from experience of criteria which relate the ideal and the real.

The local dimension, the parish church, the individual Christian, has an important part to play in this process. It is where the experience must be digested and the learning done – the sociology must be at the source of the theology if the theology is to ring true and the Church enabled to speak of the things of God to surrounding society. For this to happen the local Church's all-absorbing fight for financial survival should be undertaken on ground which enables the necessary connections to be made, rather than in terms which emphasize compartmentalism and provide protection from underlying realities by dependence upon inherited assets.

4. *Owners called by God*

One of the more intractable problems for the Church is the fact that it is still, in a post-industrial age, using concepts and precepts about money and wealth which evolved in pre-industrial society. It is difficult to make talk of trusteeship or stewardship, condemnation of usury or interest, suspicion of wealth creation or western capitalism, ring true or relevant in a world which has seen Henry Ford and the Berlin Wall come and go. Such talk is ignored as unrealistic by Christian and non-Christian alike, and the world of money is more and more divorced from theologial praxis.

This is tragic, because the Church must have some very serious questions to put concerning late twentieth-century patterns of ownership and consumption, such as questions about dependency, addiction and obsessive security-mindedness. The Church should also wish to develop and extend the altruism of its own members and to offer this as a witness to the world. Unfortunately, however, the preoccupation with its own institutional survival means that the Church is ill-equipped to give a lead or show an example of altruism training and growth.

The need is for the development of realistic concepts, metaphors and symbols, ones which relate to the aspirations, aims, values and purposes in people's lives, and which offer a discerning and qualified affirmation of economic life. Such concepts might include 'just wealth', 'responding' or 'vocational ownership', 'detached consumption', 'proportionate giving', 'just generosity'. Stewardship may remain a useful theological theme, in common use regarding the environment, but the usefulness of the steward as a defining concept or metaphor for Christian money handling is now outdated and, furthermore, has been devalued by institutional misuse.

These new concepts would need to be applied in the corporate life of the Church itself, to give them weight and to set an example, and also to ensure that the Church is not left behind by a developing generation of 'new consumers' and 'ethical investors'. The Church has sufficient wealth and material substance to have noticeable influence and effect in the market place, as well as its actions having symbolic and leadership significance. Money should be used as a means of enhancing Christians' awareness of new concepts and putting them into practice in their lives, along with their awareness of themselves as the Church, owning the Church and owning its wealth.

5. *Pastoral implications of money*

We seriously underestimate the pastoral implications of money in the life of the Church and in its relationship with society. For many, money in the life of the Church is the story of the Church as it touches them or as they see it. There is the effect on Christians and non-Christians if they feel that the Church is failing to practise what it preaches, if hypocrisy becomes the perceptible end-product of compartmentalism. There is the way that economic social division is represented in the life of the Church, particularly the need for justice as well as charity. There is the fear that condemnation of riches will upset affluent and comfortable churchgoers. There is Christian Stewardship creating a successful, inward-looking Church or a clericalised laity. There is the widely-held perception that the Church is constantly fundraising and nagging about its shortage of money.

All these situations, and many more, are pastoral in nature. The Church's attitude to money needs to be more coherent if it is to be able to speak with and through the members of its congregations as representatives of and to God's world.

What would be the features of a Church which was moving to take the pastoral implications of money more seriously in the context of contemporary economic life? It would probably be approaching funding and giving from a more associational perspective, its mission and ministry from a more communal one, and building structures and patterns of education which enable and encourage this.

It would pursue greater subsidiarity in financial responsibility, encouraging debate about idealism and realism at lower hierarchical levels, using money as a channel of identification for Christians with the Church. This could parallel teaching about society which would attempt to use individualism, responsible ownership and consumerism to enhance the common good. These matters are dealt with in more detail in my concluding chapters.

The pastoral aim would therefore be to create a cohesive and consistent network of relationship, within and beyond Church membership. This would reach across the whole of society and all financial circumstances, making contact at both the level of the structural and macro-economic and of the individual and micro-economic.

In practical terms this would mean, for example, more debate about the management of the Church's assets and thus more connections between the Church's social responsibility activists and the culture of the City. It would mean more financial responsibility and decision-making in deanery synods and PCCs. It would mean learning together, both inside and outside Church, about responsible ownership in the contemporary world. Just as money helps to define the compartment of life we call the Church, it can be used to broaden horizons and make connections.

PART THREE

The Way Ahead

17. Patterns in the Church and the World

Introduction

Various patterns have emerged from the two main parts of this study. The first part dealt with the features and changes of contemporary economic life and the Church's ethical response. The second examined the current practice of the Church itself in its handling of money and wealth. In this first chapter of the concluding part those patterns are compared and contrasted. Then in Chapter 18 the need for Christians and the Church to come to terms with economic change is emphasized as a preliminary to examining, in Chapter 19, possible ways in which the Church might become more effective and an influence for change in the world.

The power and use of money

The importance of money in the lives of people, in society at large and in the Church has been emphasized at every stage of this study. Contemporary economic circumstances do nothing to diminish that importance. Jesus detected the pressure to keep the subject of wealth well insulated and well protected from the ethical challenge he brought. He felt the need to address the subject fairly often, and developed some disarming strategies to bring people face to face with their own behaviour.

In our culture a form of compartmentalism operates to strengthen that insulation of money from morals. This is at work both in society at large and in the Church. The pressure comes at every level, from ourselves, from the Church and from the wider community – no-one wants to be put on the spot and Church people are not exempt from this. Nevertheless, if Christians and the Church can address this within themselves without retreating from the world, their social tradition and capacity for mission can be renewed and enhanced.

The patterns have appeared time and time again. The importance of 'possessive individualism' and the security of ownership, leading to greater emphasis for greater numbers of people on the acquisition of property – home, car, investments, pension, electronic labour-

169

saving aids, holidays – and on borrowing in order to achieve these aims. The investing of more and more meaning in the role of the consumer, making the point of consumption the key point of decision not only in economic life but also in self-perception and search for meaning. These features are reinforced by the now commonly held perception of the importance of the market mechanism in all economies and of the property-owning democracy as the shared aspiration of much of the world's population.

There is an irony to be noted in this victory of the western way of life, for in practice it implies a developing pattern of economic growth which may not be sustainable in a finite world. More and more nations have decided that socialism and corporatism are cul-de-sacs. But human moral maturity and political activity remains hardly further forward than the stage of development of the social contract, largely based on property rights, worked out when the potential for economic exploitation had no apparent limits.

The Church is fully participant in economic life, through the daily participation of its members and through the structural participation of its institutions. Church life and the attitudes of Church members are both strongly influenced by ownership and consumption, conforming to the general pattern in society of consumer choice, individual decision-making and financial accountability. Thus, in terms of its daily living, the Church flows in the same direction as the society around it. Yet this creates a tension with the apparent thrust of the teaching of Jesus, setting up a conflict which is for many only resolved by keeping money in one compartment of life and Christian faith in another.

The possession of money, we have seen, gives us power over our lives, makes us less vulnerable to the choices of others, and gives us power over the lives of others, makes them more vulnerable to our choices. Without making money or profit, it is not possible to exercise consumer choice, to acquire property, to spend or save or invest. These activities, for Christians and the Church just as much as anybody else, are limited only by wealth and allowed only by wealth.

Consequently, for Christians and the Church just as much as anybody else, freedom of choice in what is needed or wanted, good or bad, is up to the consumer, the spender, the investor, whose position is therefore one of responsibility which can be well or poorly exercised. The potential is there to express our values, to impart and quantify value to people and things, and to communicate that value to others – that is positive. But conflict lies in the question – is immersion in the world of market, property and consumer values inimical to the values of Christianity?

Some will want to answer that question with a straight 'yes', but that is of little help to Christians living their lives in the world or to a Church which is committed to maintaining a tangible presence in the world. The need exists to answer the question in some other way.

To answer 'no' implies ignorance of the gospel or total compartmentalism of life, so the practical answer has to be some form of 'yes, but . . .' Thus the Church is called to develop ways to undertake a difficult journey, both individual and corporate, working with flawed materials to produce good ends.

Values

The persistent question remains – how to harness self-interest and mixed motives for beneficial ends? For a western society this means working through the market system and developing ownership and consumption to engage people in a movement towards the common good. For the Church it means using similar ingredients to develop and enhance the life of the Body of Christ. In both these endeavours the ground under our feet is shifting and we sense the faltering of 'that complex web of non-contractual, moral, legal and religious bonds which capitalism both assumed and at the same time undermined.'[1]

Economic determinism is not the only way to interpret social change. Other cultural, religious and historical factors may play their part. However, there is little doubt that the combined force of economic motivation, organisation and institutions, technological innovation and entrepreneurial skill now dominates a western world which, through its wealth, dominates the world. In many ways economic determinism *is* the culture, and it tends to dismantle the restraints and structures of other value systems, religious or secular.

This ushers in an eclectic and plural post-modern world in which everything is on display for individual choice or rejection. Religious values can thus be rejected more easily than ever before, and the response to this can be an attempt, as in fundamentalism, to put up the barricades against the world – compartmentalism writ large. Values are in conflict.

Values also flow together. Economic determinism is no less

influential within the institutional structures of the Church than it is in the world outside. This can be just an intrusion of reality – the answer 'There is no money!' can be heard as frequently in the Church as it can in the National Health Service – but it can also be a consequence of intangibles such as the amount of will or motivation. The value questions begin to become complex and muddled.

It may be that a new dialectic is beginning to emerge. Economic determinism is now the thesis, and the antithesis will develop in the form of an alliance between ecological and ecumenical (not in the narrowly ecclesiastical sense) values, leading to a synthesis of some sort in the future. It may be that environmental disaster will overtake us before this can happen, or that in a plural setting these things will themselves turn out to be relative and transitory. All the same, it remains necessary to work out what to do for the time being, in the present. This means that the Church should ensure that its own values are as coherent as is possible with its actions and with the actions of its members.

Reinhold Niebuhr pointed out that religious idealism is fundamentally different from a rational system of values[2]. The religious preoccupation with motive produces a qualitative difference, which means that it is not just the logical extension or the extreme end of a series of differing levels of response. This difference can have the effect of bolstering the compartmentalism which separates faith and life, drawing Christians towards the adoption of clearly negative positions towards economic life. Solutions tend to become utopian and unrealistic: religiously beyond criticism but also literally out of this world, as in proposals to introduce the Old Testament jubilee or to apply biblical and medieval condemnations of usury to daily life in the high street.

Nevertheless, accommodating reality should not silence the utopian clarion call and its inspirational and clarifying effect. The difference must be affirmed at the same time as Christians build bridges with and for the world. What is needed is a theology which is 'about promoting the interaction between two poles or spheres of reality.'[3] Reflection on the divine economy must be combined with understanding society. Interaction is necessary between the two to illuminate, interpret and change – change which will be required in the theological reflection as well as being called for in the world upon which it is reflecting.

Christianity does emphasize motive, but it also has a high place for consideration of the fruits of action. In allowing fruits as a criterion of judgement, it offers a meeting place for the ideal and the real, for theology and economics, for faith and money. This means that the Church must look critically at its own economic behaviour. Furthermore, it means that the Church must consider the damage done to its own mission by the failure to allow economic reality to sufficiently impinge upon its processes of theological reflection.

The urgent necessity is to set about establishing networks of links between the compartments. In this generation it is money which marks the area of life where culture and faith are mutually most abrasive – it is a strong pressure point on both. Consequently it is in the area of money that we can seek to find the necessary connections between the sheltered world of 'my Church' and the real life of the world.

Charity and Justice

Many of these paradoxes are most apparent in the area of charitable giving. A way forward may be found in an examination of the ways in which the 'voluntary impulse' works, in the world, in the Church and in interaction between the two. The task is to see if 'consumer' attitudes to charity can be developed – expanded into a creative attitude to society including a greater awareness of social justice. The danger is that these attitudes remain ephemeral and impulsive, dissipated in actions which tend towards the sentimental and ultimately ineffective.

Voluntary activity in the 1980s, at its most apparent in the telethons, has sometimes shown a spirit of generosity which is an expression of true humanity. Almost any type of giving is in some way a point of contact and growth and it is good to see Christians heavily involved in charitable events, provided that these do not serve as a substitute for disciplined reflection on the state of the world and Christianity's part in it. The present moment is itself a sacrament in Christian spirituality, and it is right to be ready for a generous impulse of compassion. There must always be room for that, but it takes intellectual rigour and an open mind to produce a regular and consistent response which incorporates sharing and justice.

The rational argument for a regular and consistent reponse is an affirmation of the need for institutional structures to give effective expression to idealistic impulses. This applies both to the Church

itself and to society. There may well be a role for the Church in
extending such impulses into a training ground for citizenship, by
searching out the potential linkages to be found in generous
response. In this way people can exercise individualism by fulfilling
an expanding sense of duty as well as enjoying rights.

More than ever voluntary activity (of which, in sociological terms,
the Church is part) is an important channel both for those who need
to receive and those who wish to give. In an age in which state
welfare is no longer generally accepted as the final solution to all
problems, voluntarism is once again taking on a wider task. The
voluntary sector's capacity for flexibility, immediacy, innovation
and experimentation make it increasingly attractive in complex
modern society, but there are disadvantages. Now that more services
are delivered through the voluntary channel, many agencies lose the
very flexibility which makes them attractive because they are caught
in a spiral of competition to raise funds for a growing number of
existing commitments.

It is therefore unfortunate that non-government organisations
throughout Europe report an increase in 'giving fatigue' – an affluent
society seems to produce a shortfall, rather than an increase, in
generosity. It is just as unfortunate that direct giving in the Church
seems to suffer from the same fatigue. There is not much chance of
the Church being able, say, to give some sort of lead in the case of
some of the less popular charitable causes, or to set an example of
regular giving without strings attached. In fact, the need to be told
you are generous whatever the truth of the situation – 'Thank you
Mr and Mrs Buggins' – is at least as bad in the Church as elsewhere.

Current trends in charitable giving and fundraising are connected
with wider trends in society and the Church. Voluntarism and an
emphasis on individual salvation in religion have often run in closely
parallel tracks. In a compartmentalised society, charitable giving is
in danger of providing a compartment in which the conscience can
be contained as an activity separate from more overtly dangerous
questions such as politics, justice and wealth creation and
distribution.

The value of charitable activity can only be enhanced if those
taking part in it strive to break through and make connections
across these barriers, both in terms of perception and of generosity.
This would probably be difficult in the light of current British
charity and ecclesiastical law, which tends to strengthen this compartmentalism, but the situation in the United States indicates that

this may not have to be the case[4]. Is there an unspoken principle that tax relief on covenants buys some sort of limitation which makes it harder to build the necessary connections? Perhaps what is needed is some sort of concept of basic purpose. This could provide greater flexibility for charitable activity in a rapidly changing world, giving more realistic and appropriate criteria for such issues as ethical investment and 'political' activity.

This whole area is a striking example of the need for the Church to regard itself as the 'third kingdom' and to act accordingly, striving to link in its own life the kingdoms of God and the world. The giving of money is highly symbolic in a culture as strikingly money-oriented as ours. Work needs to be done to enhance the quality and quantity of giving in the light of both the ultimate giving shown in Christ and the penultimate efforts of human altruism and generosity.

Patterns of interdependence

A sharp dose of New Right therapy has in recent years given dependency a bad name, and it may be that some sort of tonic was needed. The model to be applauded instead has been independence, standing on your own two feet, not being a burden on society. However, it may be that this reaction back to the simplicities of puritanism has been excessive.

Everybody has periods of dependence and independence at different stages and in different states of life. The Welfare State retains great influence, and has always had more to do with *inter*dependence, and thus relationship. People give when they are able and receive when need is greatest, in childhood, illness and adversity, old age.

Christians acknowledge humanity's dependence on God and God's gifts, but the very fact that they are gifts, without strings, transforms the dependence into independence. Such is the absolute givingness of God. Human beings are left in freehold, in a state of ownership, free to acknowledge the dependence of their independence, or to ignore it. To acknowledge the dependence is to follow Christ in the offering up of independence. This leads to the way of interdependence, to God-human and human-human relationship.

Traditional Christian ways of looking at the conundrum of money and wealth start from the presumption of dependence. Consequently, somewhere a limit is drawn to human property rights, with very few exceptions, from the Fathers right through to twentieth-century Christian social thought. Human beings are trustees or stewards and the real owner hovers in the background. The sovereignty of God is not compromised.

However, it is in the nature of that real owner to be constantly giving away ownership, to be taking the risk of donating sovereignty to creatures and creation and of allowing them autonomy and independence. The social, scientific, political and philosophical movements of recent centuries have taken this gift and run with it. In western society the sense of dependence no longer resonates with daily life in the world, neither is it to be admired or sought for.

But total independence is dangerous; human moral judgement seems unable to cope with the resultant unqualified domination, and economic injustice and ecological disaster signal a warning of the most serious kind.

It might seem that the way out of this is to return to the acknowledgement of dependence, to step back from being owners and see ourselves as stewards once again. This has much to commend it, and it does need saying, but it is unlikely to be the way out of present difficulties. It simply does not speak to people where they are as owners and consumers, in concepts and patterns which have meaning in their lives. The figure of the steward remains, but it can no longer speak to the real world without mediation. To use human independence, as found in the world, to admit dependence, as found in the kingdom of God, requires a mediating structure.

To provide such a structure is the task of the Church, the 'third kingdom', but it cannot work to fulfil this task without using the symbolic, ownership-oriented, subject of money to represent and exemplify its intermediate role.

Our usual thinking about stewardship presupposes, consciously or subconsciously, a hierarchical system which involves dominion – first God, then humanity, then creation. As ecological awareness deepens, this model will increasingly be called into question. The New Testament itself offers an alternative, exemplified by the picture of God given in the Parable of the Loving Father and the Prodigal Son: 'You are with me always and all I have is yours.'[5]

The suggestion is one of co-ownership, and of a more dynamic structure than hierarchy – a structure of partnership, mutuality and interrelation between God, humanity and creation.

18. Options before the Church

Pluralism and post-industrial society

This is a plural and changing world which is dominated by the economic power, market criteria and values of advanced western society – a world where it is difficult to identify the landmarks and boundaries which have in the past helped people to find meaning, direction and purpose in their lives. This has created a period of confusion for the Church, further complicated by the tension between God as the centre of value and money as both representative and formative of our values.

To these ingredients must be added the fact that the Church is still to adjust its thinking and terminology to the post-industrial world in which it is now set and to which it now has to relate and communicate the Christian gospel. Christians feel pulled in different directions; they can be pluralist, inclusive, bridge-building, world-affirming, or they can be iconoclastic, idealistic, radical, world-denouncing. Often this tension is resolved by means of compartmentalism, rather than being properly worked through.

Many theologians have dealt with the conflict between the absolute demands of the gospel and the practical demands of life in the world by noting that Jesus' view was conditioned by an apocalyptic short-term perspective, as was that of Paul and the early Church. Later generations have had to adjust to the realities of life in the longer term, and to evolve intermediate concepts and strategies. In this century, for example, 'middle axioms' have been constructed to reconcile views of society with Christian faith and to avoid the pitfalls of moving directly from the Bible to economic prescription.

Often this has meant adopting a consensual approach which can be seen to have political parallels in the development of social democracy. However, it is questionable whether such an approach has the strength and durability to cope with the fragmented, atomistic, consumerist, pluralist, provisional and relative times in which we now live. For example, Ronald Preston has pointed out that 'ideological disagreement on interpreting "facts" and evaluating tendencies may be so great that no agreed middle axiom is possible.'[1] Such disagreement may well be increasingly likely in the future.

There are a variety of ways in which the Church can respond to this situation. Robin Gill has identified five options available for

Christian social action in a pluralistic society[2]: individual prophecy, group prophecy in or across Churches, sectarian prophecy with its strongly exclusive stance, transposition of Christian values into the structures of pluralist society, and moral praxis, the combination of 'moral insight with pastoral practice'[3]. There is a divergence between those whose emphasis is on personal salvation and individual integrity and who tend to a more exclusive view of the role of the Church, and those whose view is more inclusive and universal, working to relate to the formative structures of society.

This echoes the shifting perspectives of the nineteenth century, during which people came to realise that the social ends they sought could not be brought out solely by means of evangelism and individual conversion. The social environment and structure would itself need some sort of transformation and this could only be achieved by corporate and political action.

However, with the onset of greater pluralism the consensus implicity required by a corporate approach becomes more and more difficult to achieve, and small scale action again seems more attractive as a result. The danger is that fragmentation and compartmentalism will result within the Church itself as people take up the differing options identified by Robin Gill.

The need is to incorporate the energy, integrity and passion of individual or group prophecy, and to put backbone into Christian attitudes towards society, but without building a barrier between the committed and everyone else – the uncommitted, the wage or salary earner, the wealth creator, other faiths, other value systems.

Theologically, this means attempting to inject some redemption stiffening into a somewhat floppy incarnational consensus. Pastorally it may well involve further development of the concept of an associational Church with a communal mission. This would entail an attempt to work towards the interaction of four of Gill's five types – individual prophecy, group prophecy, transposition of values and moral praxis.

In a plural society where values are relative it is important to emphasize and clarify the God-relatedness and worship-centredness of a Christian approach, to make clear its specific nature. However, this must happen in service to the world, not in retreat from it. A worship centre of gravity can then pull on other areas of life both through the Church and through the lives of Christians in the world.

In a period of confusion for the Church as it adjusts to pluralistic society, a 'three kingdoms' approach can create a clear space or linking structure for the Church from which it can relate to, and represent to the other, both the kingdom of God and the world. Within that space (the associational Church) and moving beyond it (the communal mission) the four options for social action mentioned above would each have a part to play. One of Gill's types, sectarian prophecy, is not compatible with a 'three kingdoms' approach, because in the end it requires an exclusivist rejection of society.

Any attempt to oppose the plural spirit of the age with reruns of strategies used in previous periods is likely to be as self-defeating as Canute's efforts to stem the tide. 'What we seek is not the expulsion of pluralism but its transformation through Christian awareness and Christian criticism into a higher unity in which the various forms of plurality . . . will be mutually interrelated, mutually understood, more vulnerable to further transformations, and will be recognised precisely as a plurality in contrast to and in relation with that which is One and Undivided.'[4] Christians need to learn to relate to and seek to understand all areas of life, all views of reality, including and especially the economic view of reality in a world in which the power and influence of money is steadily increasing.

Affluence, division and 'just wealth'

In changing times the need is as, or more, important than ever to work with what we have been given to produce as good a result as is possible. There are consumers in society and consumers in religion. We all make decisions every day on this basis – these are the materials which must be used and for which a strategy must be constructed.

Christians have to work with and relate to the market, without being sure whether it is a mechanism which *can* be appropriated by another value system, or whether it always carries its own ideology along with it. Is the market system and consumer society a network which can be used to cut across the compartmentalism of post-enlightenment western culture, a possible instrument in the hands of the 'third kingdom'? Or must it be rejected as incorrigibly individualistic, divisive and spiritually and ecologically unsustainable?

In spite of these questions and anxieties Christians and the Church have little choice but to participate. Forms of withdrawal from the complexities and compromises of contemporary society, of keeping unsullied, are only possible for a very few, if that. It is difficult to see in practical terms how a completely sectarian response can be achieved at all in a modern western economy. Involvement seems inevitable, and with it the risk of consumerist addiction, of being in thrall to possessive individualism. So it is that, as security is sought in home ownership and investment, and self-expression is sought in consumer decision, the Church should examine how values and meaning can be offered and ultimate realities faced.

It is certainly time to end unthinkingly pejorative use of terms such as materialism and consumerism. These are in fact the raw materials which have to be used in the building of new strategies. A new ethos of sustainable and responsible property ownership is required for new generations inheriting material wealth from their predecessors. Perhaps the 'new consumer' and the 'ethical investor' movements, as they attain higher levels of organisation, can provide a symbolic lead and training ground for the rest of society.

However, justice must be a definitive ingredient in any Christian programme. It is, as William Temple pointed out, the social manifestation of love. If social division grows with increase in affluence, as seems to be the case, it presents a very serious problem. It may be possible to develop the role of the consumer ethically as it is enhanced economically, but the poor overall response to increased affluence in terms of charitable giving indicates that words alone will not be sufficient for this to be the case.

Structures to increase generosity and training in altruism are both required. As noted earlier, David Marquand has pointed out that the 'exchange mode' of the market must be augmented by a 'preceptoral mode'. Moral learning is needed, and it is for this that people will look to the Church, amongst others.

It has been noted that post-industrial economic life has tended towards a structure analogous with subsidiarity. Decisions are devolved to the lowest level, which tends to be that of consumer choice. Of course, this devolution can be qualified by monopoly power, especially transnationally, but the trend should be towards such power being brought under contol by legal or fiscal means. A multitude of micro-economic transactions make up the overall macro-economic pattern. Generally, Christians should welcome this encouragement of responsibility and participation, and work with others to enhance it and to control monopoly power.

However, they will also wish to ensure that such participation is not withheld from the disadvantaged. If the cumulative effect of a multiplicity of consumer decisions is economicially unjust or ecologically unsustainable, it must be possible for democratic reforms to be brought to bear, although simple majority decisions may not be adequate when the poor are a minority. For Christians, 'just wealth' is a necessity, and this means a detailed debate with society at large about criteria, means and regulations. The Church's task is therefore to build up a body of moral wisdom and to reflect upon developing practice, so that such a debate can be properly undertaken.

During the period of industrialism the Church remained outwardly committed to an ethical position on money and wealth which had been formulated in the pre-industrial period. This meant, in fact, that it was either simply negative towards capitalism, or that its moral message became compartmentalised into the private sphere. In each case it became increasingly marginalised.

It is important that the same thing does not happen again as we move into a post-industrial world. The Church can become an influence for good and an agent of change, but to do so it will need to come to terms with change itself and to contemplate change in its own structures and programmes.

This means that the unpopular subject of money and wealth must be faced. Precisely because it is the subject which can make us so uncomfortable, it is a key to advance and a more credible posture towards the world. Swift remarks that 'mankind may judge what Heaven thinks of riches by observing those upon whom it has been pleased to bestow them.'[5] We can all afford to smile at this, because no-one thinks they are rich, or, at least, very few do. But most Christians, with their ambivalent or ambiguous attitude to wealth, are themselves now part of an affluent culture. They find it as difficult as anyone to be told of the danger of riches, of the misuse of economic power, or of the desirability of detachment or even renunciation.

Before, or as, the Church answers any call for moral precepts, it has its own learning to do. Much of this will be to do with money. Money is such an important subject that it must be given high priority, and this will not simply mean delivering neat prescriptions to society. It will mean listening to society, reflecting seriously about how Christians and the Church handle wealth themselves, and seeking coherence and credibility – without reconciling differences by means of any evasive compartmentalism. Church structures themselves must be a training ground in justice and generosity if the 'third kingdom' is to have anything to say to the second.

The challenge is real both for Christians who are active in social issues and for those who remain passive. The first must take care not to leave others behind in their quest for purity, and thus suffer a long-term loss of the influence they can expect to bring to bear. The second must beware of compartmentalising their faith, shutting out the anxieties arising out of economic injustice, acquiescing in consumer addiction. Many people shelter both these types within themselves; spiritual discipline and discernment is needed to grow through this towards a more mature understanding and expression of Christian faith.

The money compartment

Opportunities are lost and potential for growth ignored because money is kept in a separate compartment of life. The Church deprives itself of a system of communication, allows itself to speak to the world in a foreign language, and consequently is not properly able to address issues concerned with acquiring and holding wealth. At local level, discussion of money is so often limited to Church-based questions of institutional maintenance. Whole areas of life, to which a discussion of money might be the entry point, are thus left unaddressed. The Church will be unable fully to come to terms with change while this continues to be the case.

The reality is that money, and what it is used for, is a powerfully active representation of our real values over and against what we claim our values to be. Popular sayings such as 'Put your money where you mouth is!' or 'Practise what you preach!' contain an important, and biblical, truth which Christians ignore at their peril. Compartmentalism means that they are often in danger of ignoring it.

One thing which is clear from the New Testament, and which can be applied to a different context, is that money is an impressive symbol and metaphor which is often able to uncover meaning and truth. So it is that Paul's second letter to the Corinthians 'leads to fresh ways of conceiving the gospel and God's activity through economic metaphors, but it also leads to ordinary economic concepts being transformed in accordance with the new metaphorical reference.'[6] An interactive process is at work. In particular, 'chapters 8 and 9 show the connection between "real" economies and the gospel's "economy of God", interweaving them inseparably in relation to the practical issue of the collection for the Jerusalem church.'[7] Here money takes on a quasi-sacramental significance, representing and signifying eternal value in financial value.

Learning processes in the Church will need to take this deep significance seriously, and to ensure that money is not treated in isolation. Each person's relationship with money is part of a complex, interactive whole. It is a crucial element in a total context which runs from personal attitudes to global structures. The Church can equip itself to address a changed and changing world by reflecting upon its own handling of money and wealth and learning from the experience.

This is why it is necessary to use some criteria along the lines of the five questions and guidelines developed in Part One of this study: Are money issues being faced? Is there a balance between idealism and realism? Is the Church acting as the 'third kingdom'? Are owners being called by God? Are the pastoral implications of money being taken into account?

In this way the Church can move towards greater integrity regarding money and greater authenticity in its relationship with the world. At present the Church is seriously baulked by its own compartmentalised thinking about money. This can lead to inaction or inadequate action on many important matters, from central investment policy through to local pastoral care and ministry.

It is true to say that the disciplines to do with money, economics and accounting have their own reality which exists independently of anything the Church might say or do. Nevertheless, the Church must test its own verities against such reality if it is to have anything useful to contribute to reflection and debate about the ways in which such disciplines are used.

Incarnation, dualism and the third kingdom

The doctrine of the incarnation, particularly as developed over the past century in the wake of F. D. Maurice and 'Lux Mundi', seeks to provide a paradigm for overcoming spirit/matter dualism and the sort of compartmentalism which can be observed in attitudes towards money and faith and ethics. The bridge between the human and the divine offers a model for the restoration of all manner of fragmentation.

However, the 'incarnationalist consensus' is not beyond criticism[8]. There is a danger of 'sacralising what already exists' and of giving insufficient weight to society's rejection of Jesus as symbolised by the cross. Rowan Williams points to the need for Christianity to be in some sense at odds with, or over against, other forms of corporate life[8]. Missionary credibility requires the Church to be able to show different, Christ-oriented patterns of belonging. Jesus creates something radically new and distinctive, essentially different from other human association, a new covenant.

This difference remains; the demands of Jesus can never be made reasonable. 'There is only one step from a rationally moderated idealism to opportunism, and only another step from opportunism to dishonest capitulation to the status quo.'[9] The absolute message of the gospel, the pure idealism of those who refuse to compromise that message, the surprises and jagged edges of Christian experience – all this is of the essence. In human terms the kingdom of God is radically other, and Jesus who announces it is radically new. This cannot be tamed.

'It seems, then, as though, for us to grasp that the event of Jesus is the act of God, the Church must first understand its distinctiveness and separateness – not from the human race but from all communities and kinships whose limits fall short of the human race. The Church's primitive and angular separateness . . . is meant to be a protest on behalf of a unified world, the world that holds together in and because of Jesus Christ. This paradox is a hard one to live out.'[8] Out of this paradox grew Augustine's two cities and Luther's two realms, offering ways of living under God in the world without compromising the unique nature of the kingdom of God itself, but ultimately proving inadequate in the face of twentieth-century totalitarianism.

It does not seem possible to find a tidy wrapping for the parcel. To emphasize the real difference of the Christian message can lead to dangerous dualism. To emphasize that dualism is bridged in the incarnation can lead to equally inadequate acceptance of what the world has to offer. The argument is circular.

How are we to steer a course between a new moralism – green, puritan, revelationist – which veers towards dualism, and an incarnational consensus which is insufficiently rigorous? Somewhere there is a creative balance which harnesses the positive element in both approaches, and which encourages interplay between opposed compartments.

Much hinges on the view that is taken of the Church's relation to the kingdom of God. Rowan Williams seems to imply that the body of Christ and the kingdom are confluent, and of course there is much in common, but it is the purpose of the body of Christ to proclaim the kingdom and they cannot therefore be the same thing.

This distinction is important because the Church itself has been instituted to be the body of Christ in the world, and to identify body and kingdom is thus to identify Church and kingdom, too. This is to fly in the face of the evidence – the Church is manifestly a human institution with human failings, it is quite obviously not the kingdom of God, however well it might be proclaiming the kingdom. In reality, the Church is a distinct entity, a 'third kingdom'.

So the Church must maintain its distinctiveness, both from the world and from the kingdom of God, so that it can show the kingdom to the world, and bring the world to the kingdom. It must be distinct from the world in order to be able to offer the good news with clarity. It must be distinct from the kingdom if its human failings are to be comprehensible.

By maintaining distinctiveness from both directions in this way the Church retains its identity as body of Christ. It continues to proclaim the possibility of an incarnational bridge between the human and the divine, and at the same time witnesses to the need for redemptive change. Both prophecy and affirmation of the material world can make their necessary contributions.

This is not a static model, but one of interaction, mutual interrogation and developing relationship, one of participation, change and development in a changing world. A Church working in this way is itself becoming an influence for change.

19. An Influence for Change

Being the Third Kingdom

'Perhaps the opportunism of early Christianity in accepting the social structures of its place and time and seeking to transform them to the service of transcendence and the benefit of the poor is the primary ethical message which it has to impart. Social institutions and social movements alike have a certain autonomy which does not require the church either to initiate or to approve them. The ancient Christians did not shrink, however, from active involvement with these autonomous phenomena in an effort, at least partially success-ful, to subordinate them to higher ends.'[1]

Christianity's claim to uniqueness lies in the incarnation. It must therefore be committed *both* to the idealistic struggle for perfection, to becoming what God calls us to be, *and* to the realistic expression of love, to accepting that God speaks to us through what is. Being the 'third kingdom' means living within the field of attraction of both these poles, and living with the ambiguity thus created.

On the one hand there is the world – economics, experience, culture, realism, wealth. On the other hand there is the kingdom of God – ethics, scripture, revelation, idealism, poverty. In interaction with both is the Church, the body of Christ – incarnation, tradition, spirituality, sacrament, sacrifice. To be in this position means to be in the business both of constructing practical programmes for action and of presenting a specifically Christian ethical position. It means living with provisionality.

Every person will need to be continually creating their own fluid casuistry as they do their own theology and economics in today's world. The 'third kingdom' is there to offer solidarity to those engaged in such a task. Within this view of the Church the five questions or guidelines identified at the end of Part One can be used in evaluation and reflection: Are money issues honestly faced? Are idealism and realism held in balance? Is the 'third kingdom' active? Are owners called by God? Is there an awareness of the pastoral implications of money? This study has shown these guidelines being applied to key areas of money-handling in the Church, and they underlie the conclusions reached and recommendations made.

I have noted that economic culture tends towards compartmental-ism. It sets into opposition the quantifiable judgement and the qualitative; the short-term benefit and the long-term common good; market relations and personal relationships; the individual's contribution to society and society's contribution to the individual; and measurable means and conceptual ends. The need is to connect these, for the Church to do this in its actions (not just to emphasize the opposite pole) and thus to provide a structure for values in market conditions. A 'three kingdoms' approach is needed to connect the moral and economic circuits, and yet to leave an appropriate autonomy to each.

Such interaction acknowledges the autonomy of each kingdom. Yet, by the very activity of making connections it moves towards definitions of limits to that autonomy. This is done as criteria developed, say, in the ethical sphere are brought to bear in the area of economics. For example, the autonomy and free development of the market is limited by the requirements of justice, or by a compassionate response to social division, or by the long-term needs of the environment. Similarly, the autonomy of moral perfection will be limited by questions of feasibility and practical application. Unlimited autonomy can lead to the dangerous oversimplification of complex issues.

The Church needs its own autonomy, its own space, from which and within which it can be the Church in relation to its call to perfection and its place in contingency. As body of Christ the perfection is to be sought in relation to, and by being given up for, the world. This means building bridges, in the examples above, a justice bridge, a social bridge, a long-term bridge, engaging in mutual qualification of autonomy. To use the extreme example of Bonhoeffer's participation in an assassination attempt on Hitler – here the Church's autonomy of moral expression is deliberately limited and qualified in order to mount a feasible attack upon the perverse and exaggerated autonomy of the fascist state.

Within the space of the Church's own autonomy it will live out the vocation to be the 'third kingdom' by offering that autonomy in a constant dialectic with both perfection and contingency, with the ideal and the real, with the divine poverty and the human engagement with money. In this, money is particularly important because the world of money is so all-pervasive, interacting with political life, social life, family life and personal life in a multiplicity of ways. It forms linkages, often unrecognised, between the compartments of life which are often kept separate. It makes statements about the values of those who use it.

The gap between the two kingdoms, represented here by the exaggerated divergence between the worlds of faith and money, leaves people stuck in their quest for meaning in daily life. Hence there is a proliferation of privatised religious systems – Christian, New Age and other. If we look at the Church as a third kingdom engaged in mutual interaction with the other two, this creates a picture of a third circle which overlaps with two circles which previously had been tending to bounce off one another.

It is not possible to be in the third circle without relating to both the others. It is defined by its relationship with both the others and its call to bring both the others into closer mutual relationship. There is here an intrinsic role for the individual as representative of the communal, representing different areas from different spheres to each other. Similarly, the internal and spiritual finds clear expression in the external, the material and the institutional.

The Christian wealth creator thus represents the Church to the the world at the same time as representing the realities of money to the Church. In both directions the Christian responds to God-given individuality and personality by acting thankfully (because meaning and purpose is thus invested) as representative of the communal. This forms an interconnecting linkage across the three kingdoms of God, world and Church.

All this points to the paramount importance of worship and sacrament, thanksgiving in eucharist, in the life of the 'third kingdom'. Members of the body are dispersed in the world and are, in being so dispersed, answering the call to follow Christ, to take up the Christ-like task. Consequently the times of gathered worship, of shared solidarity and support, of sharing what it means to be going out and in, of offering what is learnt from life, are of definitive importance. The 'third kingdom' is the sacramental community par excellence, nurturing a sacramental view of the whole of life, pointing towards mystery, potential and fulfilment whilst remaining in the here and now.

Active consumers and owners

Being in the here and now, and using that as a springboard for change and development, means that attention must be given to the Church's relationship with money and economic life. The tendency is for the Church to keep this whole subject at arm's length. Individualists wish to emphasize the spiritual and are suspicious of serious talk about money. Communalists are wary of excessive individualism in contemporary economic life and consequently suspicious of any positive view of present patterns of ownership and consumption. The viewpoints are very different but, ironically, the results are very similar.

The Church therefore appears most reluctant to take up the task of improving the moral circuits in the realm of economic life, to work at making ownership and consumption an area of vocation and discipleship. Some reject the privatisation of public issues, others reject the sacralisation of secular mechanisms. In either case, no change is possible because the necessary connections are not made.

However, the Church should in fact be welcoming the enhancement of responsibility given to each person, the subsidiarity of market decisions, and seeking ways in which it can see these trends in terms of Christian vocation in the world. This will mean hard work both in terms of individual learning and of the vocational appropriation of the Church's own money responsibilities. Both Christians and the Church should consciously reflect and act upon the need to be responsible owners and consumers, and to pull together strands of values and structure, idealism and realism, purpose and practical strategy.

The current ethos of individual money-handling tends, to the extent that it is thought about at all, to regard the earning or acquiring of money as means towards ends, such as spending, saving and giving. Similarly, at the macro-economic level, it can seem that ownership and production are means towards ends such as consumption, charity and participation. The truth is more complicated, particularly as economic life moves towards a greater emphasis on services. Economic activity is cyclical, involving both production and consumption, and means and ends revolve around one another in a continuum. The Christian call is to live and express in the world an interpretation of this cyclical interdependency. For the Church this means bringing means and ends together in its own actions, and using its own resources as both laboratory and example.

Active consumers and owners are engaged in seeking a proper, connected balance between idealism and realism, holding a creative tension and moving towards feasible criteria. For the Church of England wealth must be held and used in ways appropriate to its role within the nation and to its role as the 'third kingdom'.

Market disciplines should be respected and allowed to interact with ethical priorities. Owners and consumers have a part in society *as* owners and consumers, which should be recognised and placed in dialogue with the Christian traditions of detachment and altruism. Similarly, continuity provided by the trusteeship of the Church Commissioners and others should be valued, but allowed to be tested against primary Christian purposes such as the social expression of love through justice.

If, consequently, subsidiarity and devolution becomes a growing presumption of attitudes to wealth in the Church, there will of course be an effect on its perception of authority, hierarchical structure and pastoral care. As noted at the very beginning, in the preface to this study, money is a subject which keeps popping up, even though we try to avoid it. The examples chosen, debt and credit, property and home ownership, and charitable giving, have shown money touching every area of life. In the Church, ownership, funding and giving present some of the most intractable problems to be found, at the same time as offering an opportunity to relate to the world. All this shows why it is so important to consider the implications of money in greater depth.

Stewardship or ownership?

When it was used in the early vernacular translations of the Bible the word 'steward' held resonance with the economic circumstances of the times. The feudal 'sty-ward' or 'stigweard' was not that far removed from daily experience in a highly structured society. That is no longer the case in a plural culture in which individual aspirations and endeavour are much more closely involved with the ownership of property than with the trust of position.

Somehow, 'stewardship' seems better able to express a contemporary meaning in relation to the environment, although even this is challenged in some quarters. Here personal ownership and control is not a typical experience, as it is in the case of private property. However it is to the latter, private property, that Christian Stewardship in the Church is, at its best, trying to relate.

It follows that the Church's use of the term in an effort to encourage direct giving to the Church may become increasingly anachronistic, and increasingly an attempt to reproduce a formula rather than undertake necessary reformulation. To avoid misunderstanding consideration should be given to the use of language which directly addresses the contemporary manifestation of the age-old problem of property. Owners and consumers may now need to replace stewards in our terminology.

All language carries overtones, a variety of shades of meaning which may change as time passes. All language has shortcomings. How does the language of ownership compare with the language of stewardship? Can it take us further in responding to the love of God and the needs of the world?

The overtones of stewardship imply a master/servant or an employer/employee relationship. They speak of an Old Testament pattern which looks over the shoulder towards a jealous God who may withdraw favour granted, a God whose gifts are conditional. Ownership, on the other hand, as John Cole points out, is 'the mark of being no longer servants but heirs'. It implies the unconditional giving and forgiving of God, and is thus closer to the message of the New Testament.

Ownership therefore calls for greater levels of gratitude, but perhaps runs a risk of freeing humans to play God (as if they do not do that already). This stresses the importance of not separating the gift from the giver, again calling to our attention the crucial role of thanksgiving and worship. Thus ownership is unequivocally given to us but it must always speak to us of God the giver.

Stewardship implies a long-term perspective with its overtones of care for future generations. Similarly, though less obviously, ownership too carries implications of long-term responsibility, bequest and provision, perhaps with a more individualistic tone.

In society, the emphasis is increasingly on property ownership and upon the expression of choice through consumer decision. As we have seen, this has both positive and negative aspects, the most worrying being growing social division. Nevertheless, this is the language which more and more people speak. In the Church, however, the talk is typically of stewardship. The clergy are provided with tied accommodation to look after but not to own, the laity are told of their duty to give in stewardship, and ownership of the Church's assets is not clearly focused in the perceptions of Church members.

Once again there is a tension, for moving on from stewardship to ownership, from Old Testament to New, from duty to gratitude and thankgiving, is not without risk. In reaching for a sense of ownership responding to God, we risk finding ownership playing God. This is not a risk to be taken lightly. But surely this is, on the 'wrong' side of our compartmentalised barriers, where we are already? What do we really have to lose?

Our problem is that the language of stewardship is in too many ways no longer appropriate. It does not match the reality of ownership. It is not even readily taken up by many Church members themselves. We cannot speak comprehensively or universally *except* in terms of ownership. The risk has to be taken. The alternative is to remain, increasingly beleaguered, in our Church compartment.

The concept of the 'third kingdom' provides for us the safeguards, checks and balances which are necessary as we take the risk of moving from stewardship to ownership. It calls Christians and the Church to relate life in the world to the kingdom of God, and thus to practise ownership responding to God. The 'third kingdom' provides values, criteria, structure and support within which this can happen.

In the end, all language falls short, all human metaphors fail God. Nevertheless, we have to use words. But language can begin to transcend its limitations if it is placed within the dynamic, truine model of the 'three kingdoms'. This creates a preceptoral structure within which personal and corporate development can take place.

In Practice: Responding Ownership

What are the key elements in developing an ownership which is responding to God the giver? First, a proper autonomy of secular economic life should be acknowledged, requiring a positive stance towards the position of owners and consumers and the development of criteria for the responsible ownership of property. It is necessary to start where people are in order to be able to bridge idealism and realism.

Second, theological and sociological expressions of 'responding ownership' should be harmonised, seeking to ensure that the question of giving is not looked at in isolation from a consideration of money in the two contexts of the world and the Church. As already noted, any practical model will seem inadequate in comparison with the gospel itself, but that does not dimish the importance of the task of building bridges between areas of concern which are more comfortably kept apart.

Third, the puritan attribute of personal responsibility, the right of conscience, under grace, to guide the individual, should be incorporated whilst conscious effort is made to avoid the middle class pride and self-satisfaction which often accompanies such virtue. This could be done because working within a 'three kingdoms' structure would bring out connections between the individual and the communal.

Fourth, 'responding ownership' should be a practical outworking of *metanoia*, and of worship and thanksgiving. This is basic, and necessary to guard against the danger that greater emphasis on ownership does not tip over into idolatry or narcissism.

Fifth, awareness of the relation of economic factors to individual circumstances can be developed: increases in personal wealth; greater numbers benefiting from property inheritance; tax incentives awarded by the property-owning democracy. All these should inform questions of Christian giving. The challenge of proportionate giving should be related to such factors, and will comprise an important cutting edge connecting abstract principle with the particular circumstances of individuals and families. In John Habgood's phrase, there needs to be 'more experiment in releasing people's generous impulses'. Similarly, the Church should take up responsibility for unfashionable, unattractive or unnoticed recipients.

Sixth, 'responding ownership' should enhance the self – offering a full and rounded form of self-interest incorporating social ties, religious teaching, civic duty and an affirmation of the long-term. This will include what Frank Prochaska has called the 'voluntary impulse'. Puritanism found renewal in nineteenth-century philanthropy, and required of the wealthy a restrained lifestyle combined with generosity in charitable giving. If the Church answers the call to concentrate on the moral circuits, it will have to include a restatement of the duties of wealth and their application to the majority of the population. Duties do not exist in an individualistic vacuum, they relate to some communal end or purpose, and this is what now needs to be invested in the self's role as owner or consumer. In consumer choice it is feasible to try to exercise influence, and thus to exercise duties as well as rights, to express mutuality in human relationships and thus the fullness of human personality.

So it is that the Church is called to affirm compassion and charity and in so doing to draw out those levels of sharing and justice which are inadequately expressed in the common life either of the world or of the Church. How can this vocation to bring the kingdom of God into interaction with both the Church and the world be better expressed, in practice, in the Church's structures and programmes?

In practice: structures

Traditionally much of the Church's attitude to wealth depended on individual attitudes. For example, wealth was acceptable if it was possible to maintain a state of detachment towards it. Now, however, we are more aware of the effect of social and institutional structures, and John Paul II can speak of 'structural sin' as a factor in human affairs. How can the attitudes of and in the Church be developed in positive directions by improvements in its institutional structures?

It is possible to react to the institutional shortcomings of the Church in three ways – 'renounce the institution', 'ignore the dilemma', or, preferably, seeing 'the institutional form as an opportunity for special witness and vocation'[2]. If the Church is to fulfil its role as 'third kingdom', this third way is extremely important, but it is often overlooked. When William Temple set out criteria for Church activity in society[3], he tasked it with stating principles and individual Christians with setting an example in carrying them out, but the institutional performance of the Church itself is not mentioned. We need the humility to take a long, hard look at ourselves; this study has attempted to make a start in this direction, particularly in respect of the three examples of ownership, funding and giving in the Church.

The object of any changes, seen in the light of what can be discerned from these examples, should be to reduce compartmentalism, to promote participation, to break down 'them' and 'us' attitudes, to encourage interaction between the world and Christian values, to promote the 'owning' of Church wealth by its members, to assist long-term planning, to overcome fear of addressing the issue of money felt by clergy, preachers and teachers, and to stimulate realistic giving and generosity. Various possible changes in Church structures are set out below, to exemplify rather than exhaust the sort of alterations that are required.

Buildings The historic resources held by the Church Commissioners, or accruing to diocesan pastoral accounts from the sale of property, should be swung round and applied much more than at present to the cost of maintaining church buildings. It may come as a surprise to some that this would, in fact, be a progressive reform. General Synod's follow-up to 'Faith in the City' said: 'A crucial area of concern continues to be raised by the almost universal problem of repairs to church buildings regularly used for worship. Congregations enjoying the comfort of well-maintained churches often have little understanding of the depressing situation facing UPA churchgoers . . . Rather than focusing a national appeal upon cathedrals alone we should surely be considering how any living congregation in urgent need of finance towards repairs should be eligible to seek help from a central fund.'[4]

At present the cost of repairs to church buildings falls on parishes in a totally arbitrary way (much more arbitrary than the cost of the stipendiary ministry, which *is* subsidised), and the largest bills often go to small congregations in rural or inner city areas. The result is all too frequently that the life of the Church comes to revolve negatively and disproportionately around raising funds for the building, to the detriment of the real ministry of the Church. Grants should be available to significantly ease this burden.

Parishes Of course, this would mean that much less money would be available from the Church Commissioners to underwrite the cost of stipendiary parochial ministry, stipends, pensions and housing. However, this would itself be a beneficial change, especially if the quota system were to be radically reformed as set out below. The, combined effect would then be to produce much more realism, subsidiarity and responsibility at parish level concerning the cost of current patterns of pastoral ministry. There would be a realistic parochial contribution towards the cost of full-time ministry (tempered by the operation of some form of special needs allowance), perhaps more than doubling in real terms over several years, but the haphazard building burden would be substantially ameliorated. Overall, the result would be much fairer, and many of the criteria or purposes for change listed above would be met.

The parish structure remains the most important insitutional manifestation of the Church of England, and it would benefit in various ways from such reforms in the financial subsidy available to it from historic resources. It has been noted that 'general levels of giving tend to be more a reflection of perceived needs than of church members' overall potential to give.'[5] This is regrettable and limiting, but it is encouraged by present structures. Giving tends to be worse where historic resources are higher, not where poor people live. Structural reform is required, to relate principle to necessity, before the level of giving can be encouraged to improve commensurately with churchgoers' increased affluence.

To this end the 'quota' or 'share' system should be radically changed. At present this system miraculously manages at one and the same time *both* to conceal the huge subsidy from historic resources effectively received by almost every parish Church *and* to convince almost every parish Church that it is paying something akin to a Church Tax *in spite of the fact* that it is receiving that huge subsidy. Ironically all the lengths to which we go to make quota fair only manage to convince people the more that it *is* a tax.

Instead, each parish should be fully invoiced for the resources it uses in terms of stipendiary clergy and their housing, for contributions towards training costs and pensions, and for central and diocesan costs. All these items should be accounted for separately in the PCC's books and annual statement of income and expenditure.

Of course, the amounts involved would be horrendous to many. That is precisely the point, for it emphasizes the distance from reality of the present system. The subsidy from historic resources would then also be shown separately in each parish's accounts, as a grant received. A parish paying its own bills and receiving a grant, rather than paying a quota which protects it from its real costs, will be made much more aware of its own responsibility for the ministry of the Church.

A great deal more than at present would then be out in the open: differing levels of historic resources in different dioceses; the amount of grant each parish needs in order to carry out its ministry; the stake each person has in the diocesan and central structures of the Church. It would be painful, but the end result would be a much needed shift towards interdependence, realism and subsidiarity.

Dioceses   At the levels of Diocesan and General Synods, financial responsibility is in the hands of Boards of Finance, and other councils or boards exist to deal with matters such as mission, unity, social responsibility, education and ministry. Obviously all these specialities require their own space, but present structures can often lead to a regrettable institutional dualism or compartmentalism in which policy and finance do not interact sufficiently. A recent report in the Diocese of St Edmundsbury and Ipswich[6] imaginatively recommended that the Diocesan Board of Finance be subsumed into an elected Bishop's Council. Unfortunately, this change was too radical to survive into the second stage of the consultation process.

Debates which are at present safely tucked away in the Board for

Social Responsibility should be allowed to impinge upon the Church's own financial decision making. In fact, Boards of Social Responsibility could be tasked with conducting social audits of the affairs of their own governing body and making recommendations to it.

Church Commissioners The Commissioners present the most complex area in which to propose change, but their enormous financial power and substance is at present too little 'owned' by Church members, and their potential to be an area of interaction between the worlds of faith and money is not taken up. The trust under which they operate, whilst giving them continuity and autonomy, also works to shelter one of the more arcane institutions of the British establishment – very definitely a case of 'them' and 'us'. Certainly, the shift in application of the bulk of their income to Church buildings rather than stipendiary ministry would be a big change, but it is one which should be possible within the Commissioners' overall brief.

If, as suggested above, each parish were to receive a grant from the historic resources held by the Church Commissioners – which would merely be accounting for what actually happens already – Church members would grow in awareness of their own relationship with the Commissioners as trustees of those resources.

More problematic is the debate about the Commissioners' investment policy. The Bishop of Oxford's 1991 legal action may have failed in that the Vice-Chancellor did not agree to declare that the Church Commissioners must 'have regard to the object of promoting the Christian faith', saying that this was a dangerously loose phrase. However, pressure has increased on those who claim to prefer participation to 'hand-washing', to actually participate and engage in debate with companies in which shares are held.

Within months of the case the Commissioners were putting pressure on companies over the issue of Sunday trading. The challenge is to achieve the will and the consensus to do the same on more controversial and important issues, less apparently compromised by the Church's own interests. There is a whole range of concerns where responding shareholder ownership could be exercised, from employment policies in the Third World to slow payment of debts.

Ethical investment, in the narrow sense of avoiding the unethical, is only the first step. It is an imprecise and blunt instrument. It does not cover the case of a company which behaves immorally in an approved area of operation. This makes it all the more necessary for Christians and the Church to be involved and prepared to get their hands dirty, to take risks rather than to be satisfied with being seen to be playing safe and doing the right thing. It may be a more effective witness, a greater influence on the tone of the market environment, for the Church to be publicly seen to be engaged in the process of conscientiously choosing the better of two imperfect courses of action.

It does seem important, if the Church is to bridge faith and money, to take up its role as 'third kingdom', for it to be able to debate openly the ethics of investment policy and to allow such considerations to be put in the melting pot along with other relevant criteria. Here, the law, or at least the interpretation of the law, will need to be changed to allow the Church to express its vocation in terms of its financial posture.

Any change will itself need to be provisional, to be open to adjustment in the light of experience and further change. There is a creative tension between creating new structures which will replace inadequate institutions – and this must be done for change to be effective – and creating a new problem of institutions for later generations. The question of trusteeship exemplifies this, from the grand scale of the Church Commissioners to the smallest parish charity. On the positive side, this provides valuable stability and continuity of purpose. However, the resulting inflexibility creates great difficulty in responding to the needs of a rapidly changing world. The need is for prior or underlying purpose to be given greater weight when the rights and duties of such trustees are being considered in the light of modern experience. Such purpose can be developed and defined if the Church takes up its role as 'third kingdom' and thus overcomes the difficulties created by compartmentalism.

In practice: programmes and people

The personal approach to change is as important as the structural – they must complement one another. 'Christ proved to be too hard for the religious institutions of the Judaism of his day to contain. So he cannot be contained by any religious institution which threatens to put itself, its own status, power or formulations of belief, in place of God's Spirit, to demand the obedience due only to him. But though whole churches may defect, as human institutions, the Church itself, the hidden body of Christ, will always contain the power of its own renewal. If we, as members of the Church, protest about its unthinking conformism, than we contribute, in our way, to that renewal.'[7] There has to be a place for individual idealism, dreams and visions of what could be. The Church should be a community where lives are changed and vision is deepened and broadened.

The importance of money as a catalyst for the soul should not be underestimated. Its metaphorical, symbolic, even sacramental, significance has already been discussed. A changed attitute to what is given away can signal a change in underlying attitudes and motivation towards thanksgiving, gratitude and generosity.

The question of giving in the Church is not just a question of maintaining institutional structures, it is also an area for learning about making an outgoing and generous response to God and one another. As in the philanthropic tradition, people are trained for participation and citizenship. A learning 'loop' can be constructed, moving from self-interest, to self-love, to self-giving, seeking to use the raw materials of a 'my needs', consumer- and individually-oriented religion and to turn them round to face the world.

This vital task must be attempted, however difficult it may be. In spite of the allergy of many Anglicans to anything that smacks of sectarianism, the evidence that giving is taken more seriously in Churches which are more associational cannot be ignored – 'a church which does not *at least* possess certain features of a "sect" cannot act as an agent of transformation.'[8] By building money requirements into the associational Church we may be able to produce a more communal result than we expect. But for this to happen the money requirements should not be narrowly defined to fit the needs of the Church itself – they should tackle the questions of ownership and consumption.

In an increasingly affluent society it is most important that the unpopular subject of money and wealth be faced by Christians. We should cease dressing it up with talk of 'time and talents' or whatever else to make it more acceptable, and come to realise that too much talk of the Church's need to receive money undermines its greater importance as an area for praxis.

Reform of the strategies and language of Christian Stewardship (including its renaming) is therefore required to enhance the use of money as a cutting-edge of experience and as a vital area for learning about being a Christian in the contemporary world. Subsidiarity in Church life must lead to interdependence, not independence of selfish, separate communities. This will mean that the importance of the strong helping the weak needs to be recognized as *the* crucial test of Christian generosity in giving.

A common failing of Christian Stewardship work in local Churches is the tendency to confuse teaching and accountability. This takes us back to the question with which I began: 'Why does the Church only teach about money when it wants some?' Teaching about money, I have sought to show, has an importance of its own which merits its own space and a good deal of undivided attention. This precedes issues such as accountability and institutional needs, which are secondary and dependent upon proper teaching about money for their context and adequate handling. Usually financial pressure means that needs and accountability come first; the teaching then becomes inaudible.

One way forward is the use of narrative in, for example, 'money autobiographies', involving people in identifying and telling the story of money in their own lives.[9] Asking 'What are the stories and feelings involving money and wealth in which I find myself a part?' can lead on to many other questions, not least some relating to the Church.

Programmes for parishes are required which incorporate as many of the following features as possible:

– a long-term approach aimed at increasing the use of the local Church as a forum for interrelationship and interaction between faith and life.

– use of an outside director, consultant or facilitator, particularly in the early stages, to provide a framework and structure, to open out issues, to balance and link the requirements of prophecy and pastoral care, to ensure that important challenges are not avoided, to give support and encouragement, and to be a scapegoat during times of turmoil.

– clarity and integrity of structure and teaching, to ensure that the necessary connections are made between theory and practice, faith and action, both individually and as a Christian community.

– regular challenge to self-examination and reflection on the handling of money and personal wealth, earthing faith and Christian teaching as Jesus did in the reality of how people live their lives. This should lead to a decision, about what is given away and what is given through the Church, enabling proper connections to be made with worship and the corporateness of the Christian faith. Motivations, priorities and attitudes can thus become focused and liberated so that energy and resources can be freed for the activity of the body of Christ in the world.

– an ongoing pastoral structure, undertaken by the laity, to provide the context and background for continued learning, growth, participation and interaction.

Reaction to such a challenge can often prove negative. If such good practice is to be maintained at local level, it must be supported and encouraged by the structures and hierarchies of the Church. Unfortunately, however, it is often the case that pressure to have recourse to short-term remedies, in the face of financial crises, comes from precisely those people who should be guiding the Church towards a strategic and long-term response. Stronger help and guidance is desirable. Short-term cures are unlikely to deal with a long-term illness. Hierarchies should help local Churches to avoid them.

Instead, resolve is needed at every level to state the challenge and to support one another in rising to meet it. 'People are largely unconscious of their own faith and this unconsiousness is itself part of a defensive network. Since part of the task of Christian education is to bring faith to the level of consciousness, thus increasing the responsibility and integrity of the self, one must expect that Christian education will encounter resistance.'[10] Especially if an attempt is being made to break down some effective and, in selfish terms, useful barriers between money and faith.

People will resist, and they will be baffled. Money still presents Christians with a difficult conundrum, and that difficulty will not go away. But it should be faced, and facing it will provide the arena for growth and development. A rigorous look at money is bound to make Christians aware of great tensions in and between their own view of life, their own actions in life, the views of life held by others and the ways of the world. It will set up 'direct cognitive conflict', but then 'in the image of a divine man and a crucified God Christianity presents cognitive dissonance at the very heart of its self-understanding.'[11]

It is not easy for the Church to disturb its pastoral preoccupations with thoughts of the implications of money. Nor is it easy for any person to face money issues seriously and think, in the light of Christian faith, about what it means to own and consume in today's world. However, simply an honest attempt to do so will speak volumes. It will signal a breaking down of the compartments which separate idealism from realism. It will begin a movement making more profound and more effective connections between the kingdom of God and the world.

Notes

Chapter 2. Pressure of Change

1. R H Tawney, *Religion and the Rise of Capitalism*, Pelican, 1938, p 275
2. Charles Handy, *The Future of Work*, Basil Blackwell, Oxford, 1984, p 27
3. E F Schumacher, *Small is Beautiful*, Blond and Briggs, 1976, p 75
4. John Atherton, *Faith in the Nation*, SPCK, 1988, pp 5–22

Chapter 3. Society and Economic Culture

1. R H Tawney, *Equality*, Geo Allen & Unwin, 1938, p 200
2. John Wesley, *Sermons on Several Occasions*, Epworth Press, 1944, p 584
3. Reinhold Niebuhr, *Moral Man and Immoral Society*, Scribners, New York, 1960, p 117
4. see, for example, Weber's *The Protestant Ethic and the Spirit of Capitalism* and Tawney's *Religion and the Rise of Capitalism*
5. H G Wood, *The influence of the Reformation on ideas concerning wealth and property*, in ed Charles Gore, *Property – its Duties and Rights*, Second Edition, Macmillan, 1915, p 140
6. Brian Griffiths, *Morality in the Market Place*, Hodder & Stoughton, 1982, p 29
7. Brian Griffiths, *The Creation of Wealth*, Hodder and Stoughton, 1984, pp 15–17
8. Brian Griffiths, *Morality in the Market Place*, Hodder & Stoughton, 1982, p 92
9. ibid, p 97
10. Ronald H Preston, *Religion and the Persistence of Capitalism*, SCM Press, 1979, p 35
11. Brian Griffiths, *Morality in the Market Place*, Hodder & Stoughton, 1982, p 13
12. ibid, p 109
13. R H Tawney, *Religion and the Rise of Capitalism*, Pelican, 1938, pp 273/4
14. Robin Murray, *Life after Henry (Ford)*, in *Marxism Today*, October 1988, pp 8–13
15. Brian Griffiths, *The Creation of Wealth*, Hodder & Stoughton, 1984, p 113
16. ibid, p 114
17. C B Macpherson, *The Political Theory of Possessive Individualism*, OUP, 1962
18. Brian Griffiths, *The Creation of Wealth*, Hodder & Stoughton, 1984, pp 80/1
19. John Francis Kavanaugh, *Following Christ in a Consumer Society*, Orbis Books, New York, 1984, p 6
20. ibid, p 42

21. quoted by Edward P Elchin in *Crucible*, Jan–Mar 1988
22. Brian Griffiths, *The Creation of Wealth*, Hodder & Stoughton, 1984, p 50
23. ibid, p 53
24. Ronald H Preston, *Religion and the Persistence of Capitalism*, SCM Press, 1979, p 34

Chapter 4. Christians and Economic Culture

1. G K Chesterton, *St Francis of Assisi*, Hodder and Stoughton, 1960
2. J D Davies, *On Creating Wealth*, Industrial Christian Fellowship Theme Pamphlet No 35, Dec 1987, p 9
3. F D Maurice, quoted in Peter Cornwell, *Church and Nation*, Basil Blackwell, Oxford, 1983, p 76
4. R H Tawney, *Religion and the Rise of Capitalism*, Pelican, 1938, p 245
5. ibid, p 275
6. Ulrich Duchrow, *Global Economy: a Confessional Issue for the Churches?*, WCC Publications, Geneva, 1987, pp 149–158
7. ibid, p 153
8. Brian Griffiths, *Morality and the Market Place*, Hodder & Stoughton, 1962
9. Brian Griffiths, *The Creation of Wealth*, Hodder & Stoughton, 1984, p 107
10. J P Wogaman, *Economics and Ethics*, SCM Press, 1986, p 19
11. ibid, p 110
12. John Atherton, *Faith in the Nation*, SPCK, 1988, p 60
13. R H Tawney, *Religion and the Rise of Capitalism*, Pelican, 1938, p 105
14. Ed Charles Gore, *Property – its Duties and Rights*, 2nd Ed, Macmillan, 1915, pp xv & 183
15. ibid, pp 118–126
16. ibid, pp xviii–xx
17. John Paul II, *Laborem Exercens*, Catholic Truth Society, London, 1981, par 14
18. Hastings Rashdall, in *Property – its Duties and Rights*, p 64
19. quoted in ibid, p 147
20. E F Schumacher, *Small is Beautiful*, Blond & Briggs, 1973, p 245
21. Brian Griffiths, *The Creation of Wealth*, Hodder & Stoughton, 1984, p 25
22. R H Tawney, *The Acquisitive Society*, G Bell & Sons, 1927, p 30
23. Maurice A Coombs, *A Christian Response to Possessions Wealth and Property*, Good Shepherd, Philadelphia, 1988, p 14
24. *Johnson's Dictionary*, Vol II L–Z, 8th Ed, 1799
25. C B Macpherson, *The Political Theory of Possessive Individualism*, OUP, 1962, pp 263–270.
26. R H Preston, *Religion and the Persistence of Capitalism*, SCM Press, 1979, p 76
27. J P Wogaman, *Economics and Ethics: A Christian Enquiry*, SCM Press, 1986, p 74
28. Adam Smith, *Theory of Moral Sentiments*, quoted by John Atherton in

Christianity and the Market in the 1990s, Industrial Christian Fellowship Theme Pamphlet No 39, Dec 1988

29. Reinhold Niebuhr, *Moral Man and Immoral Society*, Scribners, New York, 1960
30. R H Preston, *Church and Society in the Late Twentieth Century*, SCM Press, 1983, p 47
31. H G Wood, in ed Charles Gore, *Property – its Duties and Rights*, 2nd ed, Macmillan, 1915, p 154
32. William Laud, quoted by R H Tawney, *Religion and the Rise of Capitalism*, Pelican, 1938, p 176
33. John Atherton, *Faith in the Nation*, SPCK, 1988, Chapter 2, pp 24–46
34. R H Preston, *Religion and the Persistence of Capitalism*, SCM Press, 1979, p 154
35. ibid, p 70
36. Gustavo Gutierrez, *A Theology of Liberation*, SCM Press, 1974, p 166
37. ibid, p 165
38. Brian Griffiths, *Morality and the Market Place*, Hodder & Stoughton, 1982, p 98
39. ibid, p 79
40. ibid, p 91
41. Brian Griffiths, *The Creation of Wealth*, Hodder and Stoughton, 1984, p 47
42. ibid, p 62

Chapter 5. Debt and Credit

1. reported in *The Guardian*, 11th November 1991, p 15
2. Roy McCloughy & Andrew Hartropp, *Debt*, Grove Ethical Studies No 71, Bramcote, 1988, p 15
3. reported in *The Observer*, 23rd February 1992, p 3
4. National Association of Citizens Advice Bureaux, *Annual Report*, 1988
5. R H Tawney, *Religion and the Rise of Capitalism*, Pelican, 1938, pp 41–42
6. ibid, p 116
7. ibid, pp 116–117
8. ibid, p 186
9. ibid, p 238
10. Roy McCloughy and Andrew Hartropp, *Debt*, Grove Ethical Studies No 71, Bramcote, 1988, p 13
11. Paul Mills, *Neither a borrower nor a lender be?*, ICF Theme Pamphlet No 38, September 1988, p 3

Chapter 6. Property and Home Ownership

1. See Jim Hart and Neville Black, *Housing Tenure and the Gospel*, *Crucible*, Oct–Dec 1987, pp 161–167, for a trenchant defence of the merits of council housing
2. R H Tawney, *The Acquisitive Society*, G Bell & Sons, 1927, p 66

3. ibid, p 92
4. Brian Griffiths, *Morality and the Market Place*, Hodder & Stoughton, 1982, p 62
5. Max L Stackhouse, *Public Theology and Political Economy*, Eerdmans, Grand Rapids, 1987, p xiii
6. Ulrich Duchrow, *Global Economy*, WCC Publications, Geneva, 1987, p 94

Chapter 7. Charitable Giving

1. see, for example, Deut 15: 7–10
2. Frank Prochaska, *The Voluntary Impulse*, Faber & Faber, 1988, p 23. My brief survey of the voluntary tradition in this country owes much to this excellent book.
3. ibid, p 49
4. Clement Attlee, quoted in Briggs and Macartney, *Toynbee Hall*, pp 35–36
5. reported in *Charity*, November 1988, p 29
6. Speaking at the Charities Aid Foundation Annual Charity Conference 1988, quoted in *Charity*, Dec 1988, p 4
7. Judith McQuillan ed, *Charity Trends: 14th Edition*, 1991, p 92
8. ibid, p 110
9. ibid, p 113
10. giving the second annual lecture of the Per Cent Club, quoted in *Charity*, January 1989, p 20
11. Judith McQuillan ed, *Charity Trends: 14th Edition*, 1991, p 18
12. Frank Prochaska, *The Voluntary Impulse*, Faber & Faber, 1988, p 63
13. *The Guardian*, 11th March 1989, "Barefaced cheek and red noses net £15 million", p 2
14. quoted by Janet Hodley, "Cashing in on the freak-show", *New Statesman and Society*, 10th March 1989, p 24
15. Simon Fanshawe, speaking at 'Charities Forum', 27th June 1988
16. Frank Prochaska, *The Voluntary Impulse*, Faber & Faber, 1988, p 30
17. F J Gladstone, *Voluntary Action in a Changing World*, London, 1979, p 100
18. Reinhold Niebuhr, *Moral Man and Immoral Society*, Scribners, New York, 1960, p 127
19. reported in *The Guardian*, 11th March 1989, p 2
20. John Posnett, in Judith McQuillan ed, *Charity Trends: 11th Edition*, Charities Aid Foundation, Tonbridge, 1988, p 44
21. examined by Peter Halfpenny, in ibid, *14th Edition*, 1991, pp 115–118
22. Peter Halfpenny, in ibid, p 118
23. Robin Guthrie, *Charity and the Nation: The 5th Arnold Goodman Charity Lecture*, Charities Aid Foundation, Tonbridge, 1988, pp 12–13
24. reported in *Charity*, November 1988, p 6
25. Charles Gore, in Charles Gore ed, *Property – Its Duties and Rights*, 2nd Edition, Macmillan, 1915, p xviii
26. Vernon Bartlett, in ibid, pp 91–92

27. A J Carlyle, in ibid, p 122–130
28. H Scott Holland, in ibid, p 180
29. Duncan B Forrester, in *Christian Action Journal*, Spring 1988, p 11
30. William Temple, *Christianity and Social Order*, Shepheard-Walwyn/ SPCK, 1976, p 78
31. Robin Guthrie, *Charity and the Nation: The 5th Arnold Goodman Charity Lecture*, Charities Aid Foundation, Tonbridge, 1988, p 17
32. Berdyaev, *The Destiny of Man*, quoted in Ronald H Preston, *Church and Society in the Late Twentieth Century*, SCM Press, 1983, p 114
33. Frank Prochaska, *The Voluntary Impulse*, Faber & Faber, 1988, p 44
34. ibid, p 76
35. Judith McQuillan ed, *Charity Trends: 11th edition*, Charities Aid Foundation, Tonbridge, 1988, p 43
36. Ken Young, *Meeting the Needs of Strangers*, Gresham College, 1991, p 34

Chapter 8. An Emerging Pattern

1. Brian Griffiths, *Morality and the Market Place*, Hodder & Stoughton, 1982, pp 83–84
2. R H Tawney, *The Acquisitive Society*, G Bell & Sons Ltd, 1927, p 96
3. William Temple, *Christianity and Social Order*, Shepheard-Walwyn/ SPCK, 1976, p 53
4. David Marquand, *The Unprincipled Society: New Demands & Old Politics*, Fontana Press, 1988, p 81
5. see, for example, Rosemary Radford Reuther, *Sexism and God-Talk*, SCM Press, 1983, pp 79–82
   or Sara Maitland, *A Map of the New Country*, Routledge & Kegan Paul, 1983, pp 7, 19, 20, 21
6. Ulrich Duchrow, *Global Economy: A Confessional Issue for the Churches?*, WCC Publications, Geneva, 1987, p 11
7. Ronald H Preston, *Church and Society in the Late Twentieth Century*, SCM Press, 1983, p 54
8. Paul Ekins, *Sustainable Consumerism*, New Consumer, Newcastle-upon-Tyne, 1989, p 16

Chapter 9. Issues before the Church

1. Karl Rahner, in Karl Rahner/Paul Imhof, *Ignatius of Loyola*, Collins, 1979, p 17
2. P F Strawson, in *Language, Truth and Candour*, in an obituary of Sir Alfred Ayer, *The Guardian*, 29th June 1989, p 39
3. John Habgood, *The Bonds of Freedom*, in the *Observer*, 19th May 1988, p 12
4. Ronald Preston, *The Kingdom and the Church*, in *Theology*, November 1989, p 524

5. David Jenkins, at a William Temple Foundation seminar, 11th March
   1988
6. Luke 17:21

Chapter 10. Money and the Church: Introduction

1. David Jenkins, at a William Temple Foundation seminar, 10th March
   1988
2. John Atherton, *Faith in the Nation*, SPCK, 1988, p 130
3. J P Wogaman, *Economics and Ethics*, SCM Press, 1986, p 129

Chapter 11. Background to Ecclesiastical Economics

1. L Wm Countryman, *The Rich Christian in the Church of the Early
   Empire: Contradictions and Accommodations*, Edwin Mullen Press, New
   York & Toronto, 1981
2. Clement of Alexandria, *The Rich Man's Salvation*
3. L Wm Countryman, *The Rich Christian in the Church of the Early
   Empire*, Edwin Mullen Press, New York & Toronto, 1981, p 173
4. Dietrich Bonhoeffer, *Letters and Papers from Prison*, The Enlarged
   Edition, SCM Press, 1971, p 382
5. Dietrich Bonhoeffer, *The Communion of Saints*, Harper & Row, 1963,
   p 123
6. J P Wogaman, *A Christian Method of Moral Judgement*, SCM Press,
   1976, pp 67–69
7. Dietrich Bonhoeffer, *Ethics*, SCM Press, 1955, p 114
8. Ronald H Preston, *Religion and the Persistence of Capitalism*, SCM
   Press, 1979, p 18
9. The European Value Systems Study Group, quoted in *LandMARC*,
   Publication of MARC Europe, Summer 1989
10. reported by Leslie Francis, *Discovering the Identity of Anglicanism: The
    Canadian Experience*, in *Crucible*, Apr/June 1989, p 69
11. See Lesslie Newbigin, *Foolishness to the Greeks*, SPCK, 1986, and
    Alasdair MacIntyre, *After Virtue: a Study in Moral Theory*, 2nd Edition,
    Duckworth, 1985
12. Robin Gill, *Beyond Decline: A challenge to the churches*, SCM Press,
    1988, p 11
13. ibid, pp 20–32
14. ibid, p 22
15 Giles Ecclestone ed, *The Parish Church?*, Mowbray, London/Oxford,
   1988, p 16
16. David Marquand, *The Unprincipled Society*, Fontana Press, 1988,
    pp 228–231
17. Neville Black, *Housing Tenure and the Gospel*, in *Crucible*, Jan–Mar
    1988, p 16

Chapter 12. Land and Property Ownership

1. Douglas McKean, *Money Matters: a guide to the finances of the Church of England*, Church House Publishing, 1987, p 67
2. *The Historic Resources of the Church of England*, GS 563, Church Commissioners, 1983
   The Historic Resources of the Church of England – Second Report by the Church Commissioners, GS 563, 1986
3. *The Church Commissioners for England; Report and Accounts*, 1990, p 44
4. ibid, 1990, p 9
5. ibid, 1988, p 6
6. Elizabeth Cairns, in *Charity*, January 1990, p 6
7. reported in *The Tablet*, 9th November 1991, p 1366
8. *The Church Commissioners for England: Report and Accounts*, 1988, p 26
9. ibid, 1988, p 29
10. ibid, 1990, p 31–32
11. reported, for example, in *Church Times*, 17th March 1989
12. *The Ethical Investor*, EIRIS, Apr/May 1989, p 7
13. *The Church Commissioners for England: Report and Accounts*, 1990, p 62
14. *The Objects and Investment Powers of the Church Commissioners*, Christsian Ethical Investment Group, February 1990
15. Douglas McKean, *Money Matters: a guide to the finances of the Church of England*, Church House Publishing, 1987, pp 65–71
16. *The Church Commissioners for England: Report and Accounts*, 1988, pp 6–7
17. ibid, 1984, p 6
18. see, for example, ibid, 1988, p 27
19. Michael Bourke, *The Archdeacon's Dilemma*, in *Theology*, May 1989, p 197
20. ibid, p 198
21. ironic statement in John Hammersley, *Christianity and the MetroCentre Do Not Mix . . . ?*, in *Crucible*, Apr–June 1988, p 60
22. D Perman, *Change and the Churches: An Anatomy of Religion in Britain*, Bodley Head, 1977, p 148
23. Sir Douglas Lovelock, July 1988, quoted by the Christian Ethical Investment Group

Chapter 13. Responsibility for Funding

1. *The Church of England Year Book*, Church House Publishing, 1990, p 175
2. *Church Statistics*, Central Board of Finance of the Church of England, 1991, pp 6–7
3. Douglas McKean, *Money Matters: a guide to the finances of the Church of England*, Church House Publishing, 1987, p 97
4. *The Parochial Expenses of the Clergy*, Church House Publishing, 1989, p 5
5. ibid, p 17

6. *Money and Mission*, Dr M. Sheard for the Diocese of Lichfield, 1989, p 2
7. Nigel Sharp, *Survey concerning Church attendance and Non-churchgoers' attitudes towards the Church and Christian Faith*, Media Services Agency, Swindon, 1987
8. David Collins, Peter Cotton, Otto Germann, *The Political Economy of the Church*, Portsmouth Diocesan Council for Social Responsibility, 1988. Further work is being done to incorporate pastoral and societal information, and to update the system following the 1991 census. It is hoped that this will be completed during 1993 so that a new Adjustment Factor can be implemented in the parishes for 1994. For further information contact Portsmouth 821137.
9. ibid. afterword
10. *The Church Commissioners for England: Report and Accounts*, 1990, p 10

Chapter 14. Voluntary Giving

1. *Financial Trends in Christian Organisations*, MARC Europe Monograph No 10, Bromley, 1987, p 5
2. for historical details of the Christian Stewardship movement and examples of the methods employed, see Gordon Strutt, *A Handbook of Parish Stewardship*, Mowbray, London and Oxford, 1985
3. *Christian Stewardship in the 1980s*, British Council of Churches' Stewardship Committee, 1980, p 3
4. ibid, p 5
5. Clive Barlow, *Clergy Attitudes towards Christian Stewardship*, St George's House, Windsor Castle, 1986, following an article in *New Christian*, August 1968, by Charles Davis
6. Hugh Buckingham, *How to be a Christian in Trying Circumstances*, Epworth Press, 1985, p 33
7. Clive Barlow, *Clergy Attitudes towards Christian Stewardship*, St George's House, Windsor Castle, 1986, p 3
8. ibid, p 22
9. *Faith in the City*: Report of the Archbishop of Canterbury's Commission on Urban Priority Areas, Church House Publishing, 1985, p 363
10. *The Church Urban Fund: Progress Report*, General Synod GS 799, October 1987, p 4
11. ibid, p 6
12. *Stewardship*, Issue No 44, Spring 1990, p 3
13. see, in particular, 2 Cor 8 & 9
14. Reinhold Niebuhr, *Moral Man and Immoral Society*, Scribners, New York, 1960, p 13
15. Sir Douglas Lovelock in *A Sharing Church*, Church Commissioners and Central Board of Finance of the Church of England, 1985, p 1
16. reported in *The Independent*, 6th February 1990
17. Maurice Coombs, *Where Moth and Dust Corrupt: A Theology of Stewardship*, Forward Movement Publications, Cincinnati, 1989, p 28
18. ibid, p 9

NOTES

NOTES 211

Chapter 15. An Emerging Pattern

1. Ben Whitney, *Keeping it Local – Social Responsibility and the Churches*, in *Crucible*, Jan–Mar 1989, p 3
2. David Jenkins, at a William Temple Foundation seminar, 11th March 1988
3. Ulrich Duchrow, *Global Economy – a confessional issue for the churches?*, WCC Publications, Geneva, 1987, p 14
4. Douglas Hurd, *God versus Caesar?*, in *Church Times*, 9th September 1988, p 12
5. John V Taylor, *Conversion to the World*, in ed Giles Ecclestone, *The Parish Church?*, Mowbray, London/Oxford, 1988, p 129
6. ibid, p 133
7. *Living Faith in the City*: a progress report by the Archbishop of Canterbury's Advisory Group on Urban Priority areas, General Synod, 1990, pp 131–132
8. Ruth Page, *Divine Grace and Church Establishment*, in *Theology*, July 1988, pp 284–8
9. John Tiller, *The Associational Church and its Communal Mission*, in ed. Giles Ecclestone, *The Parish Church?*, Mowbray, London/Oxford, 1988, p 90

Chapter 16. Facing Questions and Guidelines

1. Alan Chesters, at the annual conference of Church of England Diocesan Stewardship Advisers, 16th July 1990

Chapter 17. Patterns in the Church and the World

1. Ronald H Preston, *Religion and the Persistence of Capitalism*, SCM Press, 1979, p 14
2. Reinhold Niebuhr, *Moral Man and Immoral Society*, Scribners, New York, 1960, p 263
3. John Atherton, *Faith in the Nation*, SPCK, 1988, p 136
4. Brian Cordingley, *USA and El Salvador Sketches*, William Temple Foundation, Occasional Paper No 18, Manchester, 1990
5. Luke 15: 11–32

Chapter 18. Options before the Church

1. Ronald H Preston, *The Future of Christian Ethics*, SCM Press, 1987, p 109
2. Robin Gill, *Beyond Decline: a challenge to the churches*, SCM Press, 1988, pp 44–63
3. ibid, p 59
4. John M Hull, *What Prevents Christian Adults from Learning?*, SCM Press, 1985, p 34
5. R H Tawney, *Equality*, Geo Allen & Unwin, 1938, p 10

6. Frances Young and David F Ford, *Meaning and Truth in 2 Corinthians*, SPCK, 1987, p 167
7. ibid, pp 169–170
8. Rowan Williams, *Incarnation and Social Vision*, 1989 Gore Lecture, Westminster Abbey, November 1989
9. Reinhold Niebuhr, *Moral Man and Immoral Society*, Scribners, New York, 1960, p 222

Chapter 19. An Influence for Change

1. L Wm Countryman, *The Rich Christian in the Church of the Early Empire*, Edwin Mullen Press, New York & Toronto, 1981, p 214
2. Sara Maitland (following Anne Scheibner), *A Map of the New Country: Women and Christianity*, Routledge & Kegan Paul, 1983, pp 139 & 146
3. William Temple, *Christianity and Social Order*, Shepheard-Walwyn/ SPCK, 1976, p 43
4. *Living Faith in the City*: a progress report by the Archbishop of Canterbury's Advisory Group on Urban Priority Areas, General Synod, 1990, pp 57–58
5. ibid, p 60
6. *Demanding Renewal: The Needs and Resources Working Party Report*, Diocese of St Edmundsbury & Ipswich, 1989
7. Keith Ward, *Holding Fast to God*, SPCK, 1982, p 113
8. Rowan Williams, *Incarnation and Social Vision*, 1989 Gore Lecture, Westminster Abbey, November 1989
9. Elizabeth O'Connor, *Letters to Scattered Pilgrims*, Harper & Row, and Ministry of Money leaflet *Why should I write a Money Autobiography?*, available from South Park Community Trust, Chobham, Surrey
10. John M Hull, *What Prevents Christian Adults from Learning?*, SCM Press, 1985, p 55
11. ibid, p 101

Bibliography

General

Richard Adams, Jane Carruthers, Charlie Fisher *Shopping for a Better World* (Kogan Page 1991)

Richard Adams, Jane Carruthers, Sean Hamil *Changing Corporate Values* (Kogan Page 1991)

John Atherton *Faith in the Nation* (SPCK 1988)

Dietrich Bonhoeffer *Letters and Papers from Prison* (Enlarged Edition SCM Press 1971)

Hugh Buckingham *How to be a Christian in Trying Circumstances* (Epworth Press 1985)

Charity Commissioners *Oxfam: Report of an Enquiry* (HMSO 1991)

G K Chesterton *St Francis of Assisi* (Hodder & Stoughton 1960)

Maurice Coombs *Where Moth and Dust Corrupt* (Forward Movement Publications 1989)

L Wm Countryman *The Rich Christian in the Church of the Early Empire* (Edwin Mellen Press 1981)

Ulrich Duchrow *Global Economy: A Confessional Issue for the Churches?* (WCC Publications 1987)

Avery Dulles SJ *Models of the Church* (Gill & Macmillan 1976)

Giles Ecclestone ed *The Parish Church?* (Mowbray 1988)

Paul Ekins *Sustainable Consumerism* (New Consumer 1989); *A New World Order: Grassroots movements for social change* (Routledge 1992)

Robin Gill *Beyond Decline: A challenge to the churches* (SCM Press 1988)

Charles Gore ed *Property – Its Duties and Rights* (2nd edition Macmillan 1915)

John Gosling *Clergy Housing, Pay and Morale* (Edward King Institute)

George Goyder *The Just Enterprise* (Andre Deutsch 1987)

Brian Griffiths *Morality and the Market Place* (Hodder & Stoughton, 1982); *The Creation of Wealth* (Hodder & Stoughton, 1984)

Robin Guthrie *Charity and the Nation* (Charities Aid Foundation 1988)

Gustavo Gutiérrez *A Theology of Liberation*, Revised Edition, (SCM Press 1988)

Adrian Hastings *A History of English Christianity 1920–1985* (Collins 1986)

Martin Hengel *Property and Riches in the Early Church* (SCM Press 1974)

John M Hull *What Prevents Christian Adults from Learning?* (SCM Press 1985)

John Francis Kavanaugh *Following Christ in a Consumer Society*, Revised Edition, (Orbis Books 1991)

Alix Love *Determinants of Charity Giving* (Charities Aid Foundation 1991/2)

Alasdair MacIntyre *After Virtue: a study in moral theory* (Second edition Duckworth 1985)

John Macquarrie *Principles of Christian Theology* (Revised Edition SCM Press 1977)

Ed Judith McQuillan *Charity Trends: 11th–14th Editions* (Charities Aid Foundation 1988–91)

214   BIBLIOGRAPHY

Sara Maitland *A Map of the New Country: Women and Christianity* (Routledge & Kegan Paul 1983)

David Marquand *The Unprincipled Society: New Demands and Old Politics* (Fontana Press 1988)

Jürgen Moltmann *Theology Today* (SCM Press 1988)

Redmond Mullin *The Wealth of Christians* (Paternoster Press 1983)

Owen Nankivell *All Good Gifts* (Epworth Press 1978)

Lesslie Newbigin *Foolishness to the Greeks* (SPCK 1986)

H Richard Niebuhr *Christ and Culture* (Harper and Row 1975)

Reinhold Niebuhr *Moral Man and Immoral Society* (Scribners 1960)

Oxfam Trustees *Oxfam's Public Education and Campaigning Programme* (Oxfam 1990)

Wolfhart Pannenberg (*Christianity in a Secularized World* (SCM Press 1988)

David Potter and Philip Sarre eds *Dimensions of Society* (Hodder & Stoughton/Open University Press 1974)

Ronald H Preston *Religion and the Persistence of Capitalism* (SCM Press 1979); *Church and Society in the Late Twentieth Century* (SCM Press 1983); *The Future of Christian Ethics* (SCM Press 1987)

Frank Prochaska *The Voluntary Impulse* (Faber & Faber 1988)

Edward Schillebeeckx *Jesus in our Western Culture* (SCM Press 1987)

E F Schumacher *Small is Beautiful* (Blond & Briggs 1973)

W J Sheils and Diana Wood eds *The Church and Wealth* (Basil Blackwell 1987)

Max L Stackhouse *Public Theology and Political Economy* (Wm B Eerdmans 1987)

Gordon Strutt *A Handbook of Parish Stewardship* (Mowbray 1985)

R H Tawney *Religion and the Rise of Capitalism* (1937 edition Pelican 1938); *The Acquisitive Society* (G Bell & Sons 1927); *Equality* (Geo Allen & Unwin 1938)

William Temple *Christianity and Social Order* (Shepheard-Walwyn/SPCK 1976)

Sue Ward *Socially Responsible Investment* (Directory of Social Change 1991)

Phil Wells & Mandy Jetter *The Global Consumer* (Victor Gollancz 1991)

John Wesley *Sermons on Several Occasions* (Epworth Press, 1944)

Rowan Williams *Incarnation and Social Vision* (Gore Lecture Westminster Abbey 1989)

J Philip Wogaman *A Christian Method of Moral Judgement* (SCM Press 1976); *Economics and Ethics: A Christian Enquiry* (SCM Press 1986)

Frances Young & David F. Ford *Meaning and Truth in 2 Corinthians* (SPCK 1987)

Ken Young *Meeting the Needs of Strangers* (Gresham College 1991)

Church Reports and Publications

Archbishop of Canterbury's Commission on Urban Priority Areas *Faith in the City* (Church House Publishing 1985)

Archbishop of Canterbury's Advisory Group on Urban Priority Areas *Living Faith in the City*: a progress report (General Synod 1990)

Archbishop of Canterbury's Commission on Rural Areas *Faith in the Countryside* (Churchman Publishing 1990)

Clive Barlow *Clergy Attitudes Towards Christian Stewardship* (St George's House, Windsor 1986)

Board of Education *All are Called* (General Synod 1987); *Called to be Adult Disciples* (General Synod 1987)

Board for Social Responsibility *Changing Britain: Social Diversity and Moral Unity* (Church House Publishing 1987)

British Council of Churches *Christian Stewardship in the 1980s* (C in W Publications 1980)

Central Board of Finance of the Church of England, *Church Statistics 1989, 1990, 1991*

Central Stipends Authority *The Parochial Expenses of the Clergy* (Church House Publishing 1989)

Christian Ethical Investment Group *The Church Commissioners and the case for Disinvestment* (ELTSA/CAN)

Church Commissioners *Central Stipends Authority Report* (General Synod 1989); *The Assets Committee and Other Constitutional Matters* (General Synod 1990); *Report and Accounts 1984, 1988, 1989, 1990*

Church of England Pensions Board *Report and Accounts 1988*

Church of Scotland *Special Commission on the Ethics of Investment and Banking 1988*

Church Urban Fund *Report to General Synod* (General Synod 1990)

Peter Cotton, David Collins, Otto Germann *The Political Economy of the Church* (Portsmouth Diocesan Council for Social Responsibility 1989)

abridged Michael Crowther-Green, after Douglas John Hall *The Steward: A Biblical Symbol for Today* (Diocese of Oxford 1985)

EIRIS *Ethical Investment Dilemmas: the Church of England as a case study* (Second Edition EIRIS 1987)

General Synod Standing Committee *The Proposed Church Urban Fund* (General Synod 1986); *The Church Urban Fund: Progress Report* (General Synod 1987); *Infrastructure Review Follow-up: Policy & Finance* (General Synod 1989)

General Synod Working Party *State Aid for Churches in Use* (General Synod 1989)

Mark Hayes *Social Investment: a new option for the poor* (CEIG & Traidcraft Exchange 1991)

Joint Liaison Committee *A Responding Church* (Central Board of Finance of the Church of England/Church Commissioners 1982); *A Sharing Church* (Central Board of Finance of the Church of England/Church Commissioners 1985); *Giving in Faith* (Central Board of Finance of the Church of England/Church Commissioners 1988)

Lichfield Diocese Working Party *Money and Mission* (Diocese of Lichfield Board for Mission and Unity 1989)

Douglas McKean *Money Matters: A Guide to the Finances of the Church of England* (Church House Publishing 1987)

Francis P McHugh & Peter F Askonas *The Root of All Evil?* (CTS Publications 1990)

St Edmundsbury & Ipswich Diocesan Needs and Resources Working Party *Demanding Renewal* (Diocese of St Edmundsbury & Ipswich 1989)

St Edmundsbury & Ipswich Diocesan Synod Standing Committee *Demanding Renewal: The Next Stage* (Diocese of St Edmundsbury and Ipswich 1990)

John Smallwood *Slothful Stewards? Giving in the Church of England* (John Smallwood 1987)

Various *Theme Pamphlets* (Industrial Christian Fellowship)

Various *MARC Monographs* (MARC Europe)

Various *Occasional Papers* (William Temple Foundation) *Being in the World* (William Temple Foundation 1986)

Journals

British Journal of Theological Education
Charity
Charities Aid Foundation Newsletter
Crucible
Ethical Investor
Grove Ethical Studies
Grove Pastoral Series
Industrial Christian Fellowship Quarterly
Marxism Today
Ministry
New Consumer
Stewardship
Studies in Christian Ethics
Theology
Trust Monitor

Index

217